D0497357

STAR WARS
COLLECTOR'S
POCKET
COMPANION
2000 Edition

by Stuart W. Wells III

Copyright 2000 by Stuart W. Wells III

All Rights Reserved.
Written, photographed, and designed by Stuart W. Wells III

Printed in the United States of America

Star Wars, and the Star Wars stories and characters are registered trademarks of LUCASFILM, LTD.

No portion of this publication may be reproduced or transmitted in any form or by any means, electronic or mechanical, including photocopy, recording, or any information storage and retrieval system, without permission in writing from the publisher, except by a reviewer who may quote brief passages in a critical article or review to be printed in a magazine or newspaper, or electronically transmitted on radio, television or the Internet.

Trademarks and copyrights of all products listed in this book are the sole property of their respective trademark and copyright owners. Copyrights for items depicted in photographs and illustrations are reserved to their respective owners, and the items are depicted here for the sole purpose of identification. The content of this book is the work of the author, and is not authorized, approved or endorsed by any manufacturer, licensee, or trademark or copyright owner listed herein. This book is published without warranty, solely for the educational and informational benefit of the reader. None of the information, advice, or pricing data presented is guaranteed in any way.

Published by

**krause
publications**

700 E. State Street • Iola, WI 54990-0001
Telephone: 715/445-2214
www.krause.com

Please call or write for our free catalog. Our toll-free number to place an order or obtain a free catalog is 800-258-0929. Or please use our regular business telephone 715-445-2214 for editorial comment and further information.

Library of Congress Catalog Number: 99-68139

ISBN: 0-87341-889-1

CONTENTS

ACKNOWLEDGMENTS

A number of avid Star Wars collectors were kind enough to let me photograph their collections. Thanks especially to: Rob Rintoul, Rob Johnson, Wats Wacker, Morgan McClain, and Harry Rinker Jr. Thanks also to Sam Pagano for letting me photograph his sticker books and other toys.

Many manufacturers of Star Wars items supplied information, catalogs or photographs. Thanks to: Don Post Studios, Alan Payne at Icons, Don Schmidt at Tiger Electronics, Tracy at Illusive Originals, Chaz Fitzhugh at Applause, Jim Schneider at Star Jars, Joshua Izzo at Topps, and Matt Mariani at Decipher, Inc. Thanks also to Kenner, Galoob, and JusToys for all the trips through their showrooms during Toyfair for many years.

Several local retailers were kind enough to let me photograph inventory in their stores. Thanks to:

Todd Testa and Larry Russo at Castle Comics, Milford, Conn. (Comics, Toys, Model Kits and Statues) 203-877-3610, Website: www.castlecomics.com

David Kruseski and Steven Bryant at Heroes Comics & Cards, Norwalk, Conn. (Comics and CCGs) 203-750-0505

THIS BOOK COVERS

Star Wars Collectibles
Made Between 1976 and 2000

This book covers Star Wars collectibles from the beginning, through the end of March 2000, with additional information on forthcoming items. This is from the very beginning of the first or classic age of Star Wars through the end of the second age of Star Wars collectibles, perhaps destined to be called the "Silver Age" and the first year of *The Phantom Menace*, which may well become known as the "red tag year." The veritable flood of items beginning in 1999 based on the new movie has led to a glut of collectibles in the stores; almost all of which are available at substantial discounts. It's a great time for bargain hunting!

Distribution in the United States

This book covers Star Wars collectibles distributed in the United States. While just about every foreign item makes its way to a few collectors in the United States, the only items listed here are ones which were distributed in enough quantity to be generally available. The most significant of these are the "Tri-Logo" action figures. These figures came on header cards with logos for "Return of the Jedi" in three languages (thus the name) and were intended for foreign markets. However, they were widely distributed in the United States as the Star Wars phenomenon was winding down in 1984–86. A few foreign figures, such as the Power of the Force Yak Face, are listed for completeness. Although never distributed in the United States, it is a necessary and expensive figure for collectors who want to complete their collections. Other figures on foreign header cards are worth less than their U.S. counterparts and are more likely to be bought by a collector as a temporary measure, until the more desirable American figure can be acquired.

Categories

The book is divided into sections based on the categories which collectors most frequently use in organizing their collections. The amount of coverage given to any category depends on its popularity. Action figures are the most popular Star Wars collectible and so they are given the most coverage—56 pages, with additional sections on the vehicles, accessories and the 12-inch dolls. Actually, many of the less popular categories could just as well have been grouped in a section called "Other Stuff" because that is how most collectors view the items. However, this would have made it hard to use the book.

Pocket Guide

This is a pocket guide, and is based on my 1998 book titled *The Galaxy's Greatest Star Wars Collectibles Price Guide, 1999 edition*. This book has been updated with **new material** covering collectibles issued in the last two years and with **current prices**. However, the previous book had more space, and therefore more detail and also a lot more **color pictures**. It's still available at your local bookstore or from the publisher. ISBN 0-930625-97-8, $26.95. Buy two copies and give one to a friend!

Grading

Most Star Wars items are graded on a 10-point scale from C-10 (the best) down to C-1. Hardly any-

The Galaxy's Greatest Star Wars Collectibles Price Guide, 1999 Edition (Landmark, 1998)

thing old qualifies as a C-10 and nobody admits that anything they are trying to sell is a C-1, so the actual number of categories is probably less than 10. Prices in this book are for items in their original packaging in "near mint" condition, which corresponds to about C-9 or C-9.5. The occasional extraordinary item that is actually "mint" (i.e. C-10) commands a slightly higher price. How much higher depends on how much better than an ordinary near mint copy it actually is. Mint means the same thing, regardless of age and type of product. It is not the same thing as "new." Many, probably most, new action figure header cards are not mint. They have been handled when they were put in the shipping box, taken out of the box and hung on a rack, maybe dropped on the floor, handled by the check-out clerk, etc. This leaves an item which is a defect-free collectible, acceptable anywhere at the near-mint price. The figure inside is most likely mint, but rarely the package. "Near mint" does vary somewhat with the type of product. Some kinds of things are simply more durable than others and do not normally show any wear from normal handling. For those things, there is very little difference between the ordinary, (i.e. near mint) and the extraordinary, (i.e. mint) and probably very little difference in price.

Prices

A single price is given for each listed item. This represents the full retail price or asking price. Prices vary from one dealer to another and from one location to another, so prices actually fall into a range. But even though no single price can be perfect for all situations, a price range of, for example, $40 to $100 is no more meaningful than a single price, and even less satisfying. The single price given in this book should be used as a guideline or baseline. If you can find the item that you want to buy for 10% to 25% less than this price you are getting a good deal. If you are paying more, but you really want the item, that's okay too. Just shop around a little first to see if you can do better.

This book is based on the author's research. The author is not a dealer in Star Wars collectibles and not associated with any dealer or manufacturer nor with Lucasfilms or any of its licensees.

INTRODUCTION

The Star Wars Phenomenon

The Star Wars phenomenon started in 1977, and, after a little slump in the late 1980s, it is still going strong, fueled by great expectations for the new movies. Collectibles from the movie were available beginning in late 1976—first a poster and a book, then the comics in early 1977, and finally, after the movie opened, a few games and puzzles. The real flood didn't start until 1978, when the action figures actually arrived.

Before *Star Wars,* action figures (really dolls) were either 8" or 12" tall, but Kenner made their figures 3¾" tall so that they could fit in vehicles of a reasonable size. The idea was so successful that most action figures became small and most action movies had action figure lines thereafter. It took the toy industry almost a decade to grow action figures back up to 5" to 6" tall, the current standard, and almost two decades to bring out any significant number of new 8" to 12" action dolls for boys. And, in a sense, the toy industry has never recovered from basing action figures on the summer's hot new movie.

What Might Have Been

In *Star Wars* collecting, Kenner (now Hasbro) is King. Almost anything made by Kenner, and a lot of things they never quite made, is collected more intensely than anything, however attractive, made by anyone else. Was this inevitable? It didn't seem to be so at the time.

The first *Star Wars* collectible available to the general public was the original paperback book. I call it "*Star Wars* collectible #1." There was also a poster, which was available at the San Diego Comics Convention, held earlier that fall, but it was available only at the convention. The book appeared in November 1976, a full seven months before the movie opened, and it was available at bookstores everywhere. Later book editions had a different cover and can easily be distinguished by the date on the copyright page. Unlike some of the most valuable action figures, the original paperback cannot be faked. Nevertheless, this paperback is not as valuable as any of the early action figures.

Star Wars collectible #2 is the first issue of the comic book series from Marvel. It's worth a lot more than the paperback book, and the 35¢ test issue of this comic is more valuable than many of the early action figures. A couple of issues of the comic came out before the movie opened. Other pre-opening collectibles include articles in movie magazines about the forthcoming movie. The week the movie opened, *Time* magazine ran a two page spread calling it the best movie of the year. Then there are ticket stubs to the movie. Stubs from opening day would be the most valuable, with stubs from the first anniversary being a strong contender.

Movie photos, autographed by the stars, could be prime collectibles. Other significant movie anniversary events also yielded some items to collect. After the movie was finally out of the theaters, Lucas and company sent a high quality studio copy of the film to Noreascon II, the 1980 World Science Fiction convention in Boston, for a free showing. The movie was accompanied by the world premiere of *The Making of The Empire Strikes Back*. There must have been something to collect at the convention. (I was there collecting autographs for the science fiction books in my collection.)

Star Wars opened May 25, 1977. By November 19, it was the largest grossing picture of all time, doing $200 million domestic and $400 million worldwide by that time. It received a special Hugo award in 1977 from the World Science Fiction Convention. *The Empire Strikes Back* grossed $23 million in the first 3 weeks. These were huge numbers for pictures that cost $10 million to $20 million to make, not $100 million to $200 million like today.

Ten-year-olds were not the only people who saw the movie 10 times in the theater. A lot of older kids and adults did too. Fans and potential collectors who liked movies of this type were the people who read the cinema magazines about forthcoming science fiction, fantasy, horror and action pictures.

They were more likely to read the comics and the books, and less likely to play with action figures. These were the people Lucas was thanking when he sent the movie to the World Science Fiction Convention. A convention of authors and book readers, who also happen to like science fiction movies.

During all of this, *Locus*, the "Newspaper of the Science Fiction Field" had a *Star Wars* picture on its first page exactly one time. The movie was mentioned from time to time. Once was to report that Leigh Brackett, a respected science fiction writer, would do the screen play for the sequel, and another time was to indicate that the success of *Star Wars* had convinced Paramount that they shouldn't do a *Star Trek* movie.

Fans had been begging Paramount to make a *Star Trek* for years, but they didn't figure there was any money in it. Now they concluded that George Lucas had captured all the money, so there still wouldn't be any money in it. Of course, they eventually did make one, but talk about being "clueless!" I estimate that they could have had about a billion dollars in revenue if they had made a *Star Trek* movie every couple of years in the 1970s, with a budget and schedule similar to the James Bond movies. On the other hand, they probably would have farmed the project out to someone who would have destroyed the entire *Star Trek* franchise by the mid 1970s. With all this on their minds, perhaps it's not surprising that science fiction fans didn't become today's *Star Wars* collectors.

Many of today's *Star Wars* collectors were kids filled with wonder when they first saw the movie. They saw the movie 10 times in the theater and now they are grown up, have some money, and want to collect the neat toys that they played with in their youth. Even these fans might have collected the comic books and the earliest toys, by Kenner and others, who hastily scrambled to get licenses. Many of these items came out before the first action figures, which did not appear until 1978. Nevertheless, it's the action figures that everyone collects and that have the highest prices. Every tiny variation in the figures is noticed, found, analyzed, evaluated, and collected.

Prices of most other *Star Wars* items are fairly reasonable, especially by comparison to the action figures. This has little to do with scarcity. Millions of action figures were produced, while only tens of thousands of most other items were ever made. When many other classic *Star Wars* collectibles were completely gone, action figures, especially those from the *Return of the Jedi*, were still available.

What Happens to Star Wars Things?

Did you ever wonder what happens to leftover *Star Wars* stuff after the stores can't sell it any more? You probably assumed that the stores just leave it hanging around until the last one is sold and then they are all gone. This may even be true for the items that have been unpacked from their boxes. But what about the boxes still in the store room, not to mention the ones back in some warehouse somewhere?

What stuff? Unsold action figures, and toys of all kinds; leftover fast food and other promotional figures. Just about everything yields leftovers.

Excess stuff back at the factory can be repackaged for overseas. The Orient is a great place for this, because that is where a lot of the factories are. In the case of *Star Wars*, some excess action figures became the cheap (then, not now) three packs.

One place excess stuff goes is KayBee. KayBee Toys has made a business of buying the tail-end of action figure series and selling them at discount. They have only been doing this for the last few years, so the original *Star Wars* merchandise didn't get there, but the tail end of the new or "silver age" action figures arrived in late March, 2000. Even Toys "R" Us got in the act this year with a large selection of excess vehicles for and deluxe creatures for under $10.

Second, there are surplus dealers who buy up toys at pennies on the dollar and sell them to variety stores and other surplus merchandise outlets. You can get extraordinary bargains at these stores, but it all depends on what happens to show up.

One other place merchandise can show up is a lot closer to home—your local comic shop. Enterprising dealers who have acquired enough warehouse stock can sell it to comic shops through Diamond Distribution Company, by offering it in *Previews Magazine*. In the early and mid 1990s, leftover Mego figures such as the 8" Kirk, Spock, and the Klingon *Star Trek* figures, and the 12" Batman, Spider-Man, and Wonder Woman figures were advertised periodically. The price reflected the collector market, so no shop bought a huge supply, but these figures were still available, in the original package.

Quite a number of left over *Star Wars* figures were also advertised in *Previews Magazine* in the early 1990s. Most were on *Return of the Jedi* header cards, which is hardly surprising, but a few were even from *The Empire Strikes Back*. Typically, the figures carried a $15.00 retail price tag and the comic shop would have paid about $9.00 to $10.

While writing this book, I looked through most of the back issues of *Previews Magazine,* starting with 1991. I found all of the action figures listed below for sale on the original header cards. I have only listed the ones which had their first appearance in the *Return of the Jedi* series (and Lobot from *The Empire Strikes Back*). There were also a number of reissue figures offered.

In addition, there were assorted Droids figures and assorted Ewoks figures, including Dulok Scout, Urgah Lady Gorneesh, Dulok Shaman, and King Gorneesh. You could also buy a group of ten 1" metal, hand-painted micro figures from 1983 for $30.

What does this all mean? For one thing, if you are operating on the assumption that all of the action figures, vehicles, and other items being sold by dealers are from private collections and that there can't be too

---

Classic *Return of the Jedi* figures distributed to comic shops in the early 1990—Partial Checklist

Admiral Ackbar	$15.00
Bib Fortuna	15.00
Biker Scout	15.00
C-3PO, removable arms and legs	30.00
bagged (*still available in 1997!*)	10.00
Chief Chirpa	15.00
Emperor's Royal Guard	15.00
General Madine	15.00
Klaatu	15.00
Lando Calrissian, Skiff Guard	20.00
Lobot (*The Empire Strikes Back*)	18.00
Logray	15.00
Nikto	15.00
Nien Nunb	15.00
Rancor Keeper	15.00
R2-D2 with pop-up sensorscope	30.00
Ree-Yees	15.00
Squid Head	15.00
Weequay	15.00
Many reissue figures, each	15.00

many of them around, you might be mistaken. There was enough leftover stock from 1983 and 1984 for it to be distributed in quantity to comic shops just a few years ago. That's probably why the prices are still somewhat reasonable for many of these figures.

What to Look For

The red tag specials for the 1997 to 1998 toys from the classic movies and for the overstocked toys from *The Phantom Menace* started a little after Christmas 2000 and are in full swing. This means that some of the prices in this book are more guess work than observation. Hasbro opened up its warehouse(s) and shipped a large number of Freeze Frame action figures to Toys "R" Us and Kay-Bee stores for sale at about $3.00 each. Toys "R" Us got figures originally sold in early 1998, many of which were the Collection 1 ".00" figures with "Saelt-Marae" misspelled "Sealt-Marie." This should reduce the previous premium price for this packaging variation from $8.00 to around $3.00, at most. On the other hand, Kay-Bee stores got many of the same figures, but they were from later assortments and none had this error. However, Kay-Bee's figures included some previously scarce Collection 1 figures, most notably the R2-D2 with new features. Most examples of this figure have a slide which reads "Shutting down the Death Star trash compactor," but a few had a slide which said "Shutting down the Imperial trash compactor." This variation was worth as much as $200 according to most guides. However, I saw 30 figures with this scarce variation in one store and several more in two others. Everyone thought that the earliest versions of these figures were scarce, and long gone from the warehouse, but every-

one was wrong! It's very difficult to estimate the final price that this figure will command (I picked $50 for the listings), but people who paid $200 or more will be kicking themselves. In fact, at one local store, one such irate collector bent and creased the corner of several of these figures.

R2-D2 "Imperial" slide from Freeze Frame figure (Kenner 1998)

1998 Freeze Frame Figures with "Sealt-Marie" error
Endore Rebel Soldier (#69716)
Han Solo in Carbonite (#69817)
Bespin Han Solo (#69719)
Han Solo in Endore Gear (#69621)
Hoth Rebel Soldier (#69821)
Lando Calrissian as Skiff Guard (#69622)
Lando Calrissian in General's Gear (#69756)
Bespin Luke Skywalker (#69713)
Luke Skywalker in Stormtrooper Disguise (#69819)
Obi-Wan (Ben) Kenobi (#69576)
Princess Leia Organa, Ewok Celebration Outfit (#69714)
Princess Leia Organa as Jabba's Prisoner (#69683)
Rebel Fleet Trooper (#69696)
All 13 were available again in March and April 2000 at under $3.00 each, mixed in with spelling-corrected versions. When this happens, prices must, and did, fall.

As if that wasn't enough, the big sell-off also featured such previously scarce, and valuable, items as Mynock Hunt "cinema scene" packs, Darth Vader Gunner Station figures, AT-ATs for $10 to $20 each, etc. etc. These bargains were not to be missed and I saw a lot of collectors in the stores who weren't missing them.

The best lesson to draw from this is not to pay $50 or $100 or $200, or whatever, for a recent figure. No matter how scarce the variation seems to be, you can't

*Electronic Imperial AT-AT Walker with AT-AT Commander
and AT-AT Driver (Kenner 1997)
Collectors were able to buy these for $10 to $30 in April, 1999.*

Kyle Katarn and Imperial Sentinel Expanded Universe
3-D PlayScene figures (Kenner 1998) Collectors were looking
for these figures in May, 1999, without success.

really know for sure until all the warehouses are empty
and the guys who bought all 25 of them at some local
store finally sell off their stock. By then, most collectors will be looking for some new, seemingly scarce
item, and the price will be more reasonable anyway.

As this book went to press, collectors were not
"waiting for the other shoe to drop." Rather, they were
checking local stores frequently, "hoping for an entire
shoestore to drop." The top items on their wish list were
case assortments containing some very scarce Freeze
Frame, and Expanded Universe action figures (see
pages 36 to 40). If a large quantity of them appear, most
the prices for these figures will drop sharply, at least in
the short run.

What should a savvy collector do to build a prime
collection? Look for those bargains! Go to a lot of
stores until you find the items you are missing. Use
your feet (to go to a lot of places) and your eyes (to look
through all the racks) and don't pay through the nose
unless you have to.

Savvy collectors will be looking in the bargain
bins for vehicles and ships, both common and deluxe
action figures, carry cases, and role play weapons.
Deluxe creatures, 12" dolls, and store exclusives
shouldn't last long enough to get there, but you never
know.

ACTION FIGURES

STAR WARS
Kenner (1977)

The very first *Star Wars* action figures arrived in 1978, in the mail, if you bought the famous Early Bird Package. The figures came in a white plastic tray in a white mailer box. In the very earliest packages, Chewbacca has a dark green plastic rifle instead of the later black plastic, and Luke has a telescoping lightsaber which not only extends out of his arm, it telescopes out of the middle of the blade and almost reaches the floor. This version lightsaber can occasionally be found on carded Luke Skywalker and also Darth Vader and Ben (Obi-Wan) Kenobi figures.

Early Bird "Figures" (1977)
Early Bird Package, 19" x 9½" flat envelope with
    certificate to purchase soon-to-be released
    figures and scenes to be used with them
    (#38140) Star Wars logo. $300.00
Early Bird figures **R2-D2**, **Luke Skywalker**,
    Princess Leia and **Chewbacca**, in box 450.00

Star Wars action figures are heavily collected, both on their original header cards and loose. Every tiny variation in the figure or the packaging makes a difference in the price, and Star Wars figures have many of both kinds of variations. The chief variation comes about because Kenner continued to produce the original figures for many years, but changed the movie logo to "*The Empire Strikes Back*" and then to "*Return of the Jedi*" as each of those new movies premiered. After the movies, figures were issued on *Power of the Force* header cards with a collectible coin as a premium.

In addition, most of the figures were available in the United States on foreign "Tri-Logo" header cards which had *Return of the Jedi* movie logos in three languages. There are

Star Wars Early Bird Certificate Package (Kenner 1977)

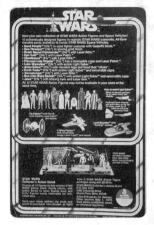 

Star Wars original 12-back card and 48-back card with
Revenge of the Jedi figure offer (Kenner 1978 & 1982)

variations among Tri-Logo header cards as well, but all are lumped together for pricing purposes. This means that there are four or five different packages for most figures, before you even consider the normal variations that occur in any action figure line, such as hair color or other changes to the figure, and photo or text changes to the card. Figures are grouped by the series in which they first appeared, and all of the different versions of the figure are listed together so that you can easily compare their prices.

The most significant of the header card changes involves the first group of figures to be produced, which includes all of the major characters. The cards for these figures have a picture and list on the back that shows just the original 12 figures and are called "12 backs." When more figures were produced later, their cards reflected all 20 or 21 then existing figures, and the cards for the original 12 got new backs as well, called "20/21 backs." Original figures on 12 back cards are scarce and desirable, so they are worth a lot more money—$75.00 to $100.00 more at current prices. There are two slightly different 12-backs, eight different 20-backs, and two or more versions of most of the others, for a total of 45 different U.S. header cards. The only ones with any extra collector value are the 48-back cards which contain a *Revenge of the Jedi* offer.

The most significant of the figure variations was with the Jawa, where the original version had a vinyl cape. This was quickly changed to cloth, which was used for all the rest of the figures. The few vinyl-caped Jawas are the most valuable of all the Star Wars figures and currently sell in the $1,500.00 range, with loose figures going for $250.00 to $300.00. Care in buying is essential, because a loose Jawa in cloth cape is only worth $15.00 and a fake vinyl cape is not hard to make.

All Star Wars action figure prices are volatile and generally increasing. This will almost certainly continue with the release of *Star Wars, The Phantom Menace* and other movies in the series.

3¾" Figures (1978)
Artoo-Detoo (R2-D2) (#38200) 2¼" figure

Original *Star Wars* "12 back" card	$200.00
Reissue on *Star Wars* "20/21 back" card	200.00
Reissue on *Empire Strikes Back* card	75.00
Reissue on *Return of the Jedi* card	35.00
Reissue on Tri-Logo card	35.00
Loose, no accessories	15.00

Ben (Obi-Wan) Kenobi (#38250) **white hair**

Original *Star Wars* "12 back" card	300.00
Reissue on *Star Wars* "20/21 back" card	160.00
Reissue on *Empire Strikes Back* card	100.00
Reissue on *Return of the Jedi* card	50.00
Reissue on Tri-Logo card	50.00
Reissue on *Power of the Force* card	100.00
Loose, with lightsaber	15.00

Ben (Obi-Wan) Kenobi (#38250) **gray hair**

Original *Star Wars* "12 back" card	300.00
Reissue on *Star Wars* "20/21 back" card	150.00
Reissue on *Empire Strikes Back* card	100.00
Reissue on *Return of the Jedi* card	50.00
Reissue on *Return of the Jedi* card new photo	45.00
Reissue on *Power of the Force* card	115.00
Reissue on Tri-Logo card	50.00
Loose, with lightsaber	15.00

Chewbacca (#38210) 4¼" figure

Original *Star Wars* "12 back" card	300.00
Reissue on *Star Wars* "20/21 back" card	200.00
Reissue on *Empire Strikes Back* card	100.00
Reissue on *Return of the Jedi* card	50.00
Reissue on *Return of the Jedi* card, new photo	45.00
Reissue on *Power of the Force* card	100.00
Reissue on Tri-Logo card	35.00

Artoo-Detoo (R2-D2) & Ben (Obi-Wan) Kenobi (Kenner 1978)

Death Squad Commander & Han Solo (Kenner 1978)

Loose, with rifle	12.00
Darth Vader (#38230) 4¼" figure	
Original *Star Wars* "12 back" card	400.00
Reissue on *Star Wars* "20/21 back" card	300.00
Reissue on *Empire Strikes Back* card	100.00
Reissue on *Return of the Jedi* card	50.00
Reissue on Tri-Logo card	40.00
Reissue on *Return of the Jedi* card, new photo	45.00
Reissue on *Power of the Force* card	90.00
Loose, with lightsaber	12.00
Death Squad Commander (#38290)	
Original *Star Wars* "12 back" card	275.00
Reissue on *Star Wars* "20/21 back" card	150.00
Reissue on *Empire Strikes Back* card as **Star Destroyer Commander**	100.00
Reissue on *Return of the Jedi* card	75.00
Reissue on Tri-Logo card	75.00
Loose, with pistol	15.00
Han Solo with small head (#38260) brown hair	
Original *Star Wars* "12 back" card	650.00
Reissue on *Star Wars* "20/21 back" card	550.00
Reissue on *Empire Strikes Back* card	300.00
Reissue on *Return of the Jedi* card	175.00
Reissue on *Return of the Jedi* card, new photo	185.00
Reissue on Tri-Logo card	125.00
Loose, with pistol	35.00
Han Solo with large head (#38260) dark brown hair	
Original *Star Wars* "12 back" card	700.00
Reissue on *Star Wars* "20/21 back" card	650.00
Reissue on *Empire Strikes Back* card	250.00
Reissue on *Return of the Jedi* card, new photo	175.00
Reissue on Tri-Logo card	175.00
Loose, with pistol	25.00
Jawa (#38270) vinyl cape, 2¼" figure	
Original *Star Wars* "12 back" card	3,500.00
Loose, with weapon	300.00
Jawa (#38270) cloth cape	
Original *Star Wars* "12 back" card	275.00

Luke Skywalker & Princess Leia Organa (Kenner 1978)

Reissue on *Star Wars* "20/21 back" card.	200.00
Reissue on *Empire Strikes Back* card.	100.00
Reissue on *Return of the Jedi* card.	45.00
Reissue on *Power of the Force* card.	100.00
Reissue on Tri-Logo card	75.00
Loose, with weapon	13.00

Luke Skywalker (#38180) **blond hair**

Original *Star Wars* "12 back" card.	600.00
Reissue on *Star Wars* "20/21 back" card.	250.00
Reissue on *Empire Strikes Back* card.	250.00
Reissue on *Return of the Jedi* card.	225.00
Reissue on *Return of the Jedi* card, new photo.	175.00
Reissue on Tri-Logo card	200.00
Loose, with lightsaber.	35.00

Luke Skywalker (#38180) **brown hair**

Original *Star Wars* "12 back" card.	650.00
Reissue on *Star Wars* "20/21 back" card.	275.00
Reissue on *Empire Strikes Back* card.	300.00
Reissue on *Return of the Jedi* card.	300.00
Reissue on *Return of the Jedi* card, new photo.	175.00
Reissue on Tri-Logo card	250.00
Loose, with lightsaber.	75.00

Princess Leia Organa (#38190) 3½" figure

Original *Star Wars* "12 back" card.	400.00
Reissue on *Star Wars* "20/21 back" card.	275.00
Reissue on *Empire Strikes Back* card.	300.00
Reissue on *Return of the Jedi* card.	425.00
Reissue on Tri-Logo card	150.00
Loose, with pistol	45.00

Sand People (#38280)

Original *Star Wars* "12 back" card.	300.00
Reissue on *Star Wars* "20/21 back" card.	150.00
Reissue on *Empire Strikes Back* card as **Sandpeople** (#38280)	100.00
Reissue on *Return of the Jedi* card as **Tusken Raider** (Sand People)" (#38280)	75.00
Reissue on Tri-Logo card	75.00
Loose, with cloak and weapon	15.00

See-Threepio (C-3PO) (#38220)
    Original *Star Wars* "12 back" card. 300.00
    Reissue on *Star Wars* "20/21 back" card. 100.00
    Reissue on *Empire Strikes Back* card. 50.00
    Reissue on *Return of the Jedi* card. 35.00
    Reissue on Tri-Logo card 45.00
    Loose, no accessories 15.00
Stormtrooper (#38240)
    Original *Star Wars* "12 back" card. 250.00
    Reissue on *Star Wars* "20/21 back" card. 150.00
    Reissue on *Empire Strikes Back* card. 100.00
    Reissue on *Return of the Jedi* card. 50.00
    Reissue on *Power of the Force* card as
        Imperial Stormtrooper 275.00
    Reissue on Tri-Logo card, new photo 60.00
    Loose with weapon 15.00

Second Release (1978–79)
Boba Fett (#39250)
    Original *Star Wars* card $1,500.00
    Reissue on *Empire Strikes Back* card. 400.00
    Reissue on *Return of the Jedi* card. 300.00
    Reissue on *Return of the Jedi* card, new photo. . 350.00
    Reissue on Tri-Logo card. 350.00
    Loose, with pistol 45.00
Boba Fett *see also mail-in figures section below*
Death Star Droid (#39080)
    Original *Star Wars* card 150.00
    Reissue on *Empire Strikes Back* card. 150.00
    Reissue on *Return of the Jedi* card. 75.00
    Reissue on Tri-Logo card. 75.00
    Loose, no accessories 10.00
Greedo (#39020)
    Original *Star Wars* card 200.00
    Reissue on *Empire Strikes Back* card. 125.00
    Reissue on *Return of the Jedi* card. 75.00
    Reissue on Tri-Logo card. 75.00
    Loose, with pistol 10.00

See-Threepio (C-3PO) & Greedo (Kenner 1978–79)

Hammerhead (#39030) 4" figure
Original *Star Wars* card 225.00
Reissue on *Empire Strikes Back* card. 125.00
Reissue on *Return of the Jedi* card. 75.00
Reissue on Tri-Logo card 75.00
Loose with pistol 12.50
Luke Skywalker X-Wing Pilot (#39060)
Original *Star Wars* card 200.00
Reissue on *Empire Strikes Back* card as
Luke Skywalker (X-Wing Pilot) 125.00
Reissue on *Return of the Jedi* card as
Luke Skywalker (X-Wing Fighter Pilot) 50.00
Reissue on *Power of the Force* card. 100.00
Reissue on Tri-Logo card 80.00
Loose, with pistol 15.00
Power Droid (#39090) 2¼" figure
Original *Star Wars* card 145.00
Reissue on *Empire Strikes Back* card. 135.00
Reissue on *Return of the Jedi* card. 55.00
Reissue on Tri-Logo card 75.00
Loose, no accessories 10.00
R5-D4 (#39070) 2½" figure
Original *Star Wars* card 150.00
Reissue on *Empire Strikes Back* card. 140.00
Reissue on *Return of the Jedi* card. 65.00
Reissue on Tri-Logo card 75.00
Loose, no accessories 10.00
Snaggletooth (**red**) (#39040) 2¾" figure
Original *Star Wars* card 175.00
Reissue on *Empire Strikes Back* card. 150.00
Reissue on *Return of the Jedi* card. 55.00
Reissue on Tri-Logo card 75.00
Loose, with pistol 10.00
Snaggletooth (**blue**) (Sears Exclusive) 3¾" figure
loose only, from Cantina Adventure Set 200.00
Walrus Man (#39050)
Original *Star Wars* card 175.00
Reissue on *Empire Strikes Back* card. 125.00

Power Droid & R5-D4 (Kenner 1978–79)

Reissue on *Return of the Jedi* card. 60.00
Reissue on Tri-Logo card 75.00
Loose, with pistol 12.50

STAR WARS:
THE EMPIRE STRIKES BACK
Kenner (1980–82)

In the second movie of the series we learn the secret of Luke's parentage and meet Yoda, played by a puppet, and Lando Calrissian, played by Billy Dee Williams. There are lots of new figures. Luke loses his hand, C-3PO gets chopped into pieces, Han Solo gets to cool off on the way to Jabba's palace, and Lando gets his ship and favorite Wookie back. Not to worry, though, because before the movie is over Luke gets a new hand, C-3PO gets put back together, and Lando turns out to be a good guy and not a traitor.

The first Empire Strikes Back figures appeared on 31-back cards, but the earlier 21 figures were re-released on 21-back cards with the Empire Strikes Back Logo.

Lots of neat figures and vehicles were produced. They are cheap by the standards of the first series, but valuable by any other standard.

3¾" Figures (1980)
Bespin Security Guard (#39810) **white**
    Original *Empire Strikes Back* card $75.00
    Reissue on *Return of the Jedi* card. 35.00
    Reissue on Tri-Logo card 25.00
    Loose, with pistol 10.00
Bossk (Bounty Hunter) (#39760)
    Original *Empire Strikes Back* card 125.00
    Reissue on *Return of the Jedi* card. 75.00
    Reissue on Tri-Logo card 55.00
    Loose, with rifle 10.00

Han Solo (Hoth Outfit) & IG-88 (Kenner 1980)

Lando Calrissian & Leia Organa (Bespin Gown) turtle neck (Kenner 1980)

FX-7 (Medical Droid) (#39730)
    Original *Empire Strikes Back* card 75.00
    Reissue on *Return of the Jedi* card. 40.00
    Reissue on Tri-Logo card. 60.00
    Loose, no accessories 10.00
Han Solo (Hoth Outfit) (#39790)
    Original *Empire Strikes Back* card 100.00
    Reissue on *Return of the Jedi* card. 75.00
    Reissue on Tri-Logo card 40.00
    Loose, with pistol 15.00
IG-88 (Bounty Hunter) (#39770) 4½" figure
    Original *Empire Strikes Back* card 150.00
    Reissue on *Return of the Jedi* card. 75.00
    Reissue on Tri-Logo card 75.00
    Loose, with rifle and pistol 15.00
Imperial Stormtrooper (Hoth Battle Gear) (#39740)
    Original *Empire Strikes Back* card 100.00
    Reissue on *Return of the Jedi* card. 50.00
    Reissue on Tri-Logo card 50.00
    Loose, with rifle 10.00
Lando Calrissian (#39800) **no teeth** version
    Original *Empire Strikes Back* card 75.00
    Loose, with pistol 12.50
    white teeth version
    Original *Empire Strikes Back* card 75.00
    Reissue on *Return of the Jedi* card. 45.00
    Reissue on Tri-Logo card 45.00
    Loose, with pistol 15.00
Leia Organa (Bespin Gown) (#39720) **crew neck**
    Original *Empire Strikes Back* card 200.00
    Original *Empire Strikes Back* card, new photo . . 175.00
    Reissue on *Return of the Jedi* card. 125.00
    Loose, in cloak with pistol. 20.00
Leia Organa (Bespin Gown) (#39720) **turtle neck**
    Original *Empire Strikes Back* card, ... 200.00
    Original *Empire Strikes Back* card, new photo . . 175.00
    Reissue on *Return of the Jedi* card. 150.00
    Reissue on Tri-Logo card 125.00

Loose, in cloak with pistol. 20.00
Luke Skywalker (Bespin Fatigues) (#39780)
    Original *Empire Strikes Back* card 200.00
    Reissue on *Return of the Jedi* card, new photo,
      yellow hair 140.00
    Reissue on Tri-Logo card 125.00
    Loose, with pistol and lightsaber. 20.00
    Reissue on *Empire Strikes Back* card, **brown
      hair**, new photo 150.00
    Reissue on *Return of the Jedi* card. 90.00
    Reissue on Tri-Logo card 125.00
    Loose, with pistol and lightsaber. 20.00
Rebel Soldier (Hoth Battle Gear) (#39750)
    Original *Empire Strikes Back* card 75.00
    Reissue on *Return of the Jedi* card. 35.00
    Reissue on Tri-Logo card 25.00
    Loose, with pistol 10.00

IG-88 & AT-AT Driver (Kenner 1981)

Second Release (1981)
2-1B (#39399)
    Original *Empire Strikes Back* card. $100.00
    Reissue on *Return of the Jedi* card as **Too-
      Onebee (2-1B)** (#71600) 50.00
    Reissue on Tri-Logo card 40.00
    Loose, with weapon 10.00
AT-AT Driver (#39379)
    Original *Empire Strikes Back* card 90.00
    Reissue on *Return of the Jedi* card. 35.00
    Reissue on *Power of the Force* card, foreign only 500.00
    Reissue on Tri-Logo card 75.00
    Loose, with rifle 10.00
Dengar (#39329)
    Original *Empire Strikes Back* card 60.00
    Reissue on *Return of the Jedi* card. 35.00
    Reissue on Tri-Logo card 25.00
    Loose, with rifle 10.00
Han Solo (Bespin Outfit) (#39339)
    Original *Empire Strikes Back* card 125.00

Reissue on *Return of the Jedi* card. 75.00
Reissue on Tri-Logo card 40.00
Loose, with pistol 15.00
Imperial Commander (#39389)
Original *Empire Strikes Back* card 50.00
Reissue on *Return of the Jedi* card. 35.00
Reissue on Tri-Logo card 25.00
Loose, with pistol 10.00
Leia Organa (Hoth Outfit) (#39359)
On original *Empire Strikes Back* card 125.00
Reissue on *Return of the Jedi* card. 100.00
Reissue on *Return of the Jedi* card, new photo. . . 75.00
Reissue on Tri-Logo card 60.00
Loose, with pistol 20.00
Lobot (#39349)
Original *Empire Strikes Back* card 45.00
Reissue on *Return of the Jedi* card. 35.00
Reissue on Tri-Logo card 25.00
Loose, with pistol 8.00
Rebel Commander (#39369)
Original *Empire Strikes Back* card 50.00
Reissue on *Return of the Jedi* card. 30.00
Reissue on Tri-Logo card 25.00
Loose, with rifle 10.00
Ugnaught (#39319)
Original *Empire Strikes Back* card 50.00
Reissue on *Return of the Jedi* card. 35.00
Reissue on Tri-Logo card 25.00
Loose, in blue smock with case 10.00
Yoda (with **orange snake**) (#38310)
On original *Empire Strikes Back* card 150.00
Loose, with snake 20.00
Yoda (with **brown snake**)
Original *Empire Strikes Back* card 250.00
Reissue on *Return of the Jedi* card. 100.00
Reissue on *Return of the Jedi* card as **Yoda,
The Jedi Master** 100.00
Reissue on *Power of the Force* card. 400.00

Lobot & Yoda, with orange snake (Kenner 1981)

AT-AT Commander & Cloud Car Pilot (Kenner 1982)

    Reissue on Tri-Logo card 90.00
    Loose, with snake 25.00

Third Release (1982)
4-LOM (#70010)
    Original *Empire Strikes Back* card. $175.00
    Reissue on *Return of the Jedi* card. 50.00
    Reissue on Tri-Logo card 25.00
    Loose, with weapon 15.00
Artoo-Detoo (R2-D2) (with Sensorscope) (#69590)
    Original *Empire Strikes Back* card 75.00
    Reissue on *Return of the Jedi* card (#69420) 40.00
    Reissue on Tri-Logo card 28.00
    Loose, with scope 12.50
AT-AT Commander (#69620)
    Original *Empire Strikes Back* card 60.00
    Reissue on *Return of the Jedi* card. 45.00
    Reissue on Tri-Logo card 25.00
    Loose, with pistol 10.00
Bespin Security Guard (#69640) **black**
    Original *Empire Strikes Back* card 65.00
    Reissue on *Return of the Jedi* card. 55.00
    Reissue on Tri-Logo card 25.00
    Loose, with pistol 10.00
C-3PO (Removable Limbs) (#69600)
    Original *Empire Strikes Back* card 90.00
    Reissue on *Return of the Jedi* card as **See-
        Threepio (C-3PO)** (#69430) "now with re-
        movable arms, legs and back pack" 35.00
    Reissue on *Power of the Force* card as **See-
        Threepio (C-3PO)** with removable limbs 75.00
    Reissue on Tri-Logo card 25.00
    Loose, with back pack and limbs 10.00
Cloud Car Pilot (Twin Pod) (#69630)
    Original *Empire Strikes Back* card 125.00
    Reissue on *Return of the Jedi* card. 45.00
    Reissue on Tri-Logo card 30.00
    Loose, with pistol and light 20.00

Imperial TIE Fighter Pilot (#70030)
    Original *Empire Strikes Back* card 100.00
    Reissue on *Return of the Jedi* card. 60.00
    Reissue on Tri-Logo card 90.00
    Loose, with pistol 15.00
Luke Skywalker (Hoth Battle Gear) (#69610)
    Original *Empire Strikes Back* card 75.00
    Reissue on *Return of the Jedi* card. 40.00
    Reissue on Tri-Logo card 30.00
    Loose, with rifle 10.00
Zuckuss (#70020)
    Original *Empire Strikes Back* card 125.00
    Reissue on *Return of the Jedi* card. 50.00
    Reissue on Tri-Logo card 25.00
    Loose, with rifle 10.00

Biker Scout & Gamorrean Guard (Kenner 1983)

STAR WARS:
RETURN OF THE JEDI
Kenner (1983)

The third movie in the series had the distinct advantage of being able to tie up all the loose ends and have the Rebels win. Solo is rescued, Jabba gets his just deserts, the new, improved, even bigger Death Star is blown up and the Ewoks steal the show. Everybody went home happy.

Collectors were happy too, with plenty of figures and vehicles to collect. They were even happier a couple of years later when the series had finally run its course with kids, and the figures finally became red tag specials. Super Powers figures were red tag specials around the same time. You just couldn't go wrong, no matter what you bought.

3¾ Figures (1983)
Admiral Ackbar (#70310?)
    Original *Return of the Jedi* card $30.00
    Reissue on Tri-Logo card 25.00

Loose, with staff 10.00
Bib Fortuna (#70790)
    Original *Return of the Jedi* card 30.00
    Reissue on Tri-Logo card 25.00
    Loose, with brown cloak and staff 10.00
Biker Scout (#70820)
    Original *Return of the Jedi* card 35.00
    Reissue on *Power of the Force* card 80.00
    Reissue on Tri-Logo card 25.00
    Loose, with pistol 15.00
Chief Chirpa (#70690)
    Original *Return of the Jedi* card 30.00
    Reissue on Tri-Logo card 25.00
    Loose, with long club 10.00
Emperor's Royal Guard (#70680)
    Original *Return of the Jedi* card 40.00
    Reissue on Tri-Logo card 60.00
    Loose, with staff 10.00
Gamorrean Guard (#70670)
    Original *Return of the Jedi* card 25.00
    Reissue on *Power of the Force* card, foreign only 250.00
    Reissue on Tri-Logo card 25.00
    Loose, with axe 10.00
General Madine (#70780)
    Original *Return of the Jedi* card 30.00
    Reissue on Tri-Logo card 20.00
    Loose, with staff 10.00
Klaatu (#70730) with **tan arms** or **gray arms**
    Original *Return of the Jedi* card 30.00
    Reissue on Tri-Logo card 20.00
    Loose, with apron and spear 10.00
Lando Calrissian (Skiff Guard Disguise) (#70830)
    Original *Return of the Jedi* card 45.00
    Reissue on Tri-Logo card 25.00
    Loose, with spear 15.00
Logray (Ewok Medicine Man)
    Original *Return of the Jedi* card 30.00
    Reissue on Tri-Logo card 25.00

General Madine & Klaatu (Kenner 1983)

Logray (Ewok Medicine Man) &
Luke Skywalker (Jedi Knight Outfit) (Kenner 1983)

Loose, with mask, staff and pouch 10.00
Luke Skywalker (Jedi Knight Outfit) (#70650)
    With **green lightsaber**
    Original *Return of the Jedi* card 100.00
    Reissue on *Power of the Force* card. 250.00
    Reissue on Tri-Logo card 60.00
    Loose, with cloak, pistol and green lightsaber. . . . 40.00
    With **blue lightsaber**, scarce
    Original *Return of the Jedi* card 175.00
    Reissue on Tri-Logo card 90.00
    Loose, with cloak, pistol and blue lightsaber 60.00
Nien Nunb (#70840)
    Original *Return of the Jedi* card 35.00
    Reissue on Tri-Logo card 50.00
    Loose, with pistol 9.00
Princess Leia Organa (Boushh Disguise) (#70660)
    Original *Return of the Jedi* card 60.00
    Reissue on Tri-Logo card 75.00
    Loose, with helmet and weapon 15.00
Rebel Commando (#70740)
    Original *Return of the Jedi* card 30.00
    Reissue on Tri-Logo card, new photo 20.00
    Loose, with rifle 10.00
Ree-Yees (#70800)
    Original *Return of the Jedi* card 30.00
    Reissue on Tri-Logo card 25.00
    Loose, with weapon 10.00
Squid Head (#70770)
    Original *Return of the Jedi* card 30.00
    Reissue on Tri-Logo card 25.00
    Loose, with pistol and cloak 10.00
Weequay
    Original *Return of the Jedi* card 30.00
    Reissue on Tri-Logo card 25.00
    Loose, with spear 15.00

Action Figures

Second release (1984)

8D8 (#71210)
Original *Return of the Jedi* card $30.00
Reissue on Tri-Logo card 20.00
Loose, no accessories 10.00

AT-ST Driver (#71330)
Original *Return of the Jedi* card 30.00
Reissue on *Power of the Force* card 60.00
Reissue on Tri-Logo card 20.00
Loose, with pistol 10.00

B-Wing Pilot (#71280)
Original *Return of the Jedi* card 30.00
Reissue on *Power of the Force* card 30.00
Reissue on Tri-Logo card 20.00
Loose, with pistol 10.00

The Emperor (#71240)
Original *Return of the Jedi* card 35.00
Reissue on *Power of the Force* card 75.00
Reissue on Tri-Logo card 20.00
Loose, with cane 10.00

Han Solo (in Trench Coat) (#71300)
Original *Return of the Jedi* card 50.00
Reissue on *Power of the Force* card 500.00
Reissue on Tri-Logo card 25.00
Loose, with camo coat and pistol 15.00

Klaatu (in Skiff Guard Outfit) (#71290)
Original *Return of the Jedi* card 30.00
Reissue on Tri-Logo card 25.00
Loose, with weapon 10.00

Lumat (#93760)
Original *Return of the Jedi* card 40.00
Reissue on *Power of the Force* card 50.00
Reissue on Tri-Logo card 25.00
Loose, with bow 15.00

Nikto (#71190)
Original *Return of the Jedi* card 30.00
Reissue on *Power of the Force* card, foreign only 500.00
Reissue on Tri-Logo card 25.00

The Emperor & Han Solo (in Trench Coat) (Kenner 1984)

Nikto & Sy Snootles and the Rebo Band (Kenner 1984)

```
        Loose, with staff . . . . . . . . . . . . . . . . . . . . . . . .  10.00
Paploo (#93680)
        Original Return of the Jedi card . . . . . . . . . . . . .  40.00
        Reissue on Power of the Force card. . . . . . . . . .  45.00
        Reissue on Tri-Logo card . . . . . . . . . . . . . . . . . .  50.00
        Loose, with staff . . . . . . . . . . . . . . . . . . . . . . . .  15.00
Princess Leia Organa (in Combat Poncho) (#71220)
        Original Return of the Jedi card . . . . . . . . . . . . .  60.00
        Reissue on Power of the Force card. . . . . . . . . . 100.00
        Reissue on Tri-Logo card . . . . . . . . . . . . . . . . . .  25.00
        Loose in poncho with pistol . . . . . . . . . . . . . . . .  15.00
Prune Face (#71320)
        Original Return of the Jedi card . . . . . . . . . . . . .  30.00
        Reissue on Tri-Logo card . . . . . . . . . . . . . . . . . .  25.00
        Loose, with cloak and rifle . . . . . . . . . . . . . . . . .  10.00
Rancor Keeper (#71350)
        Original Return of the Jedi card . . . . . . . . . . . . .  30.00
        Reissue on Tri-Logo card . . . . . . . . . . . . . . . . . .  45.00
        Loose, with prodd. . . . . . . . . . . . . . . . . . . . . . . .  10.00
Teebo (#71310)
        Original Return of the Jedi card . . . . . . . . . . . . .  40.00
        Reissue on Power of the Force card. . . . . . . . . . 200.00
        Reissue on Tri-Logo card . . . . . . . . . . . . . . . . . .  25.00
        Loose, with club, mask and pouch . . . . . . . . . . .  15.00
Wicket W. Warrick (#71230)
        Original Return of the Jedi card . . . . . . . . . . . . .  50.00
        Reissue on Power of the Force card. . . . . . . . . . 200.00
        Reissue on Tri-Logo card . . . . . . . . . . . . . . . . . .  25.00
        Loose, with spear. . . . . . . . . . . . . . . . . . . . . . . .  12.50
```

Multi-Pack

```
Sy Snootles and the Rebo Band
        Original Return of the Jedi card . . . . . . . . . . . . $150.00
        Reissue on Tri-Logo card . . . . . . . . . . . . . . . . . .  95.00
        Loose: Sy Snootles, Droopy McCool or Max
            Rebo, each. . . . . . . . . . . . . . . . . . . . . . . . . . .  15.00
```

Amanaman & A-Wing Pilot (Kenner 1985)

STAR WARS:
THE POWER OF THE FORCE
Kenner (1985)

The Power of the Force figures were produced after all three movies had come and gone. Without a new movie to pump-up sales, fewer of these figures were ordered, and many that were scheduled were never made. As sales slowed, collector interest waned and the figures became red tag specials. When the collectors finally realized that they didn't have these figures, it was too late, and so now they are among the most valuable of Star Wars figures. Several were released only overseas.

There are 15 new figures in this series, plus 22 figures that were reissued, and are listed above. All of them came with coins, making a total of 37 figures that came with coins. However, two foreign release figures (AT-AT Driver and Nikto) came with coins from other figures, so only 35 different coins came with these 37 figures.

However, coins were also available as a mail-in premium with a proof of purchase from some prior *The Empire Strikes Back* and *Return of the Jedi* figures, and so there are actually 62 coins in the series to collect.

3¾" Figures (1985) with silver colored aluminum coin
Amanaman (#93740) 5"
      Original *Power of the Force* card $275.00
      Reissue on Tri-Logo card 150.00
      Loose, with something 100.00
Anakin Skywalker (#93790) foreign release
      Original *Power of the Force* card 2,000.00
      Reissue on Tri-Logo card 125.00
      Loose, no accessories 30.00

Artoo-Detoo (R2-D2) with Pop-up Lightsaber (#93720)
    Original *Power of the Force* card 175.00
    Reissue on Tri-Logo card 150.00
    Loose, with lightsaber. 90.00
A-Wing Pilot (#93830)
    Original *Power of the Force* card 100.00
    Reissue on *DROIDS* card. 175.00
    Reissue on Tri-Logo card 75.00
    Loose, with pistol 50.00
Barada (#93750)
    Original *Power of the Force* card 100.00
    Reissue on Tri-Logo card 60.00
    Loose, with staff. 40.00
EV-9D9 (#93800)
    Original *Power of the Force* card 150.00
    Reissue on Tri-Logo card 125.00
    Loose, no accessories 75.00
Han Solo (in Carbonite Chamber) (#93770)
    Original *Power of the Force* card 250.00
    Reissue on Tri-Logo card, figure on top 200.00
    Loose, with carbonite sheet 100.00
Imperial Dignitary (#93850)
    Original *Power of the Force* card 75.00
    Reissue on Tri-Logo card 50.00
    Loose, no accessories 30.00
Imperial Gunner (#93760)
    Original *Power of the Force* card 150.00
    Reissue on Tri-Logo card 125.00
    Loose, with pistol 80.00
Lando Calrissian (General Pilot) (#93820)
    Original *Power of the Force* card 110.00
    Reissue on Tri-Logo card 75.00
    Loose, with cape and pistol 60.00
Luke Skywalker (in Battle Poncho) (#93710)
    Original *Power of the Force* card 125.00
    Reissue on Tri-Logo card 90.00
    Loose, with poncho and pistol 60.00

EV-9D9 & Luke Skywalker, Imperial Stormtrooper Outfit
(Kenner 1984)

Luke Skywalker, Imperial Stormtrooper Outfit (#93780)
> Original *Power of the Force* card 425.00
> Reissue on Tri-Logo card 225.00
> Loose, with removable helmet and pistol 175.00

Romba (#93730)
> Original *Power of the Force* card 50.00
> Reissue on Tri-Logo card 30.00
> Loose, with spear. 20.00

Warok (#93810)
> Original *Power of the Force* card 75.00
> Reissue on Tri-Logo card 60.00
> Loose, with bow and pouch 25.00

Yak Face (#93840) foreign release
> Original *Power of the Force* card 1,900.00
> Reissue on Tri-Logo card 325.00
> Loose, with staff. 250.00

Admiral Ackbar & Dengar (Kenner 1984–86)

TRI-LOGO (RETURN OF THE JEDI)
Kenner (1984–86)

Tri-Logo is just the universally used collector's short-hand name for figures on header cards with *Return of the Jedi* logos in three languages. Different Tri-Logo cards were made for different countries, but collectors generally ignore such differences and all such cards for a given figure have the same value—generally a lower value than the same figure on any other type of card. Tri-Logo figures are often in lesser condition than those from other series, which further reduces their value. Figures on beat-up cards are often worth little more than the corresponding loose figure. There are no new figures in this "series." so all of the prices and figures are listed under the previous series.

Artoo-Detoo R2-D2 & King Gorneesh (Kenner 1985)

(THE TV ANIMATED SERIES) DROIDS
"THE ADVENTURES OF R2-D2 AND C-3PO"
Kenner (1985)

The real movies were gone from the theaters, but there was still money to be made, so a couple of Ewok movies (*The Ewok Adventure* and *Ewoks: The Battle For Endor*) were produced, along with both an Ewoks and a Droids animated ABC television series. We didn't see any of them when they came out and they put us to sleep when we try to watch them on television. They must do the same to just about everybody, because the figures haven't attained much of a collector following. This may be undeserved, because, judged on their own, the figures are not too bad. So far, anyway, these figures haven't gotten much of a boost in value from the incredible popularity of the Star Wars series, and the recent re-releases and hype. Maybe they will, or maybe all the money will chase the huge pile of new figures and other collectibles and these will be completely overlooked.

3¾" Figures (1985) with copper or gold colored coin
Artoo-Detoo R2-D2 (#71780) with pop-up lightsaber . $100.00
  Loose. 50.00
Boba Fett (#39260) 1,000.00
  Loose. 50.00
Jann Tosh (#71840) 20.00
  Loose. 10.00
Jord Dusat (#71810) 20.00
  Loose. 10.00
Kea Moll (#71800) 20.00
  Loose. 10.00
Kez-Iban (#71850) 20.00
  Loose. 10.00
See-Threepio C-3PO (#71770) 125.00
  Loose. 50.00

Sise Fromm (#71820) 100.00
    Loose. 50.00
Thall Joben (#71790) 20.00
    Loose. 10.00
Tig Fromm (#71830?). 100.00
    Loose. 50.00
Uncle Gundy (#71880) 15.00
    Loose. 9.00
See also A-Wing Pilot, listed previously.

EWOKS
Kenner (1985)

3¾" Figures (1985) with copper or gold colored coin
Dulok Shaman (#71150). $15.00
    Loose. 9.00
Dulok Scout (#71160). 15.00
    Loose. 9.00
King Gorneesh (#71180) 15.00
    Loose. 9.00
Logray (Ewok medicine man) (#71260) 15.00
    Loose. 9.00
Urgah Lady Gorneesh (#71170) 15.00
    Loose. 9.00
Wicket W. Warrick (#71250). 20.00
    Loose. 10.00

*Sise Fromm & Dulok Shaman, loose figures, with coins
(Kenner 1985)*

LOOSE FIGURES

A lot of *Star Wars* figures are collected as loose figures. This is a popular type of collecting for persons whose mothers did not throw away all their *Star Wars* figures when they left home. There's nothing like finding half the figures for your collection in a box in your own attic. The condition of the figure, and finding the correct weapons and accessories is usually the challenge. The prices above are for near mint figures complete with original weapons and accessories.

*Boba Fett mail-in figure with box and Note to Consumers
(Kenner 1979)*

MAIL-INS

Mail-in offers

Early Bird Kit, 4 figures (1977). . . . . see page 1
Boba Fett with "Rocket Launcher," unpainted blue/gray
    with red missile, mailer box and letter (1979) . . $200.00
Bossk, Boba Fett, Darth Vader, IG-88 in plastic bags,
    Kenner logo, plus mailer box (#38871, 1980) . . . 200.00
Bossk (1980) 25.00
Display Arena (1981). . . . . see Display Stands, page 54
4-LOM (1982) 25.00
Admiral Ackbar (1983) 20.00
Nien Nunb (1983) 20.00
The Emperor (1984). 20.00
Anakin Skywalker (1985) 40.00
Coins (1986) . . . . See Coins section

TWO PACKS, THREE PACKS
AND SIX PACKS

In addition to all the different versions of the figures previously listed, Kenner also produced various multi-packs from time to time. "Action Figure Sets" of three figures were issued for each of the three movies. They were subtitled "Hero Set," "Villain Set," "Rebel Set," etc. They are quite scarce, and worth about $400.00 to $500.00 each, regardless of movie. Some *Star Wars* sets came with a back-drop scene and they are worth about $100.00 extra.

Two six-pack sets of figures were issued for *The Empire Strikes Back* movie. They are worth about $300.00 today. Last, and least, *Return of the Jedi* two-packs were issued with leftover figures. They are worth the price of the two loose figures contained in the pack (if they have their weapons) and maybe an additional dollar or two for oddity.

Action Figures

Classic Edition 4-Pack (Kenner 1995)

STAR WARS (NEW)

THE POWER OF THE FORCE
Kenner (1995–96)

Kenner reintroduced the *Star Wars* figures starting in 1995. The first item to appear was the Classic Edition 4-Pack and, in some ways, it is the functional equivalent of the Early Bird Figures from the original series—an initial four figures which are not on their own header cards. They caused some initial controversy because they were quite similar to the originals (which, loose, sell for over $25.00 each) but just enough differences were discovered so that collectors could tell them apart.

Star Wars Power of the Force Classic Edition 4-Pack, including Luke Skywalker, Han Solo, Darth Vader and Chewbacca with 4 Topps "Star Wars" widevision special cards (#69595, 1995). $55.00

When the carded figures appeared, collectors quickly got hot on the trail of variations in the other figures, and in the packaging. The lightsabers were shortened, yielding variations for Darth Vader, Luke Skywalker, and Ben (Obi-Wan) Kenobi. The later figure also had a packaging change with his original head photo being replaced by a full-figure photo. If short lightsabers were not enough, some figures were found with short lightsabers in the plastic slots designed for long sabers. These are scarce and highly collectible.

Packaging Variations
The most significant packaging changes in the new series is in the color of the header card. The 1995 and 1996 header cards have a red or orange laser blast running diagonally across them, while the 1997 cards have a green laser blast. Shadows of the Empire figures, from late 1996, are on

Action Figures

*Red Card and Green Card package revision numbers
(Kenner 1995 & 1997)*

purple laser blast cards. In 1998, the cards remained green, but all figures have a "Freeze Frame Action Slide."

Package Printing numbers

Sometime in 1996, collectors noticed that packaging changes could be tracked by a small "revision number" printed on the back. The first six digits of the number are unique to the particular figure and do not change even if the UPC code or the figure's name are changed. However, it's the two digits after the decimal point that collectors look at. The first version of each package is numbered ".00" and each time there is a printing change this number is increased, so that if there have been three changes, the number will read ".03" and so on. However, this number only works for *printing* changes, not for variations in the figure itself. Throughout this section, these numbers are reported in [brackets] so as to distinguish them from UPC codes, which are listed in (parentheses).

Collection Numbers

When Kenner switched to Green Cards in early 1997, they put "collection numbers" on the cards. The idea was to sort the action figures into groups so that "Collection 1" would be the Rebel Alliance, "Collection 3" would be the Galactic Empire and "Collection 2" would be the various non-aligned aliens.

Unfortunately, there weren't equal numbers of each type, and new figures were not added at uniform rates in each group, but all boxes have to contain 16 figures. The result has been that a lot of figures came out in the "wrong" collection and later in the "right" collection. The five most important, i.e. valuable, collection "errors" are Grand Moff Tarkin, Ponda Baba, Weequay Skiff Guard, Yoda, and Rebel Fleet Trooper, all of whom came out first in Collection 2, but were soon switched to other collections.

Other Packaging Variations

A holo sticker picture was added to the header cards about the time that Kenner switched from red/orange to green. and in early 1998 a number of the figures could be found without stickers, so many figures are available both with and without the sticker. The peg holes used for hanging the figure were widened in mid-1997 and the bubble was changed so that the carded figure would stand up. None of these changes has had much effect on value, but the difference in holo stickers might be significant some day.

Other Figure Variations

Luke Skywalker (Jedi Knight) originally came with a brown vest, but this was switched to black, matching the rest of his costume. Boba Fett now comes with a black circle on the back of each hand. Originally he had a bar across this circle, forming two "half-circles." Late in 1997 a variation occurred in Han Solo in Endor Gear. His pants changed color from Navy blue (almost black) to brown. These changes have had a significant effect of value.

RED CARD SERIES

3¾" Figures (Kenner 1995–96)
Ben (Obi-Wan) Kenobi with "Lightsaber and Removable Cloak" (#69576) head photo, long
lightsaber $45.00
    Full-figure photo on package, long lightsaber 50.00
    Loose, with long lightsaber 12.50
    Full-figure photo, short lightsaber 7.50
Boba Fett with "Sawed-Off Blaster Rifle and Jet Pack" (#69582) with half circle on one hand and
full circle on other hand [.00] 250.00
    Loose, with half circle on both hands 50.00
    Full circle on both hands [.01] 15.00
Chewbacca with "Bowcaster and Heavy Blaster
Rifle" (#69578) 6.00
C-3PO with "Realistic Metalized Body" (#69573) 10.00
Darth Vader with "Lightsaber and Removable Cape"
(#69572) with long lightsaber [.00] 25.00
    Loose, with long lightsaber 10.00

Boba Fett & Darth Vader (short lightsaber) (Kenner 1995 & 1996)

Action Figures

Lando Calrissian & Princess Leia Organa (Kenner 1995 & 1996)

Short lightsaber in long package slot	40.00
Short lightsaber version	7.50
Han Solo with "Heavy Assault Rifle and Blaster" (#69577)	9.00
Han Solo in Carbonite with "Carbonite Freezing Chamber" (#69613) back says "Carbonite freezing chamber"	15.00
Variation, back says "Carbonite Block"	7.50
Han Solo in Hoth Gear with "Blaster Pistol and Assault Rifle" (#69587) closed hand	6.00
Variation with open hand	25.00
Loose, with open hand	8.00
Jedi Knight Luke Skywalker with "Lightsaber and Removable Cloak" (#69596) with brown vest	75.00
Loose, with brown vest	12.00
Black vest	8.00
Lando Calrissian with "Heavy Rifle and Blaster Pistol" (#69583) [.00]	10.00
Luke Skywalker with "Grappling-Hook Blaster and Lightsaber" (#69571) with long lightsaber	40.00
Loose, with long lightsaber	12.50
Short lightsaber version	10.00
Luke Skywalker in Dagobah Fatigues with "Light-saber and Blaster Pistol" (#69588) with long lightsaber	30.00
Loose, with long lightsaber	6.00
Short lightsaber in long package slot	25.00
Short lightsaber	20.00
Luke Skywalker in X-Wing Fighter Pilot Gear with "Lightsaber and Blaster Pistol" (#69581) with long lightsaber	25.00
Loose, with long lightsaber	6.00
Short lightsaber in long package slot	20.00
Short lightsaber	15.00
Princess Leia Organa with "Laser Pistol and Assault Rifle" (#69579) [.00]	10.00
R2-D2 with "Light Pipe Eye Port and Retractable Leg" (#69574)	6.00

Stormtrooper with "Blaster Rifle and Heavy Infantry
      Cannon" (#69575) 8.00
TIE Fighter Pilot with "Imperial Blaster Pistol and
      Rifle" (#69584) with small-parts warning printed
      on sticker [.00] 30.00
      Warning printed on card [.01] 6.00
      Reissue [.02] 5.00
Yoda with "Jedi Trainer Backpack and Gimer Stick"
      (#69586) [.00] 7.50
      Reissue [.01] 6.00

Dash Rendar & Prince Xizor (Kenner 1996)

STAR WARS:
SHADOWS OF THE EMPIRE
Kenner (1996)

Shadows of the Empire figures appeared in September 1996 and were very popular. All the collectors bought them, and then looked at every minute detail in an effort to spot some valuable variation. Unfortunately, none were found, and the figures were all available at retail prices. All come with a holographic or reflective picture on a sticker pasted on the card. They are based on the book series, not on any of the movies. Then, in early 1998, a Leia in Boushh Disguise figure turned up with "Collection 1" on it. This variation has proven to be quite elusive.

In early 1999, leftover figures from this series appeared at Kay-Bee stores, giving collectors a chance to grab any that they had missed, and keeping the collector price down for the time being.

PURPLE CARD

3¾" Figures (Sept. 1996)
Chewbacca in Bounty Hunter Disguise, with "Vibro
      Axe and Heavy Blaster Rifle" (#69562) $7.00
Dash Rendar, with "Heavy Weapons Pack" (#69561) . . . 7.00

Leia in Boushh Disguise, with "Blaster Rifle and
    Bounty Hunter Helmet" (#69602) 8.00
       Variation "Collection 1" on card. 150.00
Luke Skywalker in Imperial Guard Disguise, with
    "Taser Staff Weapon" (#69566). 7.00
Prince Xizor, with "Energy Blade Shields" (#69594) 7.00

Two-Packs, with special comic book
Darth Vader vs. Xizor (#69567) without "vehicle of
    choice". 20.00
       Variation, with "*Vehicle of Choice Slave I*". 15.00
Boba Fett vs. IG-88 (#69568). 30.00

RED CARD TRANSITION FIGURES

    The fourth batch of Power of the Force figures
appeared in December 1996 with the captions "Collection 1"
or "Collection 2" at the top. The two collections appeared at
the same time, and the earliest versions came on a header card
with an red laser blast, the same color used on the other
"Power of the Force" figures from 1995–96. Later header
cards had a green laser blast.

    The Tatooine Stormtrooper (red-carded) and the
Sandtrooper (green-carded) are identical—only the name had
been changed to confuse the weary collector. That figure, and
most of the other figures in collections 1 and 2, also had
changes in the name of their weapon. Just as collectors were
digesting these changes, holographic sticker pictures were
added to the cards, making a third or fourth version of some
figures. All this was happening at the end of 1996 and early
in 1997—by early 1998 no one cared any more. Plain picture
and holographic sticker sell for the same price. Holographic
pictures do not reproduce well in black and white so the pictures in this section are of figures with plain pictures. See the
color section for pictures of green card figures with holographic stickers.

Tatooine Stormtrooper (Red Card, Collection 1)
& Sandtrooper (Green Card, Collection 3 (Kenner 1996 & 1997)

Action Figures

*Luke Skywalker in StormtrooperDisguise (Collection 2, Red Card)
& (Collection 1, Green Card) (Kenner 1996 & 1997)*

3¾" Figures (1996–Early 1997) Red Cards—Green Cards
Death Star Gunner with "Radiation Suit and Blaster
    Pistol" (#69608) on original red Col. 1 card [.00] . $25.00
    Reissue now with "Imperial Blaster and Assault
       Rifle" (#69608) on green Col. 1 card [.01]. 12.00
    Reissue with holo picture 10.00
Greedo, with "Rodian Blaster Pistol" (#69606) on
    original red Col 1. card [.00] 25.00
    Reissue with "Blaster Pistol" on green Col. 1
       card [.01] 12.00
    Reissue with holo picture 10.00
Jawas with "Glowing Eyes and Ionization Blasters"
    (#69607) on original red Col. 2 card [.00] 25.00
    Reissue, now with "Glowing Eyes and Blaster
       Pistols" on green Col. 2 card (#69607) [.02] . . . 15.00
    Reissue with holo picture 12.00
Luke Skywalker in "Stormtrooper Disguise with
    Imperial Issue Blaster" (#69604) On original
    red Col. 2 card [.00] 35.00
    Reissue on green Col. 2 card (#69604) [.01]. 12.00
    Reissue with holo picture 10.00
Momaw Nadon "Hammerhead" with "Double-Barrel-
    ed Laser Canon" (#69629) On original red Col. 2
    card [.00] 20.00
    Reissue, now with "Double-Barreled Blaster
       Rifle" on green Col. 2 card (#69629) [.01]. 12.00
    Reissue with holo picture 10.00
R5-D4 with "Concealed Photon Missile Launcher"
    (#69598) On original red Col. 2 card, no small
    parts warning [.00] Straight Latch 20.00
    Reissue, with small parts warning, straight latch . . 20.00
    Reissue, with "Concealed Missile Launcher"
       (#69598) on green Col. 2 card with warning
       [.01] hooked latch 12.00
    Reissue with holo picture, Hooked Latch 10.00
Tatooine Stormtrooper with "Concussion Grenade
    Cannon" (#69601) original red Col. 1 card [.00] . . 25.00
    Reissue as **Sandtrooper**, with "Heavy Blaster

Action Figures

    Rifle" (#69601) on green Col. 1 card [.01] 15.00
    Reissue with holo picture [.01] 10.00
Tusken Raider with "Gaderffi Stick Battle Club"
    (#69603) on original red Col. 2 card [.00] closed
    left hand. 25.00
    Variation, open left hand 75.00
    Reissue, now with "Gaderffii Stick" on green
    Col. 2 card (#69603) [.01] open hand. 12.00
    Reissue (#69603) with closed hand 45.00
    Reissue with holo picture 10.00

2-1B Medic Droid & ASP-7 Droid (Kenner 1997)

STAR WARS
Kenner (1997)

    About sixty figures and vehicles were released in 1997, starting with the transition figures listed above. Highlights among these included the first figure of Grand Moff Tarkin, large creature figures of Jabba the Hutt, Dewback, Tauntaun and the new Ronto plus the one 3¾" figure every red-blooded collector wanted: Princess Leia as Jabba's Prisoner, brass bikini top and all.

GREEN CARD SERIES

3¾" Figures (1997) Plain or Holographic Picture
2-1B Medic Droid with "Medical Diagnostic
    Computer" (#69618) Col. 2 [.00] $10.00
    Reissue (#69618) Col. 2 [.01] 8.00
4-Lom with "Blaster Pistol and Blaster Rifle"
    (#69688) Col. 2 [.00] 12.00
Admiral Ackbar with "Comlink Wrist Blaster"
    (#69686) Col. 2 [.00] 10.00
ASP-7 Droid with "Spaceport Supply Rods" (#69704)
    Col. 2 [.00] 10.00
AT-ST Driver with "Blaster Rifle and Pistol" (#69623)
    Col. 2 [.00]. 12.00
    Reissue? [.01?] *Does not seem to exist*
    Reissue (#69823) Col. 3 [.02] 10.00

Bossk & Grand Moff Tarkin (Kenner 1997)

Ben (Obi-Wan) Kenobi with "Lightsaber and
  Removable Cloak" (#69576) Col. 1 [.02] 12.00
Bib Fortuna with "Hold-Out Blaster" (#69634) **Col. 1**
  [.00]. 12.00
  Reissue (#69812) Col. 2 [.01]. 10.00
Boba Fett with "Sawed-off Blaster Rifle and Jet
  Pack" (#69582) **Col. 1** [.02] 30.00
  Variations, **Black circle** one hand, or **no circle** . . . 750.00
  Reissue (#69804) Col. 3 [.03]. 20.00
Bossk with "Blaster Rifle and Pistol" (#69617) Col. 2
  [.00]. 13.00
  Reissue (#69617) Col. 2 [.01] 10.00
C-3PO with "Realistic Metalized Body" (#69573)
  Col. 1 [.01]. 12.00
Chewbacca with "Bowcaster and Heavy Blaster
  Rifle" (#69578) Col. 1 [.01]. 12.00
Darth Vader with "Lightsaber and Removable Cape"
  (#69572) **Col. 1** [.01] 14.00
  Reissue (#69802) Col. 3 [.02] 10.00
  Variation (#69802) Darth Vader figure from
    Shadow of the Empire two-pack 200.00
Death Star Gunner with "Imperial Blaster and Assault
  Rifle" (#69809) Col. 3 [.02] 10.00
  [.00] & [.01] *See Transition Figures Listed Above*
Dengar with "Blaster Rifle" (#69687) Col. 2 [.00]. 12.00
Emperor Palpatine with "Walking Stick" (#69633)
  Col. 1 [.00]. 12.00
  Reissue (#69811) Col. 3 [.01] 10.00
Emperor's Royal Guard with "Force Pike" (#69717)
  Col. 3 [.00] 10.00
EV-9D9 with "Datapad" (#69722) Col. 2 [.00] 12.00
Gamorrean Guard with "Vibro Ax" (#69693) Col. 2 [.00] 10.00
Garindan (Long Snout) with "Hold-Out Pistol"
  (#69706) Col. 3 [.00] 10.00
Grand Moff Tarkin with "Imperial Issue Blaster Rifle
  and Pistol" (#69702) **Col. 2** [.00]. 40.00
  Reissue (#69702) Col. 3 [.01]. 10.00
Greedo, *See Transition Figures Listed Above*

*Bespin Han Solo & Luke Skywalker in Ceremonial Outfit
(Kenner 1997)*

Han Solo with "Heavy Assault Rifle and Blaster"
(#69577) Col. 1 [.01] 15.00
Bespin Han Solo with "Heavy Assault Rifle and
Blaster" (#69719) Col. 1 [.00] 10.00
Han Solo in Carbonite with "Carbonite Block"
(#69613) **Col. 2** [.02] 13.00
Reissue Col. 1 [.03] (#69613) 11.00
Han Solo in Endor Gear with "Blaster Pistol"
(#69621) Col. 1 [.00] blue pants 12.00
Reissue (#69621) Col. 1 [.00] **brown pants** 25.00
Hoth Rebel Soldier with "Survival Backpack and
Blaster Rifle" (#69631) **Col. 2** [.00] 12.00
Reissue (#69821) Col. 1 [.01] 10.00
Jawas, *See Transition Figures Listed Above*
Lando Calrissian with "Heavy Rifle and Blaster
Pistol" (#69583) Col. 1 [.01] *from club 3-packs* . . . 45.00
Lando Calrissian as Skiff Guard with "Skiff Guard
Force Pike" (#69622) Col. 1 [.00] 10.00
Luke Skywalker in Ceremonial Outfit with "Medal of
Valor and Blaster Pistol" (#69691) **Col. 2** [.00] . . . 40.00
Reissue (#69691) Col. 1 [.01] 12.00
Luke Skywalker in Hoth Gear with "Blaster Pistol
and Lightsaber" (#69619) **Col. 2** [.00] 12.00
Reissue (#69822) Col. 1 [.01] 10.00
Jedi Knight Luke Skywalker with "Lightsaber and
Removable Cloak" (#69816) **Col. 2** [.00] 25.00
Reissue (#69816) Col. 1 [.02] 15.00
Luke Skywalker in Stormtrooper Disguise with
"Imperial Issue Blaster" (#69819) Col. 1 [.02] 10.00
[.00] & [.01] *See Transition Figures Listed Above*
Luke Skywalker in X-wing Fighter Pilot Gear with
"Lightsaber and Blaster Pistol" (#69581) Col. 1 [.02] 15.00
Malakili (Rancor Keeper) with "Long-Handled Vibro-
Blade" (#69723) Col. 2 [.00] 10.00
Momaw Nadon, *See Transition Figures Listed Above*
Nien Nunb with "Blaster Pistol and Blaster Rifle"
(#69694) Col. 2 [.00] 10.00
Ponda Baba with "Blaster Pistol and Rifle" (#69708)

Col. 2 [.00] Black beard.	40.00
Variation, **Col. 2** [.00] Grey beard	60.00
Reissue (#69708) Col. 3 [.01] Black beard	10.00
Princess Leia Organa with "Laser Pistol and Assault Rifle" (#69579) Col. 1 [.01] 2-bands or 3-bands . .	12.00
Princess Leia Organa as Jabba's Prisoner (#69683) Col. 1 [.00].	12.00
Princess Leia in Boushh Disguise with "Blaster Rifle and Bounty Hunter Helmet" (#69818) Col. 1 [.02] .	18.00
R2-D2 with "Light-Pipe Eye Port and Retractable Leg" (#69574) Col. 1 [.01]	18.00
R5-D4, *See Transition Figures Listed Above*	
Rebel Fleet Trooper with "Blaster Pistol and Rifle" (#69696) Col. 2 [.00]	30.00
Reissue (#69696) Col. 1 [.01].	10.00
Saelt-Marae (Yak Face) with "Battle Staff" (#69721) Col. 2 [.00].	12.00
Sandtrooper with "Heavy Blaster Rifle" (#69808) Col. 3 [.02].	10.00
[.00] & [.01] *See Transition Figures Listed Above*	
Snowtrooper with "Imperial Issue Blaster Rifle" (#69632) Col. 3 [.00]	10.00
Stormtrooper with "Blaster Rifle and Heavy Infantry Cannon" (#69803) Col. 3 [.01]	10.00
TIE Fighter Pilot with "Imperial Blaster and Rifle" (#69673) **Col. 2** [.03]	12.00
Reissue (#69806) Col. 3 [.04].	11.00
Tusken Raider, *See Transition Figures Listed Above*	
Weequay Skiff Guard with "Force Pike and Blaster Rifle" (#69707) **Col. 2** [.00].	30.00
Reissue (#69707) Col. 3 [.01].	12.00
Yoda with "Jedi Trainer Backpack and Gimer Stick" (#69672) **Col. 2** [.02]	12.00
Reissue (#69586) Col. 1 [.03].	10.00

Specials

Four figure set of Han Solo in Endor Gear, Lando Calrissian as Skiff Guard, AT-ST driver and Darth Vader (J.C. Penney catalog 1997).	20.00

Ponda Baba & Princess Leia as Jabba's Prisoner (Kenner 1997)

*Slide from Princess Leia Organa as Jabba's Prisoner
(Kenner 1998)*

POWER OF THE FORCE 1998

The new header card packaging for 1998 adds a 35mm "Freeze Frame Action Slide" as an in-package premium. This series features the first Biggs Darklighter, Captain Piett, and other figures, along with Darth Vader in removable helmet, with his finely sculpted head revealed.

COLLECT ALL THESE *STAR WARS* ACTION FIGURES

■ HAN SOLO
   IN ENDOR GEAR
   IN CARBONITE
■ LUKE SKYWALKER
   BESPIN

■ LANDO CALRISSIAN
   GENERAL'S GEAR
■ SEALT-MARIE (YAK FACE)
■ EV-9D9
■ DARTH VADER

Card back showing "Sealt-Marie" printing error

The first batch of "Freeze Frame Action Slide" "Collection 1" figures arrived on schedule in February 1998. Happily or unhappily, they all had a printing error and so corrected versions, with new printing numbers, arrived quickly as well. The error is on the back of the header card, under the picture of Jabba and Han, where weary collectors are advised to "Collect all these *Star Wars* Action Figures." In the list that follows, "Saelt-Marae" is misspelled as "Sealt-Marie"—two errors in just 10 letters. The error is the same on all packages, and the corrected version has the higher printing number.

This series of figures has been very popular with collectors. Distribution has been spotty and some reissue figures have been very hard to track down. Prices are generally higher than prices for the 1997 figures. However, a large supply of many of the figures appeared at local stores in March and April 2000, just as the book was being completed. Prices fell as all of the Collection 1 figures with the "Sealt Marie" printing error were available, along with such scarce figures as the new R2-D2 with the "Imperial trash compactor" slide. I have tried to **estimate** the effect of this new supply in the prices below, but further price changes are almost certain to occur.

GREEN CARD—
FREEZE FRAME SERIES
Kenner (1998)

3¾" Figures (1998) with Freeze Frame Action Slides
8D8 with "Droid Branding Device" (#69834) Col. 2 [.00]. $10.00
Admiral Ackbar with "Wrist Blaster" (#69686) Col. 2
    [.01] 12.00
AT-AT Driver *see Fan Club Exclusives below*
AT-ST Driver with "Blaster Rifle and Pistol" (#69623)
    Col. 3 [.03] scarce 100.00
Ben (Obi-Wan) Kenobi *renamed Obi-Wan (Ben) Kenobi*
Biggs Darklighter with "Blaster Pistol" (#69758)
    Col. 2 [.00] 15.00
Boba Fett with "Sawed-Off Blaster Rifle and Jet
    Pack" (#69804) Col. 3 [.04]. 45.00
    Variations, **Black circle** on one hand or **no circle**. 750.00
C-3PO with "Realistic Metalized Body and Cargo
    Net" (Pull-Apart Feature) (#69832) Col. 1 [.00] . . . 15.00
Captain Piett with "Blaster Rifle and Pistol" (#69757)
    Col. 3 [.00] 22.00
    Reissue with "Blaster Pistol and Baton" [.00] 100.00
Chewbacca as Boushh's Bounty, with "Bowcaster"
    (#69882) Col. 1 [.00] 15.00
Darth Vader with "Lightsaber and Removable Cape"
    (#69802) Col. 3 [.03] 20.00
Darth Vader with "Removable Helmet and Light-
    saber" and with "Detachable Hand" (#69836)
    Col. 3 [.00]. 40.00
Death Star Droid *see Fan Club Exclusives below*
Death Star Trooper with "Blaster Rifle" (#69838)
    Col. 3 [.00] 40.00

Biggs Darklighter & Captain Piett (Kenner 1998)

Action Figures

Darth Vader with Removable Helmet & Lak Sivrak (Kenner 1998)

Emperor Palpatine with "Walking Stick" (#69811)
Col. 3 [.02]. 8.00
Emperor's Royal Guard with "Force Pike" (#69717)
Col. 3 [.01]. 25.00
Endor Rebel Soldier with "Survival Backpack and
Blaster Rifle" (#69716) Col. 1 [.00] error 12.00
Reissue, "Saelt-Marae" corrected [.01] 8.00
EV-9D9 with "Datapad" (#69722) Col. 2 [.01] 12.00
Ewoks: Wicket & Logray with "Staff, Medicine Pouch
and Spear" (#69711) Col. 2 [.00]. 12.00
Gamorrean Guard with "Vibro Ax" (#69693) Col. 2 [.01] 12.00
Garindan with "Hold-Out Pistol" (#69706) Col. 3 [.01] . . 40.00
Grand Moff Tarkin with "Imperial Blaster Rifle and
Pistol" (#69702) Col. 3 [.02] 12.00
Han Solo with "Blaster Pistol" (#69577) Col. 1 [.02] . . . 15.00
Han Solo in Carbonite with "Carbonite Block"
(#69817) Col. 1 [.04] misspelling 12.00
Reissue, "Saelt-Marae" corrected [.05] 8.00
Bespin Han Solo with "Heavy Assault Rifle and
Blaster Pistol" (#69719) Col. 1 [.01] misspelling . . 12.00
Reissue, "Saelt-Marae" corrected [.02] 8.00
Reissue, "Unbeknownst" corrected [.03] 15.00
Han Solo in Endor Gear with "Blaster Pistol"
(#69621) Col. 1 [.01] misspelling 12.00
Reissue, "Saelt-Marae" corrected [.02] 8.00
Hoth Rebel Soldier with "Survival Backpack and
Blaster Rifle" (#69821) Col. 1 [.02] misspelling . . . 12.00
Reissue, "Saelt-Marae" corrected [.03] 8.00
Ishi Tib with "Blaster Rifle" (#69754) Col. 3 [.00]. 20.00
Lak Sivrak with "Blaster Pistol and Vibro-Blade"
(#69753) Col. 2 [.00] 12.00
Lando Calrissian as Skiff Guard with "Skiff Guard
Force Pike" (#69622) Col. 1 [.01] misspelling 12.00
Reissue, "Saelt-Marae" corrected [.02] 8.00
Lando Calrissian in General's Gear with "Blaster
Pistol" (#69756) Col. 1 [.00] 12.00
Reissue, "Saelt-Marae" corrected [.01] 8.00

Lobot with "Blaster Pistol and Transmitter" (#69856)
    Col. 1 [.00]. 20.00
Bespin Luke Skywalker with "Detachable Hand" and
    with "Lightsaber and Blaster Pistol" (#69713)
    Col. 1 [.00] with misspelling 12.00
    Reissue, "Saelt-Marae" corrected [.01] 8.00
Luke Skywalker in Ceremonial Outfit with "Medal of
    Valor and Blaster Pistol" (#69691) Col. 1 [.01 sic] . 15.00
Luke Skywalker in Stormtrooper Disguise with "Im-
    "perial Blaster" (#69819) Col. 1 [.03] misspelling . . 12.00
    Reissue, "Saelt-Marae" corrected [.04] 8.00
Luke Skywalker with "Blast Shield Helmet and Light-
    saber" (New Likeness) (#69691) Col. 1 [.00]. 15.00
Malakili (Rancor Keeper) with "Long-Handled Vibro-
    Blade" (#69723) Col. 2 [.01] 15.00
Mon Mothma with "Baton" (#69859) Col. 1 [.00] 25.00
Nien Nunb with "Blaster Pistol and Blaster Rifle"
    (#69694) Col. 2 [.01] 20.00
Obi-Wan (Ben) Kenobi with "Lightsaber Cloak"
    (#69576) Col. 1 [.03] misspelling 12.00
    Reissue, "Saelt-Marae" corrected [.04] 8.00
Orrimaarko (Prune Face) with "Blaster Rifle"
    (#69858) Col. 1 [.00] 25.00
Pote Snitkin *see Fan Club Exclusives below*
Princess Leia Organa with "Blaster Rifle and Long-
    Barreled Pistol" (New Likeness) (#69824)
    Col. 1 [.00]. 15.00
Princess Leia Organa in Ewok Celebration Outfit
    (#69714) Col. 1 [.00] misspelling 12.00
    Reissue, "Saelt-Marae" corrected [.01] 8.00
Princess Leia Organa as Jabba's Prisoner (#69683)
    Col. 1 [.01] misspelling. 12.00
    Reissue, "Saelt-Marae" corrected [.02] 8.00
Princess Leia in Hoth Gear *see Fan Club Exclusives below*
Rebel Fleet Trooper with "Blaster Pistol and Rifle"
    (#69696) Col. 1 [.01] misspelling 12.00
    Reissue (#69696) Col. 1 [.01 sticker] 20.00
    Reissue, "Saelt-Marae" corrected [.02] 8.00
Ree-Yees with "Blaster Pistols" (#69839) Col.3 [.00] . . 40.00

Mon Mothma and Orrimaarko (Prune Face) (Kenner 1998)

R2-D2 with "Spring-Loaded, Pop-Up Scanner, Re-
mote-Action, Retractable Scomp Link, Grasper
Arm and Circular Saw" (# 69831) Col. 1 [.00] 20.00
    Variation, "Imperial trash compactor" on slide..... 50.00
Saelt-Marae (Yak Face) with "Battle Staff" (#69721)
Col. 2 [.01] 15.00
Sandtrooper with "Heavy Blaster Rifle" (#69808)
Col. 3 [.03] scarce 125.00
Snowtrooper with "Imperial Issue Blaster Rifle"
(#69632) Col. 3 [.02] 20.00
Stormtrooper with "Blaster Rifle and Heavy Infantry
Cannon" (#69803) Col. 3 [.02] 15.00
TIE Fighter Pilot with "Imperial Blaster and Rifle"
(#69806) Col. 3 [.05] 40.00
Ugnaughs with "Tool Kit" (#69837) Col. 2 [.00] 12.00
Weequay Skiff Guard with "Force Pike and Blaster"
(#69707) Col. 3 [.02] scarce 275.00
Zuckuss with "Heavy Assault Blaster Rifle" (#69747)
Col. 3 [.00] 20.00

Fan Club exclusives (early 1999) sold in sets of two
AT-AT Driver with "Imperial Issue Blaster" (#69864)
Col. 3 [.00] 25.00
Death Star Droid with "Mouse Droid" (#69862) Col. 3
[.00} 25.00
Pote Snitkin with "Force Pike and Blaster Pistol"
(#69863) Col. 3 [.00} 25.00
Princess Leia Organa in Hoth Gear with "Blaster
Pistol" (#84143) Col. 3 [.00] 25.00

Expanded Universe. These figures are from the
comics, video games, and novels figures, and not from the
movies. They were released in November 1998, and include
Mara Jade and Grand Admiral Thrawn, from *Heir to the
Empire*, and Kyle Katarn, from *Dark Forces*. They are very
popular with collectors. No one has reported finding figures
with ".00" revision numbers, and the numbers lised are the
earliest known.

*Grand Admiral Thrawn and Mara Jade, Expanded Universe
3-D PlayScene figures (Kenner 1998)*

Expanded Universe, 3-D PlayScene figures
Dark Empire comics
Clone Emperor Palpatine (#69886) [.02]. $20.00
Imperial Sentinel (#69887) [.01] 20.00
Luke Skywalker (in Black Cloak) (#69883) [.01] 20.00
Princess Leia (in Black Cloak) (#69884) [.03] 20.00

Heir to the Empire novels
Grand Admiral Thrawn (#69888) [.02] 25.00
Mara Jade (#69891) [.03]. 60.00
Spacetrooper (#69892) [.03]. 35.00

Dark Forces video game
Darktrooper (#69894) [.01]. 40.00
Kyle Katarn (#69893) [.02] 45.00

Aunt Beru & Princess Leia in Ceremonial Dress,
Flashback Photo series (Kenner 1998)

Flashback Photo figures came with a detachable pull-down photo which showed the figure from the original movies, and, when pulled down, showed the same or a related figure from the forthcoming Episode I movie. These revealed some essential plot points for that movie, such as that Queen Amidala is Luke & Leia's mother, and that Senator Palpatine becomes Emperor Palpatine.

The first wave of eight figures appeared in November 1998, and a second wave of three new figures came out in June 1999. They have four digit revision numbers, as do their Flashback Photos. Even the Flashback Photos have variations. The earlier ones have a down-arrow on the front and back of the pull-tab, while later ones have an up-arrow and a down-arrow on the front and no arrow on the back.

3¾" Figures (1998–99) with Flashback Photos
Anakin Skywalker with "Lightsaber" (#84047)
   [.0000] $15.00
Aunt Beru with "Service Droid" (#84049) [.0000]. 18.00
Ben (Obi-Wan) Kenobi with "Lightsaber" (#84037)

Action Figures

[.00] 10.00
C-3PO with "Removable Arm" (#84041) [.0000] 10.00
Darth Vader with "Lightsaber" (#84046) [.00] 10.00
Emperor Palpatine with "Force Lightning" (#84042)
　　[.00] 10.00
Hoth Chewbacca with "Bowcaster Rifle" (#84051)
　　[.00] 10.00
Luke Skywalker with "Blaster Rifle and Electro-
　　binoculars" (#84036) [.00]. 10.00
Princess Leia in Ceremonial Dress with "Medal of
　　Honor" (#84038) [.01] 10.00
R2-D2 with "Launching Lightsaber" (#84043) [.01]
　　Lightsaber packed left side. 10.00
　　Lightsaber packed right side. 100.00
Yoda with "Cane and Boiling Pot" (#84039) [.00] 15.00

Greedo & Jawa with Gonk Droid,
CommTech Chip series (Hasbro 1999)

COMMTech Chip Figures

　　COMMTech Chip Figures appeared with a new batch
of Star Wars figures in 1999. These are the same types of
chips used on the Episode I figures listed below. Hasbro has
not given up on the classic characters just because it has a
whole new movie to work with. The R2-D2 figure with holographic Princess Leia was supposed to have been omitted
briefly because of production problems. Between hoarding
and "briefly," most collectors can't find it at all.

3¾" Figures (Hasbro 1999) with COMMTech Chips
Admiral Motti with "Imperial Blaster" (#84366) $15.00
Darth Vader with "Imperial Interrogation Droid"
　　(#84203) [.00]. 20.00
Greedo with "Blaster" (#84201) [.0000]. 8.00
Han Solo with "Blaster Pistol & Holster" (#84202)
　　[.0000] 8.00
Jawa with Gonk Droid (#84198) [.0000]
　　with two foot holes 8.00
　　with no foot holes 50.00
　　with one foot hole 60.00

Luke Skywalker with T-16 Skyhopper Model
(#84211) [.0000]. 8.00
Princess Leia with "Sporting Blaster" (#84361) [.0000]. . 15.00
R2-D2 with "Holographic" Princess Leia (#84199)
[.0000] 50.00
Stormtrooper with Battle Damage and "Blaster Rifle
Pack" (#84209) [.0000] 20.00

Mace Windu, Episode I Sneak Preview (Kenner 1999)

STAR WARS EPISODE I—
THE PHANTOM MENACE
Hasbro (1999)

"A generation before Star Wars: A New Hope …. In a galaxy far, far away, an evil force is gaining strength and threatens an entire civilization. Two courageous Jedi, a young queen, a Gungan outcast, and a slave boy named Anakin, band together to save a planet under attack as the fate of the galaxy hangs in the balance."

The long, long awaited movie stars young Jake Lloyd as young Anakin Skywalker, Ewan McGregor as a younger Obi-Wan Kenobi, Liam Neeson as Qui-Gon Jinn, and Natalie Portman as the teenage Queen Amidala. Anthony Daniels and Kenny Baker are back as C-3PO and R2-D2. Jar Jar Binks is voiced by Ahmed Best, but is completely computer generated. Supporting characters include Samuel L. Jackson as Mace Windu, Terence Stamp as Supreme Chancellor Valorum, and Brian Blessed as Boss Nass.

Sneak Previews (1998–99) boxed
Stap and Battle Droid with Firing Laser Missiles
(#84069) $20.00
Mace Windu (#84138) 20.00

Action Figures

Anakin Skywalker (Tatooine) & Boss Nass (Hasbro 1999)

3¾" Figures (Hasbro 1999) with COMMTech Chips
Wave 1: (May 1999)

Anakin Skywalker (Tatooine) with "Backpack and
    Grease Gun" (#84074) Col. 1 [.00] $10.00
    Reissue [.0100] 7.00
Battle Droid with "Blaster Rifle" (#84092) [558449]
    Brown Col. 1 [.00] 25.00
    Reissue Brown [.0100] 18.00
    Reissue Brown [.0200] 7.00
    Tan Col. 1 [.00] 25.00
    Reissue Tan [.0100]. 18.00
    Reissue Tan [.0200] 7.00
    Lightsaber slashed Col. 1 [.00]. 25.00
    Reissue Lightsaber slashed [.0100] 18.00
    Reissue Lightsaber slashed [.0200]. 7.00
    Battle scars Col. 1 [.00] 25.00
    Reissue Battle scars [.0100] 18.00
    Reissue Battle scars [.0200]. 7.00
Boss Nass with "Gungan Staff" (#84119) Col.3. [.0000] . 8.00
    Reissue [.0100] 7.00
C-3PO (#84106) Col. 2 [.00]. 8.00
    Reissue [.0100]. 7.00
Chancellor Valorum with "Ceremonial Staff"
    (#84132) Col.3. [.0000]. 10.00
    Reissue [.0100]. 7.00
Darth Maul (Jedi Duel) with "Double-Bladed Light-
    saber" (#84088) Col. 1 [.00]. 18.00
    Reissue [.0000]. 10.00
    Reissue [.0100]. 7.00
Darth Sideous (#84087) Col. 2 [.00] 8.00
    [.0100] 7.00
Gasgano with Pit Droid (#84116) [.0000] 10.00
    Reissue Col.3. [.0100] 7.00
    Reissue [.0200]. 7.00
Jar Jar Binks with "Gungan Battle Staff" (#84077)
    Col. 1 [.00] 20.00
    Reissue [.0100]. 12.00
    [.0200] 7.00

Ki-Adi-Mundi with "Lightsaber" (#84123) Col.3. [.0000]. . 8.00
    Reissue [.0100]. 7.00
Mace Windu with "Lightsaber and Jedi Cloak"
    (#84084) Col.3. [.0000]. 8.00
    Reissue [.0100]. 7.00
Obi-Wan Kenobi (Jedi Duel) with "Lightsaber"
    (#84073) Col. 1 [.00]. 8.00
    Reissue [.0100] 7.00
Padme Naberrie with "Pod Race View Screen"
    (#84076) Col. 1 [.00] 10.00
    Reissue [.0100] 7.00
Queen Amidala (Naboo) with "Blaster Pistols"
    (#84078) Col. 1 [.00]. 10.00
    Reissue [.0100] 7.00
Qui-Gon Jinn (Jedi Duel) with "Lightsaber" (#84072)
    Col. 1 [.00]. 8.00
    Reissue [.0100] 7.00
Ric Olie with "Helmet and Naboo Blaster" (#84109)
    Col. 2 [.00]. 8.00
    Reissue [.0100] 7.00
Senator Palpatine with "Senate Cam Droid"
    (#84082) Col. 2 [.00] 8.00
    Reissue [.0100] 7.00
Watto with "Datapad" (#84093) Col. 2 [.00]. 8.00
    Reissue [.0100] 7.00

Padme Naberrie & Ric Olie (Hasbro 1999)

Later Figures
Adi Gallia with "Lightsaber" (#84124) Col. 3 [.0000]. . . . $7.00
Anakin Skywalker (Naboo) with "Comlink Unit"
    (#84112) Col. 1 [.0100]. 7.00
Anakin Skywalker (Naboo Pilot) with "Flight
    Simulator" (#84246) Col. 1 [.0000] 7.00
Captain Panaka with "Blaster Rifle and Pistol"
    (#84108) Col. 2 [.0000] 7.00
Captain Tarpals with "Electropole" (#84121) Col. 3
    [.0000]. 7.00
Darth Maul (Sith Lord) with "Lightsaber with Re-
    movable Blade" (#84247) Col. 1 [.0000] 7.00
Darth Maul (Tatooine) with "Cloak and Lightsaber"

Action Figures

R2-B1 Astromech Droid & TC-41 Protocol Droid (Hasbro 2000)

(#84134) Col. 1 [.0000] 7.00
Destroyer Droid (#84181) Col. 2 [.0000] 7.00
Naboo Royal Security with "Blaster Pistol and Rifle"
   (#84079) Col. 2 [.0000] 7.00
Nute Gunray (#84089) Col. 2 [.0000] 5.00
Obi-Wan Kenobi (Jedi Knight) with "Lightsaber and
   Comlink" (#84244) Col. 1 [.0000] 7.00
Obi-Wan Kenobi (Naboo) with "Lightsaber and
   Handle" (#84114) Col. 1 [.0100] 7.00
Ody Mandrell with "OTOGA 222 Pit Droid" (#84117)
   Col. 3 [.0100 . . . . 7.00
OOM-9 with "Blaster and Binoculars" (#84127) Col.
   3 [.0000] Binoculars packed upper left. 10.00
   Col. 3 [.0000] Binoculars packed over left hand. . . . 7.00
Queen Amidala (Coruscant) (#84111) Col. 1 [.0100] 7.00
Qui-Gon Jinn (Naboo) with "Lightsaber and Handle"
   (#84113) Col. 1 [.0100]. 7.00
R2-D2 with "Booster Rockets" (#84104) Col. 2 [.0000] . . 7.00
R2-B1 Astromech Droid with "Power Harness"
   (#84128) Col.3. [.0000] 7.00
Rune Haako (#84091) Col. 2 [.0000]. 5.00
TC-14 Protocol Droid with "Serving Tray" (#84276)
   Col.3. [.0000] 7.00
Yoda with "Jedi Council Chair" (#84086) Col. 2 [.0000] . . 7.00

Per Hasbro Web-site but not seen
Darth Sidious (Holographic) (#84081). $7.00
Naboo Royal Guard (#84083) 7.00
Jar Jar Binks (Naboo Swamp) (#84252) 20.00
Destroyer Droid (Battle Damaged) (#84126) 13.00
Qui-Gon Jinn (Jedi Master) (#84107) 7.00
Lott Dodd 7.00

Accessory Sets
Naboo Accessory Set with Retracting Grappling
   Hook Backpack (#26208) $3.00
Tatooine Accessory Set with Pull-Back Droid (#26209) . . 3.00
Underwater Accessory Set with Bubbling Backpack

(#26211) 3.00
Sith Accessory Set with Firing Backpack and 2 Droid
      Missiles (#26210) 3.00
Electronic Flash Cannon Accessory Set (#26217) 6.00
Electronic Gungan Catapult Accessory Set (#26218) . . . 6.00

MAIL-IN AND EXCLUSIVE FIGURES

There have been quite a few mail-in and exclusive figures in the new series. The first to be offered was the Froot
Loops mail-in Han Solo in Stormtrooper disguise. Both the
cereal box and the figure are collectible. Since this offer was
not tied to any Star Wars event or product, many collectors
missed it. By contrast, the Spirit of Obi-Wan Kenobi mail-in
from Frito Lay was tied to the theater release of the Special
Editions of the movies in early 1997. Hardly anyone was
unaware of it. The figure cannot truly be said to be an action
figure as it is not articulated, but Kenner treats it as one on its
website and collectors have generally considered it so, as
well.

The theater edition Jedi Knight Luke Skywalker is the
most valuable of the exclusive figures. It was given away during the first showing of the Special Edition of *Star Wars, A
New Hope* on January 31, 1997. There was no prior
announcement and not all theaters got the figure, but a number of alert movie theater ushers and ticket takers did quite
well for themselves. The figure is identical to the common
version sold in stores—only the header card is different.

Many of the Star Wars vehicles came with exclusive
figures. This practice continued in 1998, when it was hard to
find a vehicle without an exclusive figure. If you want all the
figures you will have to collect vehicles too. The most interesting of these exclusives is the Wedge Antilles error figure.

*Ooola and Salacious Crumb & Han Solo Stormtrooper,
mail-in figures (Kenner 1998 & 1995)*

Action Figures

The first batches of the *Millennium Falcon* carry case came with a Wedge Antilles with a white stripe down each arm. This was clearly visible as the figure can be seen in the gun turret of the ship. Later batches of these carry cases corrected the figure. Locally, the original carry case with the error figure was available for quite a while after news of the error appeared in collector magazines. While the error figure is still the more desirable version, the price difference is not particularly large.

Mail-in Figures

Mail-in Han Solo in Stormtrooper disguise, in plastic
    bag, (Froot Loops offer) with mailer box $25.00
Spirit of Obi-Wan Kenobi, with box (Frito Lay offer,
    1997) 10.00
Cantina Band Member, Official Star Wars Fan Club
    exclusive, in plastic bag, with five musical
    instruments (#69734, 1997) in white mailer box . . 15.00
Cantina Band Set, five figures: (All five figures are
    the same as above. Only the instruments are
    different.) Official Star Wars Fan Club 65.00
    Loose: Doikk N'ats with Fizzz Instrument 15.00
    Loose: Figrin D'an with Kloo Horn Instrument 15.00
    Loose: Ickabel with Fanfars Instrument. 15.00
    Loose: Nalan with Bandfill Instrument. 15.00
    Loose: Techn with Omnibox Instrument 15.00
B'Omarr Monk, Hasbro Internet Website offer, in
    plastic bag, with instruction sheet (#69718,
    1997–98) in white mailer box 15.00
Oola and Salacious Crumb (Official Star Wars Fan
    Club exclusive) (#69871, 1998) in window box . . . 20.00
Kabe and Muftak (#84071) boxed, Internet exclusive . . 20.00
Aunt Beru and Treadwell (#) Internet exclusive. 20.00

Give-away figure

Jedi Knight Luke Skywalker, Exclusive Star Wars
    Trilogy Edition, carded, movie theater give-
    away (1997) 75.00
See also Freeze Frame figures, Fan Club exclusives.

B'Omarr Monk mail-in figure (Hasbro 1997–98)

Deluxe Probe Droid & Deluxe Boba Fett (Kenner 1997)

DELUXE FIGURES
Kenner (1995–99)

Deluxe figures have met with a decidedly mixed review among collectors and in collector publications. None of the weapons/accessories in these packages appeared in the movie. Only a few of the deluxe figures have been created, and they follow the basic concept behind the Mini-Rigs from the original series, which was to sell weapons and accessories that fit in with the ones featured in the film and could be envisioned as "just off camera."

DELUXE FIGURES

1st Wave (Asst. #69610, 1996) on red card
Deluxe Crowd Control Stormtrooper (#69609) with
    2 warning stickers [.00]. $30.00
    Variation, with 1 warning sticker? 8.00
    Reissue, printed warnings [.01]. 7.00
Deluxe Luke Skywalker's Desert Sport Skiff (#69611)
    [.00] 11.00
Deluxe Han Solo with Smuggler Flight Pack
    (#69612) [.00]. 11.00

2nd & 3rd Waves (1997) on green cards
Deluxe Boba Fett (#69638) [.00] card says "Weaponry: Photon Torpedo" 12.00
    Variation [.01] says "Weaponry: Proton Torpedo". . 11.00
Deluxe Probe Droid (#69677) card [.00] with red color
    scheme back picturing figures from the Shadows
    of the Empire series 25.00
    Variation [.01]. 8.00
    Variation [.02] green color scheme 6.00
Deluxe Hoth Rebel Soldier (#69744) [.00] 9.00
Deluxe Snowtrooper (#69724) [.00] 9.00

Gunner Stations (1998) on green cards
Millennium Falcon with Han Solo (#69848). 9.00
Millennium Falcon with Luke Skywalker (#69766). 9.00
TIE Fighter with Darth Vader (#69847) 15.00

Episode I Deluxe (Asst. #84045, May 1999) with
Lightsaber Handle which Triggers Battle Swing
Deluxe Darth Maul (#84144) [.0000] 7.00
Deluxe Obi-Wan Kenobi (#84152) [.0000] 7.00
Deluxe Qui-Gon Jinn (#84148) [.0000] 7.00

ELECTRONIC POWER F/X
Kenner (1997)

Electronic Power F/X (Asst. #69615, 1997) on green cards
Ben (Obi-Wan) Kenobi (#69643) [.00]. $9.00
Darth Vader (#69644) [.00]. 9.00
Emperor Palpatine (#69726) [.00] energy bolts
pictured pointing up 10.00
     Variation [.01] energy bolts pointing down. 8.00
Luke Skywalker (#69746) [.00]. 9.00
R2-D2 (Artoo-Detoo) (#69646) [.00] 9.00
     Variation [.01] blue UPC code bars. 8.00
     Variation [.02] black UPC code bars 8.00

EPIC FORCE

These 5" figures were introduced at the 1998 Toy Fair.
Other than the size, the gimmick is the rotating base, which
lets the collector see all sides of the figure without removing
it from the package.

5" Epic Force Figures with in-package rotating base.
Bespin Luke Skywalker (#69762) [.00] $10.00
Boba Fett (#69763) [.00] 10.00
C-3PO (#69764) [.00]. 10.00
Chewbacca 15.00
Darth Vader (#69761) [.00] 10.00
Han Solo Stormtrooper 15.00
Obi-Wan 15.00
Princess Leia Organa (#69843) [.00] 10.00
Stormtrooper (#69842) [.00]. 10.00

Millennium Falcon *with Luke Skywalker Gunner Station and
Electronic Power F/X Ben (Obi-Wan) Kenobi (Kenner 1997–98)*

Episode I 5" Epic Force Figures (1999)
Darth Maul (#84156) [.0000] 15.00
Obi-Wan Kenobi (#84157) [.0000] 15.00
Qui-Gon Jinn (#84179) [.0000]. 15.00

Boba Fett Epic Force figure & Bespin Han Solo
Millennium Minted Coin figure (Kenner 1998)

MILLENNIUM MINTED
COIN COLLECTION

The original Power of the Force coins are a popular collectible, and Kenner brought them back in 1998 in the
Millennium Minted Coin Collection series. Each figure in the
series comes with a gold-colored coin mounted on a display
pedestal. Figures and coins are packaged in a window box
that has a back window so you can see the back of the coin.
The back of the coin is different from the back of the original
coins, so even someone who doesn't notice that the original
coins are silver-colored should still be able to tell them apart.
The initial boxes appeared in early April, and included just
three different figures. The combination costs about $10.00,
which is about $3.00 to $4.00 more than the figure alone. This
seems about right, but a lot of collectors are reluctant to buy
still another version of a character that they already own.

4" Figures with gold coin (Asst. #69675, 1998) in window box
Bespin Han Solo (#84022) [.00] with text $25.00
    [.01] no text. 10.00
Chewbacca (#84023) [.00] with text 25.00
    [.01] no text. 10.00
C-3PO (#84024) [.00] 10.00
Luke Skywalker in Endor Gear (#84026) [.00] with text. 25.00
    [.01] no text. 10.00
Princess Leia in Endor Gear (#84027) [.00] with text . . 25.00
    [.01] no text. 10.00
Snowtrooper (#84028) [.00] with text 25.00
    [.01] no text. 10.00
Emperor Palpatine (#84029 [.00]. 10.00

MULTI-PACKS

The Cinema Scenes three-packs first appeared in June 1997 with the "Death Star Escape" group. Although Kenner calls them "Cinema Scenes" packs, this phrase doesn't appear anywhere on the package, but the back of the package contains a scene from the movie. They are collected, in part, because each one contains at least one figure that is not otherwise available. Three-packs are produced in much smaller quantities than carded figures, contain at least one exclusive figure, and retail for the same price as three figures, making them a pretty good deal.

"CINEMA SCENES"
Kenner (1997–2000)

Cinema Scenes Three-Packs in green window boxes
Death Star Escape with Chewbacca, Han Solo and
    Luke Skywalker as Stormtroopers (#69737) [.00] $40.00
    Variation [.01] box 35.00
Cantina Showdown with Dr. Evazan, Ponda Baba
    and Obi-Wan Kenobi (#69738, 1997) [.00] 20.00
    Variation [.01] box 15.00

Second and Third Batches (1998)
Final Jedi Duel with Emperor Palpatine, Darth Vader
    and Luke Skywalker (#69783) [.00]. 25.00
    Variation [.01] box 20.00
Purchase of the Droids with Uncle Owen Lars, C-3PO
    and Luke Skywalker (#69778) [.00]. 20.00
    Variation [.01] box 15.00
Jabba's The Hutt's Dancers with Rustall, Greeta and
    Lyn Me (#69849) [.00] 20.00
Mynock Hunt with Chewbacca, Princess Leia in Hoth
    Gear and Han Solo in Bespin Gear (#69868) [.00] 30.00
Jedi Spirits with deceased Anakin Skywalker, Yoda
    and Obi-Wan Kenobi (#84058) clear figures 15.00
Cantina Aliens with Labria, Takeel and Nabrun
    Leeds (#84059) 15.00

Mynock Hunt, Cinema Scenes figures (Kenner 1998)

Later Batches (1999)
Jabba's Skiff Guards with Nikto, Barada and Klaatu
    (#84061) 25.00
Rebel Pilots with Wedge Antilles, Ten Numb and
    Arvel Crynyd (#84057). 25.00
Jabba's Palace Aliens with Amanaman, Elephant
    Mon and Hermie Odle . . . . NYA
Cantina Confrontation with Virhas, Hand & Greedo . . . . NYA

Episode I (1999–2000) with COMMTech chip
Mos Espa Encounter with Sebula, Jar Jar Binks and
    Anakin Skywalker (#84161) [.0000] 15.00
Watto's Pod Race with Watto, Twi'lek Gir and Horox
    ($84159) 20.00
Tatooine Showdown with Qui-Gon Jinn, Darth Maul
    and Anakin Skywalker (#84158) 20.00

Princess Leia and Wicket the Ewok

TWO-PACKS
Princess Leia Collection (1998) on header card
Princess Leia and R2-D2 (#66936) [.00]. $20.00
Princess Leia (Medal Ceremony) and Luke
    Skywalker (#66937, 1998) [.00] 20.00
Princess Leia (Bespin) and Han Solo (#66938) [.00]. . . 20.00
Princess Leia (Endor Celebration) and Wicket the
    Ewok (#66939) [.00] 20.00

Max Rebo band pairs (WalMart) (Asst #69670)
Joh Yowza and Sy Snootles (#84018) [.00] 25.00
Barquin D'an with "Kloo Horn" and Droopy McCool
    with "Chidin Kalu" (#84019) [.01] 25.00
Max Rebo with "Red Ball Organ" and Doda Bodona-
    wieedo with "Slither Horn" (#84021) [.00] 35.00

THREE PACKS

    These are three figures, in original packages, with an
outer corrugated cardboard package with holes so that the
original packages show through. They are sold to various
"wholesale club" stores, where they generally sell to mem-
bers (customers) at a small discount from the prevailing toy

The Empire Strikes Back Collector Pack (Kenner 1997)

store price for three figures. The value of the pack is not much more than the value of the figures which were included. The primary collector interest is in The Empire Strikes Back pack from group two. It contained a green-carded Lando Calrissian which was never released separately.

Wholesale Club Three-packs
Group One, Figures on Red Cards
Set One: Han Solo, Chewbacca and Lando Cal-
rissian $35.00
Set Two: R2-D2, Stormtrooper and C-3PO.......... 35.00
Set Three: Luke Skywalker, Obi-Wan Kenobi and
Darth Vader 35.00

Group Two, Figures on Green Cards
Star Wars: Luke Skywalker in Stormtrooper Disguise,
Tusken Raider and Obi-Wan Kenobi [.00]
(#69851) 15.00
The Empire Strikes Back: Lando Calrissian, Luke
Skywalker in Dagobah Fatigues and TIE
Fighter Pilot [.00] (69852).................. 75.00
Return of the Jedi: Jedi Knight Luke Skywalker, AT-
ST Driver and Princess Leia in Boushh
Disguise [.00] (69853) 15.00

CARRY CASES AND DISPLAY STANDS

The first display stand for Kenner's *Star Wars* action figures was the one included in the Early Bird Certificate Package. Actually, the package only held the backdrop. The pegs to hold the figures came in the package with the Early Bird figures.

The *Star Wars* Action Display Stand was the first of many mail-away premiums. It was offered on *Star Wars* action figure cardbacks for two proofs of purchase plus $2.00. The stand has a plastic base and a cardboard backdrop, plus levers that rotate groups of figures. It originally came in a plain mailer box. Later, the stand was offered in *Star Wars* packaging, and finally, in *The Empire Strikes Back* packaging, with six figures, as the Special Action Display Stand.

The *Star Wars* Display Arena is also a mail-away premium, and consisted of four L-shaped plastic stands and four reversible cardboard backdrops, with pegs for display of up to 14 action figures.

DISPLAY STANDS
Kenner (1977–83)

Early Bird Package and figures. . . . . see page 1
Action Display Stand for Star Wars Figures, gray
  plastic first offered as a mail-in premium, and
  later in stores,
  Original *Star Wars* box (#38990). $350.00
  Loose, with original plain box 50.00
  Reissue as Special Action Display Stand in
    The Empire Strikes Back box, with six figures. . 550.00
  Loose, no box 40.00
Display Arena, mail-order premium (1981)
  Original *The Empire Strikes Back* box. 40.00
  Reissue in *Return of the Jedi* box 35.00
  Loose. 15.00

*Jabba's Palace with Han Solo in Carbonite
3-D Diorama (Kenner 1998)*

Display 3-D Diorama (Kenner 1998)
Cantina at Mos Eisley with Sandtrooper and Patrol
  Droid (#84063). 18.00
Jabba's Palace with Han Solo in Carbonite (#84068) . . 18.00

COLLECTOR CASES

Vinyl Collector's Cases were offered in packaging for each of the movies, in turn. The cases each have two storage trays designed to hold 12 figures each. The backsides had foot pegs, and could be used to display the figures. There were stickers for the figures so each one would know where it lived. Later, the Darth Vader and C-3PO head-shaped cases, along with the Laser Rifle carry case and even the Chewbacca Bandolier Strap, proved to be more popular designs, making

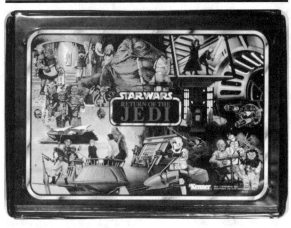

Return of the Jedi Vinyl Collector's Case (Kenner 1983)

the rather plain Collector's Case much more common in *Star Wars* packaging than in the packaging for the later two films.

CARRY CASES
Kenner (1979–84)

Carry Cases
Collector's Case, black vinyl with illustrated cover,
 holds 24 figures (1979–83)
  Star Wars package. $30.00
  The Empire Strikes Back package, Star Wars
   Pictures (#39190, 1980) 50.00
  Variation, with *The Empire Strikes Back* pictures . 50.00
  Variation, with logo centered. 50.00
  Return of the Jedi package. 100.00
Darth Vader Collector's Case, black plastic bust of
 Darth Vader, holds 31 figures (#93630, 1980)
 illustrated wrapper around base
  Original *The Empire Strikes Back* package,
   no figures. 40.00
  With **IG-88**, **Bossk** and **Boba Fett** figures in
   original *The Empire Strikes Back* package

Laser Rifle Carry Case (Kenner 1983)

Chewbacca Bandolier Strap (Kenner 1983)

(#39330) 350.00
Loose, without figures 15.00
See-Threepio Collector's Case, gold plastic bust of
    C-3PO, holds 40 figures (#70440, 1983)
    illustrated wrapper around base
      Original *Return of the Jedi* package 30.00
      Loose, without figures 15.00
Chewbacca Bandolier Strap, holds 10 figures, has
    two containers for accessories (#70480, 1983)
      Original *Return of the Jedi* box 8.00
      Loose, without figures 4.00
Laser Rifle Case, rifle-shaped, holds 19 figures
    (#71530, 1984) cardboard base with illustrations
      Original *Return of the Jedi* box 30.00
      Loose, without figures 15.00

New carry cases appeared along with the return of the
figures in 1995. Generally they have a gimmick. The
Millennium Falcon-shaped carry case came with a Wedge
Antilles figure which was visible in the gun turret. At first the
figure had white arm decorations, which did not match the
uniform in the movie. Collectors and Kenner seemed to have
noticed this about the same time and when later shipments
corrected the error, collectors searched for the original figures. However, a lot of the originals are in circulation, which
has moderated the dealer price.

CARRY CASES
Kenner (1995–2000)

Carry Cases (1995–99)
Electronic Talking C-3PO carry case, head and
    shoulders (#27609, Oct. 1996) $20.00
Millennium Falcon Carry Case with exclusive
    Wedge Antilles figure (#27728, Sept. 1997)
      with white arm stripes (error) 45.00
      Reissue, figure with no stripe on arm (1998) 25.00
      Reissue with **Imperial Scanning Crew** figure 30.00
Darth Vader box shaped carry case 20.00
R2-D2 Carryall Playset with Exclusive Destroyer
    Droid (#26226) 20.00

BOOKS

Star Wars mass market Collectible #1, the very first mass market *Star Wars* item produced, was the movie novelization paperback book which appeared in late November 1976, seven months before the movie opened. The first edition is the one to get. It can be identified by the line "First Edition: December 1976" at the bottom, on the copyright page. As the movie became a hit, the paperback was reprinted many times, with huge print runs—3.5 million copies in the first year. None of these reprintings is valuable.

The novel appeared in hardcover in the fall of 1977. The trade hardcover is scarce and valuable. It has a gold dust jacket, and says "Hardbound Ballantine Books Edition: October 1977/First Edition: December 1976" in two lines on the copyright page. Book club editions have no collector following whatever, apart from die-hard *Star Wars* fans. Consequently the book club edition of the original *Star Wars* novel, and for that matter, any *Star Wars* novel, is not valuable. The one exception might be the very first printing of the book club edition of *Star Wars*. This can be identified by the printing code "S27" in the gutter on page 183. It appeared before the trade hardcover, making it the first hardcover edition of the book.

FICTION

Movie Novelizations:
Star Wars, by Alan Dean Foster, uncredited ghost
    writer, from screenplay by George Lucas
    1st PB: $1.50, Ballantine #26061-9, Dec. 1976. . $25.00
    2nd PB: $1.95, Ballantine-Del Rey #26079-1,

Star Wars, *1st paperback and 1st hardcover*
(Ballantine Del Rey 1976 & 1977)

Books

The Empire Strikes Back, *1st paperback (Del Rey 1980)*
and Return of the Jedi, *1st Book Club edition (SFBC 1983)*

Aug. 1977, Movie tie-in, ... 10.00
1st SFBC: Del Rey #2403-4, Aug. 1977, with
   16 pages of color photos printing code S27. . . . 15.00
Later SFBC: later printing codes. 5.00
1st HC: $6.95, 183pp, Del Rey #27476-8, Oct.
   1977, with 16 pages of color photos 150.00
Recent HC: as *Star Wars: A New Hope*, Ballantine-Del Rey #40077-1, Oct. 1994, new intro . . 16.00

The Empire Strikes Back, by Donald F. Glut from
   story by George Lucas and screenplay by
   Lawrence Kasdan and Leigh Brackett
   1st PB: $2.25, 214pp, Ballantine-Del Rey
      #28392-9, May 1980. 15.00
   1st SFBC: Del Rey #3863-8, 1980, code K29. . . . 10.00
   Recent HC: 1994, new introduction 16.00

Return of the Jedi, by James Kahn, from screen
   play by Lawrence Kasdan and George Lucas
   1st PB: $2.95, 181pp, Ballantine-Del Rey
      #30767-4, June 1983, Movie Tie-in 10.00
   SFBC: $3.98, Del Rey #2144-4, code N31 . . . . . . 12.00
   HC:1994, Kazuhiko Sano cover 16.00

Star Wars Trilogy by George Lucas, Donald F.
   Glut and James Kahn
   TPB: May 1987 . . . . 10.00
   TPB: retitled: *Classic Star Wars: The Star
      Wars Trilogy*, April 1995. . . . . 10.00
   1st PB: March 1993 . . . . 6.00

Episode I: The Phantom Menace by Terry Brooks
   1st HC: $25.00 Del Rey, May 1999 . . . . 25.00
   Four different covers: Anakin Skywalker, Darth
   Maul, Obi-Wan Kenobi or Queen Amidala
   Lim. Ed. signed, slipcase, foil embossed Darth
      Maul cover with Qui-Gon Jinn pin 85.00
1st PB: $7.50 Del Rey #43411-0 , Feb. 2000. . . . . 7.50

Movie Novelizations: Illustrated Editions

The Empire Strikes Back: The Illustrated Edition, by Donald F. Glut 1980, Ralph McQuarrie illustrations and cover. 10.00

Return of the Jedi Illustrated Edition, by James Kahn, Del Rey #30960-X, June 1983 . . . . 10.00

Novels (1978–89)

Splinter of the Mind's Eye, by Alan Dean Foster
  1st HC: Del Rey #27566-7, Feb. 1978 . . . . 100.00
  1st PB: $1.95, Ballantine-Del Rey #26062-7, 1978 . 5.00

Han Solo Series, by Brian Daley

Han Solo at Stars' End
  HC: $8.95, 198pp, Del Rey #28251-5, 1979 . . . . 100.00
  1st PB: Ballantine-Del Rey #29664-8, Oct. 1979. . . 5.00

Han Solo's Revenge
  1st HC: $8.95, Del Rey #28475-5, Nov. 1979 . . . . 75.00
  1st PB: Ballantine-Del Rey #28840, June 1980. . . . 5.00

Han Solo and the Lost Legacy
  1st PB: Ballantine-Del Rey #28710-X, 1980 . . . . . 15.00

Combined edition: *The Han Solo Adventures*
  1st PB: Del Rey #37980-2, June 1992 . . . . 6.00

Lando Calrissian Series, by L. Neil Smith

Lando Calrissian and the Mindharp of Sharu
  1st PB: Ballantine-Del Rey #31158-2, 1983 . . . . . 15.00

Lando Calrissian and the Flamewind of Oseon
  1st PB: Ballantine-Del Rey #31163-9, 1983 . . . . . 15.00

Lando Calrissian and the Starcave of ThonBoka
  1st PB: Ballantine-Del Rey #31164-7, 1983 . . . . . 15.00

combined as:

Classic Star Wars: The Lando Calrissian Adventures
  1st combined PB: Del Rey #39110-1, 1994 . . . . 6.00

Novels (1990–2000)

Timothy Zahn's *Heir to the Empire* launched the current phase of *Star Wars* publishing. It appeared about six

Splinter of the Mind's Eye, *1st hardcover* & Lando Calrissian and the Flamewind of Osceon, *1st paperbaclss (Del Rey 1980 & 1983)*

months before the first Dark Horse Comic—*Dark Empire*—
and it reached #1 on the *New York Times* bestseller's list. As
the first collectible of the 1990s, after the 1985 to 1990 dark
ages, this book is highly collectible. However, it would be an
overstatement to say it caused the rebirth of *Star Wars*.
Rather, it is just the first item in a well-orchestrated plan to
bring *Star Wars* back; a plan in which we have all been entirely willing participants.

Print runs of recent *Star Wars* novels are large, and
price appreciation is unlikely. The best way to collect is to
wait for a book to appear on the remainder tables and then
look through them to find a first edition. Stay away from book
club editions. You can accumulate a handsome hardcover collection this way, at reasonable prices.

The novels and story collections are listed below in
their approximate order of appearance, based on the first book
in the series. Titles first published in hardcover are listed first,
followed by paperback series.

Books

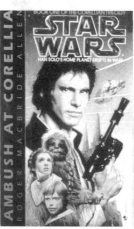

Heir to the Empire, *1st hardcover and* Ambush at Corella,
1st paperback (Bantam Spectra 1993 & 1995)

NOVELS AND STORY COLLECTIONS (1990–2000)

Hardcover originals:
Grand Admiral Thrawn series by Timothy Zahn
#1 *Heir to the Empire*
   1st HC: Bantam Spectra #07327-3, 1991 . . . . . . $35.00
   Limited Ed. HC $125.00, signed, in slipcase 175.00
#2 *Dark Force Rising*
   1st HC: Bantam Spectra #08574-3, 1992 . . . . 30.00
   Limited Ed. HC, $125.00, signed, in slipcase . . . 150.00
#3 *The Last Command*
   1st HC: Bantam Spectra #09186-7, 1993 . . . . 30.00
   Limited Ed. HC, not seen 150.00

The Truce At Bakura, by Kathleen Tyers
   1st HC: Bantam Spectra #09541-2, 1994 . . . . 30.00

The Han Solo Trilogy: The Paradise Snare *and* Rebel Dawn,
1st paperbacks (Bantam Spectra 1997 & 1998)

The Courtship Of Princess Leia, by Dave Wolverton
   1st HC: Bantam Spectra #08928-5, 1994 . . . . 30.00

The Crystal Star, by Vonda N. McIntyre
   1st HC: Bantam Spectra #08929-3, 1994 . . . . 30.00

Children of the Jedi, Barbara Hambly
   1st HC: Bantam Spectra #08930-7, 1995 . . . . 30.00

Star Wars Darksaber, by Kevin J. Anderson
   1st HC: Bantam Spectra #09974-4, 1995 . . . . . . 30.00

Shadows Of The Empire, by Steve Perry
   1st HC: Bantam Spectra #10089-0, 1996 . . . . 25.00

The New Rebellion, by Kristine Kathryn Rusch
   1st HC: Bantam Spectra #10093-9, 1996 . . . . 25.00

Planet of Twilight, by Barbara Hambly
   1st HC: Bantam Spectra #09540-4, 1997 . . . . 25.00

The Hand of Thrawn series by Timothy Zanh
#1 *Specter of the Past*
   1st HC: Bantam Spectra #09542-0, 1997 . . . . 24.00
#2 *Vision of the Future*
   1st HC: Bantam Spectra #, Sept. 1998 . . . . 25.00

I, Jedi, by Michael Stackpole
   1st HC: Bantam Spectra #10820-4, 1998 . . . . 24.00

The New Jedi Order: *Vector Prime* by R. A. Salvatore
   1st HC: $24.95, Del Rey #42844-7, 1999 . . . . 25.00

The New Jedi Order: Dark Tide by Michael A. Stackpole
#1 *Onslaught*
   1st PB: $6.99, Ballantine #, Feb 1999 . . . . 7.00

Paperback originals:
The Jedi Academy Trilogy by Kevin J. Anderson

Books

Tales From Jabba's Palace *(Bantam Spectra 1996)*
and Young Jedi Knights: Delusions of Grandeur *(Boulevard 1997)*

#1 *Jedi Search,*
    1st PB: Bantam Spectra #29798-8, 1994 . . . . 6.00
#2: *Dark Apprentice*
    1st PB: Bantam Spectra #29799-6, 1994 . . . . 5.00
#3: *Champions of the Force*
    1st PB: Bantam Spectra #29802-X, 1994 . . . . 5.00

The Corellian Trilogy by Roger McBride Allen
#1: *Ambush At Corellia*
    1st PB: Bantam Spectra #29803-8, 1995. . . . . 5.00
#2: *Assault At Selonia*
    1st PB: Bantam Spectra #29805-4, 1995 . . . . 5.00
#3: *Showdown At Centerpoint*
    1st PB: Bantam Spectra #29806-2, 1995 . . . . 5.00

Star Wars Tales edited by Kevin J. Anderson
Star Wars: Tales from the Mos Eisley Cantina
    1st PB: Bantam Spectra #56468-4 1995. . . . . 5.00
Star Wars Tales From Jabba's Palace
    1st PB: Bantam Spectra #56815-9, 1996 . . . . 5.00
Star Wars: Tales of the Bounty Hunters
    1st PB: Bantam Spectra #56816-7, 1996 . . . . 5.00

Black Fleet Crisis by Michael Kube-McDowell
#1: *Before The Storm*
    1st PB: Bantam Spectra #57273-3, 1996 . . . . 6.00
#2: *Shield of Lies*
    1st PB: Bantam Spectra #57277-6, 1996 . . . . 6.00
#3: *Tyrant's Test*
    1st PB: Bantam Spectra #57275-X, 1997 . . . . 6.00

X-Wing series
#1: *Rogue Squadron* by Michael A. Stackpole
    1st PB: Bantam Spectra #56801-9, 1996 . . . . 9.00
#2: *Wedge's Gamble* by Michael A. Stackpole
    1st PB: Bantam Spectra #56802-7, 1996 . . . . 8.00
#3: *The Krytos Trap* by Michael A. Stackpole

1st PB: Bantam Spectra #56803-5, 1996 . . . . 7.00
#4: *The Bacta War* by Michael A. Stackpole
    1st PB: Bantam Spectra #56804-3, 1997 . . . . 6.00
#5: *Starfighters of Adumar* by Aaron Allston
    1st PB: Bantam Spectra # , 1998 . . . . 6.00
#6: *Iron Fist* by Aaron Allston
    1st PB: Bantam Spectra #57897-9, 1998. . . . . 6.00
#7: *Solo Command* by Aaron Allston
    1st PB: Bantam Spectra # , Feb. 1999 . . . . 6.00
#8: *Isard's Revenge* by Michael A. Stackpole
    1st PB: Bantam Spectra #57903-7, 1999 . . . . 6.00

Han Solo Trilogy by A.C. Crispin
#1: *Star Wars The Paradise Snare*
    1st PB: Bantam Spectra #57415-7, 1997 . . . . 6.00
#2: *Star Wars The Hutt Gambit*
    1st PB: Bantam Spectra #57416-7, 1997 . . . . 6.00
#3: *Rebel Dawn*
    1st PB: Bantam Spectra #57417-5, 1998 . . . . 6.00

Bounty Hunter Wars by K. W. Jeter
#1: The Mandalorian Armor
    1st PB: Bantam Spectra #57885-5, 1998 . . . . 6.00
#2:
    1st PB: Bantam Spectra #57888-X, 1999 . . . . 6.00
#3: Hard Merchandise
    1st PB: Bantam Spectra #57891-X, 1999 . . . . 6.00

Schweighofer, Peter ed.: *Star Wars: Tales from the
Empire*, Bantam Spectra #57876-6, 1997 . . . . 5.00

YOUNG ADULT NOVELS

    Young Adult books do not draw much collector interest, while kiddie books with pictures are fairly collectible. This has little or nothing to do with the quality of the fiction.

Young Jedi Knights series by Kevin J. Anderson and
    Rebecca Moesta
#1: *Shadow Academy,* 1st PB: $6.00
#2 thru #14, each. 5.00
Combined HC: #1–#6. . . . . 20.00

Star Wars series by Paul Davids and Hollace Davids
#1: *The Glove of Darth Vader,* 1st PB 1992 . . . . 3.50
#2: thru 6, each 3.00

Galaxy of Fear series by John Whitman
#1 thru 12, each. 5.00

Junior Jedi Knights series by Nancy Richardson
#1 thru #3, each. 4.00
by Rebecca Moesta
#4 thru #6, each. 4.00

Jedi Apprentice series by Dave Wolverton & Jude Watson
#1 thru #2, each 5.00

Cruise Along Books (Fun Works 1998)
Han Solo's Rescue Mission
    TPB: with Galoob **X-Ray vehicle** 7.00

Books

Galaxy of Fear: The Swarm *(Bantam Skylark 1998) and* The Art of
Star Wars Episode V, The Empire Strikes Back *(Ballantine 1994)*

Books

Luke Skywalker's Race Against Time
    TPB: with Galoob **X-Ray vehicle** 7.00

Other Juvenile Books
Golden, Christpoher: *Shadows of the Empire: A
    Star Wars Junior Novelization*
    TPB: Dell Yearling 41303-6, Oct. 1996 . . . . 4.00
The Empire Strikes Back Shimmer Book
    HC: 24pg, 9"x9", Fun Works #860-1, 1998 . . . . 9.00

NON-FICTION

    Star Wars books come in every conceivable category of
non-fiction. There are art books, sketch books, making-of-
the-movie books, reference books, humor books, and even
"fictional" non-fiction books. Many books include elements
of several categories, making organization of the following
lists problematic. You may have to search a little for the title
you are interested in.

Art of... Books
The Art of Star Wars, edited by Carol Titelman, plus
    script by George Lucas, includes sketches,
    costume designs, blueprints, paintings and photos.
    1st HC: $17.95, Ballantine #28273-6, 1979. . . . . $25.00
    Reissue TPB: *The Art of Star Wars, Revised
        Edition*, Ballantine #30627-9, 1982. . . . . 15.00
Retitled: *The Art of Star Wars, Episode IV, A New Hope*
    TPB: $18.00, Del Rey #39202-7, 1994, 9"x12" . . . 20.00
Revised as: *Second Edition of The Art of Star Wars:
    A New Hope*, by Carol Titelman and George Lucas:
    1st TPB: $18.95, Del Rey #39202-7, 1997 . . . . . . 19.00
The Art of the Empire Strikes Back, edited by Deborah
    Call, with text by Valerie Hoffman and Vick Bullock
    1st HC: Del Rey #29335-5, 1980 . . . . 25.00
Retitled: *The Art of Star Wars, Episode V, The
    Empire Strikes Back*
    TPB: Ballantine/Del Rey 1994, repackaged 20.00
Revised as: *Second Edition of The Art of Star Wars*

The Empire Strikes Back, edited by Deborah Call
1st TPB: Del Rey #39203-5, 1997, revised 19.00
The Art of Return of the Jedi, including the film
script by Lawrence Kasdan and George Lucas
1st HC: Del Rey #30957-X, 1983, 9"x12" 25.00
Retitled: *The Art of Star Wars, Episode VI, Return
of the Jedi*
TPB: Del Rey #39204-3, 1994, repackaged 20.00
Revised as: *Second Edition of The Art of Star Wars:
Return of the Jedi*, edited by Anonymous
1st TPB: Del Rey #39204-3, 1997, revised 19.00
The Art of Star Wars Galaxy edited by Gary Cerani
TPB: 9"x12", 132p, Topps #01-5, 1993 . . . . 20.00
HC: $150.00, Underwood Miller, 1994, limited
to 1,000 copies, boxed, signed, with card . . . 150.00
The Art of Star Wars Galaxy, Volume Two by C.
Cerani and Gary Cerani
TPB: Topps #03-1, 1994,Boris Valejo cover 20.00
Star Wars: The Art of the Brothers Hildebrandt, by
Bob Woods
TPB: Ballantine #42301-1, Oct. 1997 . . . . 25.00
Star Wars: The Art of Dave Dorman, edited by
Stephen D. Smith and Lurene Haines
HC: 128p, Friedlander #38-3, 1996, signed,
limited to 2,500 copies. 75.00
TPB: $24.95, Friedlander #37-5, Dec. 1996 . . . . . 25.00
Star Wars: The Art of Ralph McQuarrie, Artbox
includes 48-page book
HC: $18.95, Chronicle #1320-7, 1996. . . . . 20.00
The Illustrated Star Wars Universe, edited by
Martha Banta
HC: Bantam #03925-4, 1995 . . . . 20.00
The Illustrated Star Wars Universe, by Kevin J.
Anderson, illustrated by Ralph McQuarrie
1st HC, Bantam Spectra #09302-9, 1995 . . . . 35.00
Industrial Light & Magic: The Art of Special Effects,
by Thomas G. Smith
1st HC: Del Rey #32263-0, 1986 . . . . 25.00
*The Art of Star Wars Episode 1, The Phantom
Menace* by Jonathan Bresman
1st HC: Del Rey #43108-1, Sept. 1999 . . . . 40.00

Books

The Art of Dave Dorman *(Friedlander 1996)*
and The Art of Star Wars Galaxy, Volume Two *(Topps 1994)*

Illustrated Screenplays
Star Wars: A New Hope Illustrated Screenplay
    TPB: Ballantine #42069-7, 1998, 5"x8" 12.00
Star Wars: The Empire Strikes Back Illustrated Screenplay
    TPB: Ballantine #42070-5, 1998, 5"x8" 12.00
Star Wars: Return of the Jedi Illustrated Screenplay
    TPB: Ballantine #42079-9, 1998, 5"x8" 12.00
Star Wars Episode 1, The Phantom Menace Illus-
    trated Screenplay by George Lucas
    1st TPB: Del Rey #43110-3, May 1999 . . . . 15.00

Guide to
A Guide to the Star Wars Universe, by Raymond L. Velasco
    1st PB, Ballantine-Del Rey #31920-6, 1984 . . . . . . 7.50
A Guide to the Star Wars Universe, Second Edition,
    Revised & Expanded, by Bill Slavicsek
    1st TPB: $10.00, 448p, Del Rey #38625-6,
        1996, 5"x8" Ralph McQuarrie cover 10.00
Star Wars: The Essential Guide To Characters, by
    Andy Mangels
    1st TPB: Del Rey #39535-2, 1995, Reference . . . 18.00
Star Wars: The Essential Guide To Vehicles and
    Vessels, by Bill Smith
    1st TPB: Del Rey #39299-X, 1996, Reference . . . 18.00
Star Wars: The Essential Guide to Weapons and
    Technology, by Bill Smith
    1st TPB: Del Rey #41413-6, 1997 . . . . 18.00
Star Wars: The Essential Guide to Droids, by Dan
    Wallace, drawings by Bill Hughes
    1st TPB: Del Rey 1998 . . . . 18.00
Star Wars Technical Journal, by Shane Johnson
    1st HC: $35.00, 192p, Del Rey #40182-4,
        Oct. 1995, combo of 3 Starlog journals. 35.00
The Secrets of Star Wars: Shadows of the Empire,
    by Mark Cotta Vaz, 7½"x9¼"
    TPB: Del Rey #40236-7, 1996 . . . . 15.00
Star Wars Episode I Who's Who: A Pocket Guide to
    the Characters in The Phantom Menace, by
    Ryder Windham

A Guide to the Star Wars Universe *(Del Rey 1984) and*
The Essential Guide to Vehicles and Vessels *(Del Rey 1996)*

1st HC: Running Press 0-76240519-8, 1999 . . . . . . 6.00
Star Wars Episode I What's What: A Pocket Guide to The Phantom Menace, by Daniel Wallace
    1st HC: Running Press 0-76240520-1, 1999 . . . . . . 6.00
Star Wars Episode I The Phantom Menace: The Visual Dictionary by David West Reynolds, Hans Jenssen & Richard Chasemore
    1st HC: DK Publishing, June 1999. . . . . 20.00
Star Wars Episode 1, Incredible Cross-Sections by David West Reynolds, oversized
    1st HC: DK Publishing #3962-X, 1999 . . . . 20.00
Star Wars Encyclopedia by Stephen J. Sansweet
    1st HC: Del Rey #40227-8, June 1998 . . . . 50.00

Making of

The Star Wars Album, edited by Anonymous
    1st TPB: Nov. 1977, $5.95, 76p, Ballantine
       27591-8, 8½"x11", Bros. Hildebrandt covers . . . 20.00
Once Upon a Galaxy: A Journal of the Making of The Empire Strikes Back, by Alan Arnold
    1st PB: Del Rey #29075-5, 1980 . . . . 10.00
The Making of Return of the Jedi, by John Philip Peecher
    1st PB, Del Rey #31235-X, 1983 . . . . 10.00
Star Wars, The Making of Episode 1, The Phantom Menace by Laurent Bouzereau and Jody Duncan
    1st HC: Del Rey #43111-1, May 1999 . . . . 40.00

Pop-Up Books

Star Wars: The Rebel Alliance, Ships of the Fleet, by Bill Smith, 10p, 11¼"x8¾"
    HC: $15.95, Little Brown #53509-5, 1995 . . . . 16.00
Star Wars: The Galactic Empire, Ships of the Fleet, by Bill Smith, 10p, 11¼"x8¾"
    HC: $15.95, Little Brown #53510-9, 1995 . . . . 16.00
Star Wars: The Mos Eisley Cantina Pop-up Book by Kevin J. Anderson and Rebecca Moesta, illustrated by Ralph McQuarrie, 16p, 8½"x12¾"
    HC: $19.95, Little Brown #53511-7, 1995 . . . . 20.00
Star Wars: Jabba's Palace Pop-up Book by Kevin

Books

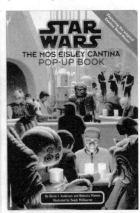

Star Wars Album *(Ballantine 1977) and* The Mos Eisley Cantina Pop-Up Book *(Little Brown 1995)*

Books

J. Anderson and Rebecca Moesta"
HC: $19.95, Little Brown #53513-3, 1995 . . . . 20.00

Scripts/Dramatizations
*Star Wars: The National Public Radio Dramatiza-
tion*, by Brian Daley
TPB: Rey #39109-8, 1994, Illustrated 12.00
*The Empire Strikes Back: The National Public
Radio Dramatization*, by Brian Daley
TPB: Del Rey #39605-7, 1995, illustrated 11.00
*Return of the Jedi: The National Public Radio
Dramatization*, by Brian Daley
TPB: Del Rey #40782-2, 1996, Illustrated. 12.00
Star Wars: The Three-In-One Annotated Scripts,
annotated by Laurent Bouzereau
TPB: Del Rey #40981-7, May 1997 . . . . 13.00
Star Wars: A New Hope, facsimile script
TPB: One Stop Publishing #306-4, 1994 . . . . 20.00
The Empire Strikes Back, facsimile script
TPB: One Stop Publishing #307-2, 1994 . . . . 20.00
Return of the Jedi, facsimile script
TPB: One Stop Publishing #304-8, 1994 . . . . 20.00
Star Wars Trilogy, facsimile scripts
TPB: 1-56693374-9, 1995 . . . . 50.00

Sketchbook
The Star Wars Sketchbook, by Joe Johnston
1st TPB: Ballantine #27380, 1977, 8½"x11" 25.00
The Empire Strikes Back Sketchbook, by Joe
Johnston and Rodis Jamero
1st TPB: Ballantine #28836-X, 1980, sketches . . 35.00
Return of the Jedi Sketchbook, by Joe Johnston
1st TPB: Ballantine, 1983. . . . . 25.00

Smithsonian
*Star Wars: The Magic of Myth: Companion to the
Exhibition at the National Air and Space
Museum*, by Mary Henderson
1st HC: Bantam Broadway #10206-0,.1997 . . . . . 50.00

Misc. Books
Most other Non-Fiction Books, each . . . . cover price

Star Wars Darth Vader Activity Book *(Random House 1979)* & The
Empire Strikes Back, Marvel Comics Version *(Marvel 1980)*

Comic
The Marvel Comics Illustrated Version of Star Wars, by Roy Thomas
  1st Comic PB: $1.50, 124p, Ballantine-Del
    Rey #27492-X, Nov. 1977, in black and white . . 10.00
The Empire Strikes Back, by Archie Goodwin, and Al Williamson
  1st Comic PB: $2.50, Marvel #02114, 1980 . . . . . 5.00

Books

Episode I: Jar Jar's Coloring Fun *(Random House 1999)*
and Star Wars Pop-Up Book *(Random House 1979)*

JUVENILE BOOKS
ACTIVITY, POP-UP, STORY

Activity Books
Artoo Detoo's *Activity Book* (Random House 1979) . . . $5.00
Chewbacca's *Activity Book* (Random House 1979). 5.00
Darth Vader's *Activity Book* (Random House 1979) 5.00
Return of the Jedi Punch-out and Make It book
    (Random House) 10.00
Activity Books (Happy House 1983)
    Various *Return of the Jedi,* Book, each. 5.00
Activity Books (Golden Book 1997)
    Various, each 4.00

Episode I Activity Books (Random House 1999)
Galactic Puzzles and Games, Darth Maul cover 3.00
Lightsaber Marker Activity Book, Jedi & Sith cover 4.00
Queen Amidala Paper Doll Book, Queen Amidala cover. 4.00
Micro-Vehicle Punchouts, Naboo Fighter cover 4.00
Jar Jar Binks or Anakin with Punch-Out(s) 10p, each . . . 8.00
*Star Wars Episode I The Phantom Menace: Sticker
    Book,* DK Publishing, May 1999 . . . . 7.00
*Star Wars Episode I The Phantom Menace: Classic
    Sticker Book,* DK Publishing, May 1999. . . . . 7.00

Coloring Books
Star Wars: The Empire Strikes Back Coloring Book,
    64 pages (Kenner 1980) various covers, each 5.00
Star Wars: Return of the Jedi Coloring Books

Books

(Kenner 1983) various covers, each 4.00
Ewoks coloring books, each 3.00
Coloring Books (Golden Book 1997) each 3.00
Episode I Coloring Books (Random House 1999) each 3.00

Pop-Up Books

Star Wars Pop-up Book illustrated by Wayne
    Barlowe, HC (Random House 1978) 15.00
The Empire Strikes Back Pop-up Book, (Random
    House 1980) 15.00
Return of the Jedi Pop-up Book (Random House 1983) 12.00

The Star Wars Storybook *and* Return of the Jedi Storybook
(Scholastic 1977 & 1983)

Movie Story Books

The Star Wars Storybook, by Geraldine Richelson,
    with color photos (Random House 1978) 12.50
Star Wars: A Storybook, by J. J. Gardner (Scholastic
    #06654-4, 1996) 6.00
Star Wars little chronicles (Chronicle #1480-7, 1997) . . 10.00
The Empire Strikes Back Storybook, by Shep Stene-
    man (Random House 84414-9, Aug. 1980) 10.00
The Empire Strikes Back Storybook by J.J. Gardner
    (Scholastic #06656-0, 1996) 5.00
The Empire Strikes Back little chronicles (Chronicle
    #4182-3, Jan. 1997) 10.00
Return of the Jedi Storybook, by Joan D. Vinge
    (Random House 1983) 12.50
Return of the Jedi Storybook by J.J. Gardner
    (Scholastic #06659-5, 1996) 6.00
Return of the Jedi little chronicles (Chronicle
    #4194-7, Jan. 1997) 10.00
Other Story Books(Random House 1979) each 6.00
Droid Story Books (Random House 1986) each 5.00
Ewoks Story Books (Random House 1984–86) each . . 5.00
Episode I Story Books (Random House 1999) each . . . 4.00

CERAMICS

BANKS

The Roman Ceramics Company was the first to manufacture ceramic banks. These, like all 1977 collectibles, appeared before the action figures, but many collectors passed them up at the time and they were available at retail for several years. Each bank came in a white box and was hand painted. Sigma made three ceramic banks for the later movies. See also plastic and metal banks under DOLLS AND FIGURES and talking banks under ELECTRONICS.

Ceramic Banks (Roman Ceramics 1977) boxed
C-3PO Ceramic Bank, 8" tall, waist up, metallic gold $75.00
Darth Vader Ceramic Bank, 7" tall, head 85.00
R2-D2 Ceramic Bank, 8" tall, full figure 75.00

Ceramic Banks (Sigma 1982)
Chewbacca Ceramic Bank, 10½" tall, kneeling. 45.00
Jabba the Hutt Ceramic Bank, 6" tall, figural. 45.00
Yoda Ceramic Bank, 8" tall, figural 45.00

COOKIE JARS

Ceramic cookie jars were another early collectible from Roman Ceramics. R2-D2 is just the right shape to hold a lot of cookies. Cookie jars have been making a comeback in the last few years from Star Jars. Only 1,000 of each are being produced, but you have to supply your own cookies.

Cookie Jars (Roman Ceramics 1977):
C-3PO, 10¾" gold metallic glaze $140.00

Yoda Ceramic Bank (Sigma 1982) &
Chewbacca Cookie Jar (Star Jars 1998)

Jabba the Hut Cookie Jar (Star Jars 1998)

Darth Vader 140.00
R2-D2 13" tall, in white cardboard box 150.00
C-3PO/Darth Vader/R2-D2 Hexagon Cookie Jar
    (Sigma 1982) 100.00

Cookie Jars by Star Jars, limited editions of 1,000 jars
Obi-Wan Kenobi (Star Jars #026, 1998) 250.00
Jabba the Hutt (Star Jars #027, 1998) 250.00
Chewbacca (Star Jars #028, 1998) 250.00
C-3PO (Star Jars #029, Sept. 1998) 250.00
Princess Leia (Star Jars 1998) 250.00
Boba Fett (Star Jars 1998) 250.00

Bookends (Sigma 1983)
Chewbacca/Darth Vader Figural Bookends 75.00

FIGURES

Sigma produced a dozen 7" ceramic bisque figures in 1983. The faces on the human figures are somewhat juvenile; the non-humans are better sculpted.

Return of the Jedi, bisque figures
Bib Fortuna (Sigma 1983) $50.00
Boba Fett (Sigma 1983) 65.00
C-3PO and R2-D2 (Sigma 1983) 60.00
Darth Vader (Sigma 1983) 60.00
Galactic Emperor, seated (Sigma 1983) 65.00
Gamorrean Guard (Sigma 1983) 60.00
Han Solo (Sigma 1983) 50.00

Klaatu (Sigma 1983) 50.00
Lando Calrissian (Sigma 1983) 50.00
Luke Skywalker, Jedi Knight (Sigma 1983) 50.00
Princess Leia, Boushh disguise (Sigma 1983) 65.00
Wicket W. Warrick (Sigma 1983) 50.00

HOUSEHOLD AND OFFICE ITEMS

These ceramic items range from bookends to tape dispensers and from toothbrush holders to music boxes.

Ceramic figural items (Sigma 1983)
Chewbacca and Darth Vader bookends $75.00
C-3PO pencil tray 40.00
C-3PO, seated figural tape dispenser 40.00
C-3PO, in pieces, "Help" picture frame 30.00
Darth Vader picture frame 45.00
Darth Vader mirror 45.00
Ewok music box radio 30.00
Gun Turret with C-3PO music box 45.00
Landspeeder soap dish, with C-3PO and Obi-Wan 40.00
Luke (Hoth Gear) and Tauntaun teapot set 150.00
R2-D2 picture frame 45.00
R2-D2 and R5-D4 figural salt and pepper shakers . . . 125.00
R2-D2 figural string dispenser, with scissors 40.00
Rebel Snowspeeder toothbrush holder 40.00
Sy Snootles & Rebo Band music box 90.00
Wicket and Kneesa music box 75.00
Yoda pencil cup 35.00
Yoda figural salt and pepper shakers 35.00
Yoda and tree figural vase 35.00
Yoda in backpack box 20.00

MUGS—FIGURAL

Ceramic Drinking Mugs
1st Batch (Sigma 1983) in white corrugated box
C-3PO $30.00
Chewbacca 30.00
Darth Vader 30.00
Han Solo 30.00

Lando Calrissian and Klaatu mugs (Sigma 1983)

Ceramics

Boba Fett Decal Mug (Applause 1998) and
Jar Jar Binks Figural Mug (Applause 1999)

Princess Leia. 30.00
Luke Skywalker 30.00
Yoda 30.00

2nd Batch (Sigma 1983) in *Return of the Jedi* color photo box
Biker Scout 30.00
Gamorrean Guard 30.00
Klaatu 30.00
Lando Calrissian 30.00
Stormtrooper 30.00
Wicket W. Warrick 30.00

Ceramic Mugs (Rawcliffe 1995)
Movies, 3 different, each 13.00
Characters or vehicles, 9 different, each 13.00
14oz. Mugs, (Applause 1995) boxed, with certificate
    Character mugs, 4 different, each. 15.00
    2nd batch, 5 different (Applause 1996) each. 15.00
    3rd batch, 4 different (Applause 1997) each 15.00
15" Decal Mugs (Applause 1998) 4 different, each 9.00

Episode I Figural Mugs (Applause 1999)
Darth Maul Ceramic Mug, 15oz (#43067) 18.00
R2-D2 Ceramic Mug, 15oz (#43050) 15.00
Jar Jar Binks Ceramic Mug, 15oz (#43068) 16.00

PLATES

The first *Star Wars* collector plates were made in the
late 1980s by the Hamilton Collection. There were eight
plates, plus a larger 10th anniversary plate in 1987. The plates
originally came in a styrofoam sandwich box.

8¼" Plates, First Series (Hamilton Collection 1985–87)
Han Solo, pictured seated in Mos Eisley Cantina $50.00
Princess Leia, pictured holding blaster 50.00
Luke Skywalker and Darth Vader 60.00
Five heroes, pictured in the *Millennium Falcon* cockpit . 50.00
Luke and Yoda, in Dagobah swamp 50.00
R2-D2 and Wicket the Ewok 50.00

AT-ATs, pictured shooting. 50.00
X-Wings and TIE Fighters in front of Death Star 50.00

10th Anniversary commemorative plate
1977–87 Commemorative 60.00

Second Series, Star Wars Trilogy, 8¼" art by
     Morgan Weistling (Hamilton Collection 1993)
Star Wars, featuring Luke Skywalke-X-Wing Pilot. 40.00
The Empire Strikes Back, featuring Luke Skywalker
     with Yoda, plus Han Solo and Leia kissing 40.00
Return of the Jedi, featuring Luke Skywalker and
     Leia in Jabba's prisoner outfit swinging on rope . . 40.00

Third Series

    These plates were originally offered at $40.00, but by
1997 Previews was still distributing them, now for $35.00.
Just about everyone who wants one of them has bought it
already, so price appreciation will be slow.

Third Series: Space Vehicles 8¼", art by Sonia Hillios
     (Hamilton Collection 1995–96) 23K gold border
Millennium Falcon (EW1MF, 1995). 35.00
Imperial Shuttle *Tyderium* and landing pad. 35.00
TIE Fighters in front of Cloud City 35.00
Red Five X-Wing Fighter vs. TIE Fighter 35.00
Imperial Star Destroyer orbiting planet 35.00
Rebel Snowspeeder circling AT-AT feet 35.00
B-wing (EW7MF, 1996) 35.00
Slave-1 (1996). 35.00

Fourth Series: Space Vehicles, 9", art by Sonia Hillios
     (Hamilton Collection 1997–98) 24K gold border
Medical Frigate (#13609) 35.00
Jabba's Sail Barge (#13602) 35.00
Y-Wing Fighter (#13604) 35.00

Star Wars Heroes and Villains, 8¼" art by Keith
     Birdsong (1997–98) bordered in 24k gold
Luke Skywalker (#, 1997). 35.00
Han Solo (#13661). 35.00
Darth Vader (#13662). 35.00
Princess Leia (#13663) 35.00
Obi Wan Kenobi (#13664) 35.00

Ceramics

Rebel Snowspeeder & Imperial Shuttle Tyderium ,
Ceramic Plates, 3nd series (Hamilton 1996)

Star Wars Stoneware Stein (Dram Tree 1995)

Emperor Palpatine (#13665) 35.00
Boba Fett (#13667) 35.00
Yoda (#13666) 35.00

STEINS

Lidded Steins 6" (Metallic Impressions 1995)
    with solid pewter lid, 3 different, each $34.00

Deep Relief Stoneware (Dram Tree 1995) boxed
    Three different, each 25.00

Lidded Steins 9½" (Dram Tree 1997–98) limited editions
Unique Darth Vader Stein. 85.00
Unique Yoda Stein. 80.00
Unique Boba Fett Stein 85.00

TANKARDS

Ceramic "Toby" Tankard, sculpted by Jim Rumph
    (California Originals 1977) in white shipping box
Chewbacca, 6¾" tall, 36oz. brown $60.00
Darth Vader 7¼" tall, 52oz. glossy black. 60.00
Obi-Wan-Kenobi, 6¾" tall, 36oz, brown 60.00

CLOTHING

You can outfit yourself from head to toe with *Star Wars* clothes, and they are listed here in that order. While many collectors own items of *Star Wars* apparel, few would consider themselves collectors of it. While some accessories, such as belt buckles or watches, have developed a collector following, the general rule can be summed up as "Don't expect to make a killing on your *Star Wars* T-shirts."

Most of the items listed here are designed for adults, and are priced accordingly. Most of the prices are the original retail price. All this really tells you is that you shouldn't pay $30.00 for a T-shirt if you can get a hundred different styles of T-shirts of the same type for under $20.00 retail at the local shopping mall.

Caps and Hats (Thinking Cap. Co. 1980–81)
The Empire Strikes Back logo cap $15.00
Imperial Guard hat, black. 25.00
Rebel Forces Logo cap 20.00
Yoda Ear Cap, cloth ears and artificial hair 20.00
Caps and Hats (Sales Corp. of America 1983)
Return of the Jedi era caps, various characters, each . 15.00
Jedi Ski cap (white with red and black trim 20.00
Ewok knit child's hat 15.00
Star Tours Hats Various styles, each . . . . 8 to 10.00
Star Wars Fan Club Hat (special promo. hat) 15.00
Newer Caps: Star Wars Trilogy era caps (1997) up to . 12.00
Episode I Caps: various styles up to 10.00

Outerwear
Poncho, children's plastic with Jedi logo (1983) 30.00
Raincoat, plastic children's with Jedi logo (1983) 30.00
C-3PO and R2-D2 blue rain jacket or poncho. 30.00
Darth Vader and Guards poncho 30.00
Episode I Rain Ponchos, in rack bag 2 different, each . . . 6.00

Rebel Forces Logo cap (Thinking Cap Co. 1981)

Clothing

Jackets
Luke Skywalker Bespin Jacket (Fan Club promotion) . . 90.00
Star Tours Jacket. 50.00
Star Tours Jacket, silver satin. 90.00
Star Wars X-Wing Squadron Bomber Jacket (1997) . . 300.00
Luke Skywalker Bespin Jacket (1997) 80.00

Sweatshirts
Sweatshirt (Star Tours). 35.00
Star Wars Galaxy Sweatshirts (AME 1995) each 28.00

Vest
Han Solo Vest (Fan Club promotion) 100.00
Han Solo Vest (1997). 60.00

AT-AT T-shirt (Liquid Blue)
and Sebula underwear (Briefly Stated 1999)

T-Shirts

Almost all T-shirts are bought to be worn, not collected. The earliest T-shirts were produced using Iron-on transfers made by Factors, Inc. Enough of these were still around in 1994 for T-shirts to be offered to comic shops with the original 1977 transfers.

In 1994, American Marketing Enterprises produced a line of T-shirts using the images from the Topps Galaxy trading cards which had appeared in 1993. Recent T-shirts have used the images from the *Star Wars Special Edition* video tape boxes and images of the Kenner action figures. I have also seen images of cards from Decipher's various collectible card games. Maybe someone is interested in using the cover of this book for a T-shirt; who knows?

Light grey T-Shirt with original 1977 Iron-On transfer
   Nine different styles (1994) each $20.00
Star Wars Galaxy card images on T-Shirt, (AME
   1994) various styles, each. 20.00
T-Shirts (Changes 1993–1998) various styles, each . . . 16.00
Embroidered T-shirt (1996) several styles, each. 19.00
Caricature T-shirt (#LUF 1997) several styles, each . . . 17.00
Ringer T-shirt (1997) several styles, each. 18.00

Tie Dye T-shirts (1997) many styles, each 25.00
Silkscreened T-shirts (Liquid Blue 1997) each 27.00

Underclothing
Underoos (Union Underwear 1983) 9 different, each . . 20.00
Star Wars: Darth Vader Repeat Silk Boxers (1998). . . . 17.00
Star Wars ships, cotton boxers. 15.00
Episode I Boys Briefs (1999) 2 styles, any size, each . . 2.00

Sleepwear
Pajamas, *Star Wars*. 20.00
Pajamas, 2 piece, kids sizes (1997) 16.50

Leg Warmers
Leg Warmers, 22" long, black (1983) 20.00

Socks
Slipper Socks (Stride Rite 1983). 15.00
Socks (Charleston Hosiery 1983) 10.00

OTHER CLOTHING ITEMS

The Ralph Marlin *Star Wars* collection started with one tie in 1992 and has now grown to a whole wardrobe of silk and polyester ties, caps, silk boxer shorts, and embroidered T-shirts. Despite the quality, most of these items are still clothing, and thus not very collectible. After all, no one will buy your used boxer shorts, even if they are silk. Ties, belts, belt buckles, and the other items listed here at least have some collector potential.

Ties
Star Wars collectors silk tie in tin litho box (Ralph
    Marlin #600020, 1995) $40.00
Collectors silk ties (Ralph Marlin 1996) each 25.00
Polyester ties (Ralph Marlin 1997) each 15.00
Star Wars Video ties (Poly Ties 1996) each 16.00

Suspenders
Suspenders, circular plastic badge with raised Em-
    pire logo and color pic. (Lee Co. 1980) 20.00
Belts
Star Wars Belts (Lee Co.1983) various styles, each . . . 25.00
Star Wars Leather Belts (Lee Co. 1983) each. 30.00

Belt Buckles
Belt Buckles (Basic Tool & Supply1977) each. 20.00
C-3PO and R2-D2 Belt Buckle (Lee Co. 1979) 15.00

Leather Belt with Yoda round buckle (Lee Co. 1983)

Clothing

Star Wars belt buckles (Leather Shop 1977) four
styles, each 20.00

Shoes and Footwear
Darth Vader Sandals, Vader head (1977) 20.00
Yoda Sandals, "May the Force Be With You" on sides . 20.00
Sneakers, cutouts of characters on sides (Stride Rite) . 25.00
Chewbacca or Darth Vader booties, per pair 25.00
Episode I Slippers (Kid Nation 1999) 3 styles, each 8.00

Shoelaces
Star Wars shoelaces (Stride Rite 1983) each pair 5.00

Umbrellas
Darth Vader Umbrella (Adam Joseph 1983) 25.00
R2-D2 Umbrella (Adam Joseph 1983) 25.00

Star Wars pins (Hollywood Pins Co.)

ACCESSORIES

PINS—JEWELRY—
WATCHES—WALLETS

Clothes make the man, but accessories make the
clothes! Also, it makes a lot more sense to collect accessories
rather than clothes. You can wear them occasionally without
damage or reduction in value.

PINS

The market for attractive pins—ones that you might
actually wear somewhere other than to a *Star Wars* fan club
meeting—has been owned by Hollywood Pins. These pins are
sold through comic shops and specialty dealers and are available over the internet. The company has not continued their
license for the original movies and, as of this writing, may or
may not make pins for the new trilogy. Existing stocks will be

Han Solo: *Christmas ornament (Hallmark 1999); 12" doll, in Hoth Gear (Kenner 1998); action figure, in Carbonite (Kenner 1982); Rebe Fighter, Power of the Force Coin (Kenner 1985); and Film Frame (Willitts Designs 1995)*

Luke Skywalker: *Action Master die-cast figure (Kenner 1995);
X-Wing Pilot action figure (Kenner 1985); in Hoth Gear, with
TaunTaun (Kenner 1981); in Ceremonial Outfit (Kenner 1997);
and with Han Solo as 12" Stormtrooper dolls (Kenner 1997)*

Princess Leia Organa: *Figural ceramic mug (Applause 1997); in Boushh Disguise (Kenner 1983); with Klaatu in two-pack (Kenner 1984); Freeze Frame slide (Kenner 1998); Keepsake Ornament (Hallmark 1998); Portrait Edition Fashion Doll (Kenner 1999)*

Obi-Wan Kenobi: *Widevision trading card (Topps 1995); Return of the Jedi action figure (Kenner 1983); Freeze Frame action figure (Kenner 1998); Electronic Obi-Wan Kenobi vs. Darth Vader 12" dolls, JC Penney exclusive (Kenner 1997)*

Darth Vader: *Parasail Kite (SpectraStar 1997); Power Talker Voice Changer (MGA 1995); Action Masters Die-Cast figure (Kenner 1994); statue (Cinemacast 1995); and Darth Vader TIE Fighter, Collector Series (Kenner 1985)*

Chewbacca: *Film Frame (Willitts Designs 1995); in AT-ST vehicle (Kenner 1995); Pez dispenser (Pez 1997); action figure (Kenner 1978); and action figure, chained (Kenner 1998)*

C-3PO & R2-D2: *C-3PO Episode 1 action figure (Hasbro 1999);
R2-D2 and C-3PO Action Master die-cast figures (Kenner 1995);
R2-D2 Giga Pet (Tiger 1997); and C-3PO bandages (Curad 1999)*

Yoda: *Yoda Shaped Puzzle (Hasbro 1999); action figure (Hasbro 1999); with Orange Snake (Kenner 1980); and Star Wars Trilogy fast food toys (Taco Bell 1997)*

Jawas: *Jawa with Wrench T-shirt, image of Star Wars Galaxy trading card (AME 1994); Star Wars Buddies figure (Kenner 1997); Jawa with Ronto (Kenner 1997); and Radio Controlled Jawa Sandcrawler (Kenner 1978)*

Tusken Raiders: *Bend-Ems figure (Just Toys 1995);cover of Star Wars Insider magazine #37 (Official Star Wars Fan Club 1997); Three classic figures (Kenner 1978); and with Bantha (Kenner 1998)*

Ewoks: *Wicket, Buddies Figure (Kenner 1997); Wicket Kid's Mug (Applause 1997); Ewok Combat Glider (Kenner 1984); Lady Gorneesh (Kenner 1985); Lumat and Paploo (Kenner 1984); and Ewok Village Playset (Kenner 1983) with added figures*

Gungans: *Femba Creature with Gungan, FAO Schwartz advertise-ment (Hasbro 1999); Boss Nass action figure (Hasbro 1999); Captain Tarpals cup topper (KFC 1999); and Gungan Patrol model (Lego 1999)*

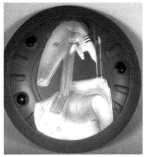

Trade Federation: *Lott Dodd Walking Throne fast food toy (Pizza Hut 1999); Battle Droid flying disk (KFC 1999); Nute Gunray Seven-up can (1999); Nute Gunray Cup Topper (Pizza Hut 1999); Armored Scout Tank with Battle Droid (Hasbro 1999)*

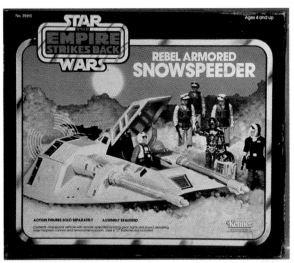

Rebel Soldiers: *Rebel Armored Snowspeeder vehicle (Kenner 1980); Rebel Soldier, Hoth Gear action figure proof card (Kenner 1985); Endor Rebel Soldier and Rebel Fleet Trooper Freeze Frame Slides (Kenner 1998); and Y-Wing Fighter vehicle (Kenner 1983)*

Imperial Troopers: *Imperial Scanning Crew Trooper from Carry Case (Kenner 1998); Stormtrooper Action Master Die-cast figure (Kenner 1995); Stormtrooper stand-up (1997); AT-AT Driver, 12" Doll (Kenner 1997); and Sandtrooper and Dewback (Kenner 1997)*

Officers & Big-Shots: *Admiral Ackbar Bend-Em (Just Toys 1995);
Prince Xizor vinyl figure, Shadows of the Empire (Applause 1996);
Imperial Commander (Kenner 1983); AT-AT Commander (Kenner
1980); arriving in style in the Shuttle Tyderium (Kenner 1983)*

available for a while, but when they are gone, prices may start to rise.

Pins & Keychains (1994–97)
Star Wars logo, theme or cut pins, many styles, price
    depends on size (Hollywood Pins) each $5–13.00
Keychains (Hollywood Pins 1994) 4 different, each 7.00
Star Wars Episode I Cloisonne Pins, 12 different
    (Applause 1999) each 5.00

JEWELRY

Star Wars head pendants (Weingeroff Ent. 1977) boxed
    Five different, each. $25.00
Star Wars earrings, three different, each 10.00
Star Wars stickpins, three different, each 8.00
The Empire Strikes Back medals, three different, each. . 8.00
Return of the Jedi pendants (Adam Joseph 1983)
    Seven different, each 8.00
R2-D2 Pendant pin and chain, sterling silver 100.00
Wicket the Ewok jewelry (Adam Joseph 1983) 7.50
Recent Jewelry (1990s) . . . . orig. retail

WALLETS

Return of the Jedi Wallets and Coin Holders
Wallets (Adam Joseph 1983) 4 different, each $15.00
Star Tours Wallet) 8.00
Pocket Pals (Adam Joseph 1983) 3 different, each. . . . 10.00
Coin Holder (Adam Joseph 1983) 3 different, each. . . . 10.00
Episode I Wallets (Pyramid Handbags 1999) each 500

WATCHES

    As with most collectibles, the best way to collect a watch is in its original packaging. Bradley Time made most of the *Star Wars* watches in the 1970s and 1980s. There are

*Darth VaderHead Pendant (Weingeroff Ent. 1977)
and Wicket the Ewok Jewelry (Adam Joseph 1983)*

Clothing

C-3PO and R2-D2 child's watch, vinyl band (Bradley Time 1977)

quite a number of styles. Digital watches generally sell for a little less than analog watches, and 1980s watches based on the second and third movies sell for a little less than those based on the first movie from the 1970s.

Recently, plastic figural head watches have been made by Hope Industries and sold in toy stores. They have not developed a following among regular watch collectors, but they are reasonably attractive as *Star Wars* toy items.

Official Star Wars Watches (Bradley Time 1977-83)
Star Wars Analog Watches

C-3PO and R2-D2 drawing, adult size analog watch, gold metal case, dark blue vinyl black strap, in plastic box.	$100.00
C-3PO and R2-D2 drawing, child size analog watch, silver metal case, light blue vinyl strap in blue plastic box with clear plastic lid.	90.00
R2-D2 & C-3PO, black face, black vinyl band.	100.00
R2-D2 & C-3PO, black face, silver bezel ring	120.00
Darth Vader, white face, red logo, black vinyl band. . .	100.00
Darth Vader, gray face, white logo, black vinyl band . .	100.00
Darth Vader, stars & planet on face	120.00

Star Wars Digital Watches

C-3PO & R2-D2 round digital, red logo, black strap . . .	90.00
C-3PO & R2-D2 oval digital, red logo, black strap . . .	100.00
C-3PO & R2-D2 rectangular digital, X-Wing and TIE fighters, musical.	125.00
C-3PO & R2-D2 oval digital, X-Wing fighters	75.00
Star Wars logo/Darth Vader round digital, blue face, black vinyl band	100.00

The Empire Strikes Back and Return of the Jedi
Analog Watches

Yoda, gray face, black vinyl band.	80.00
Yoda, white face, blue logo, black band	90.00
Jabba the Hutt, vinyl band	75.00
Ewoks, vinyl band	65.00
Wicket the Ewok, stars & planet on face.	65.00

Digital Watches

Yoda round digital	75.00
Jabba the Hutt, digital	65.00
Droids, digital.	50.00
Ewoks, digital.	50.00

Clothing

C-3PO figural plastic watch with Millennium Falcon case
(Hope Industries 1996)

Plastic Watches (Hope Industries 1990s)
Imperial Forces Collector Timepiece Gift Set, two-
    watches in Death Star Collector Case 15.00
Rebel Alliance Collector Timepiece Gift Sets 15.00
Imperial Forces Collector Timepiece 4-piece Gift Set . . 20.00
Rebel Alliance Collector Timepiece 4-piece Gift Set . . . 20.00

Watches, with face/head cover (Hope Industries 1996)
    6 different, each. 7.00

Episode I Character head collector watchs with
    Lightsaber Display Case, 4 different, each) 10.00
Episode I Die-Cast watches, metal, 4 different, each . . . 15.00

Character Watches (Nelsonic 1999)
C-3PO Skeletal Character Watch (#27588) 25.00
Darth Maul Sith Probe Droid Pocket Watch with
    Sound & Light Effects (#27591) 25.00
Podracer Pilot Compass Watch (#27583) 25.00
Queen Amidala Laser-Dial Character Watch (#27614) . 15.00
Darth Maul Laser-Dial Character Watch (#27612). 15.00
Qui-Gon Jin Character Watch (#27981) 15.00

Hologram Watches (1990s)
Darth Vader Hologram Watch (1995) 25.00
Darth Vader *Star Wars* Plastic Holographic Watch 35.00
Yoda *Star Wars* Plastic Holographic Watch. 45.00
X-Wing *Star Wars* Plastic Holographic Watch. 45.00
Boba Fett *Star Wars* Plastic Holographic Watch 40.00

Collector Watches (1990s)
Millennium Falcon Watch (Fantasma #90WA-MLF-
    LE, 1993) deluxe analog, brass case with
    flip-up lid, limited to numbered 10,000 pieces 65.00
Darth Vader Watch (Fantasma #90WA-DV-LE,

Clothing

1993) deluxe analog, black coin dial, limited to 7,500 numbered pieces	65.00
Battle of the Force Collectors Limited Edition Watch (Fantasma #90WA-DV-LE, 1993) limited to 7,500 numbered pieces	65.00
Star Wars: A New Hope quartz analog watch, gold-tone buckle (#46240, 1997)	25.00
Star Wars: The Empire Strikes Back quartz analog watch, chrome tone buckle (#46240, 1997)	25.00
Star Wars Death Star analog wristwatch, limited to 10,000 copies (1997)	90.00
Darth Vader Collector's Watch, analog, black leather band, silver bezel in Darth Vader helmet container, silver edition, limited to 15,000 copies (Fossil LI-1604)	85.00
gold edition, limited to 1,000 copies	120.00
Official limited edition Boba Fett watch, limited to 10,000 pieces, in tin case with litho image and with certificate of authenticity (Fossil #LI-1619)	75.00
23k gold plated limited to 1,000 pieces	120.00

TOTE BAGS

Tote Bags & Duffel Bags (Adam Joseph 1983)

R2-D2 and C-3PO Duffel Bag, blue	$30.00
Yoda Duffel Bag, red	30.00
Darth Vader & Imperial Guards Tote Bag, red canvas	25.00
R2-D2 and C-3PO Tote Bag, blue canvas	25.00

Star Tours Bags

Star Tours Fanny Pack, black with blue/silver	15.00
Star Tours Gym Bag	30.00
Star Tours Toilette Case	15.00
Star Tours Tote Bag	20.00

OTHER ACCESSORIES

BUTTONS, PATCHES, PINS & KEYCHAINS

Buttons are popular, but they are easy to make and most are unlicensed. As such, they can be accumulated, but no accurate list can be compiled. Just about any such button can

*May The Force Be With You Button (Unknown Mfg.)
and Star Wars Trilogy pin (1997)*

be bought for about $1.00 for regular size and about $2.00 for large size. Selling later at a profit is another matter. The most fun way to collect them is to look for free ones, which are often available at movie openings or shows.

Buttons, Badges & Tabs
Fan Club membership buttons . . . . $5.00 to 10.00
Fan Club character set, 25 buttons. 50.00
Various movie & slogan buttons . . . . 1.00 to 2.00
Revenge of the Jedi logo buttons (1982) 10.00

Patches, movies, characters. . . . . 3.00 to 10.00
Patches (**Revenge of the Jedi**) 25.00
Star Wars Trilogy Patch Set, reproduction of
    cast/crew movie patches, 5" long, limited to
    1,000 sets (1997) 12.00

KEYCHAINS

Keychains, die-cast metal (Playco 1996–98)
    16 different, each $3.00
Star Wars Keychain four-pack (Playco Toys #03120) . . 10.00
Return of the Jedi metal keychains (Adam Joseph
    1983) 4 different, each 8.00
Millennium Falcon Keyring (1983, reoffered in 1994) . . 20.00
Rebel Alliance, Pewter, Blue Card (Rawcliffe 1998)
    4 different, each 7.00
Galactic Empire, Pewter, Red Card (Rawcliffe, 1998)
    9 different, each 7.00
Episode I Metal Keychains, 2" with moveable arms,
    legs & neck (Applause 1999) 3 different, each 5.00
Episode I Vinyl Keychains, with moveable arms,
    legs & neck (Applause 1999) 2 different, each 3.00
Episode I Cloisonne Keychains (Applause 1999)
    4 different, each 4.00

Clothing

*Millennium Falcon Pewter keychain (Rawcliffe 1998)
and R2-D2 die-cast keychain (Playco 1996)*

COINS

There were two ways to get one of the Kenner Power of the Force coins—with a figure, or by mailing in a proof of purchase. The figures came with a coin which related to the figure, but when you mailed in a proof of purchase, you got a random coin. Consequently, the coins that came with a figure are a lot more common than the ones that did not. The action figure section in this book lists both the new and reissued figures which came on Power of the Force header cards, with coins. More of the new figures were issued, so their coins are the most common. The exceptions are the Anakin Skywalker and Yak Face coins, since their figures were only available overseas. There are a total of 37 Power of the Force figures, but only 35 coins. The AT-AT Driver and Nikto had Warok coins.

Kenner planned to issue Power of the Force figures for Chief Chirpa, Emperor's Royal Guard, Luke, Logray, and TIE Fighter Pilot, but did not. The coins for these figures were probably struck in anticipation of this, because they were commonly used to fulfill the mail-in requests. Interest in the *Star Wars* line was waning in 1985, and thus relatively few people mailed-in, so these coins are still scarce.

The more expensive coins were rarely used to fulfill the mail-in offer. They mostly got on the market from sources within Kenner. There was one other way, however, to get them all. Collectors who pestered Kenner about the missing coins were eventually given the right to buy a whole set, for $29.00! The offer was never made to the public. It turned out to be one of the better purchases of all time, as a complete set is worth more than 100 times that amount today.

All these coins are from the collection of Rob Johnson. Thanks again, Rob!

Star Wars Coins, Silver Color (Kenner 1985) Set . $3,000.00
Amanaman 15.00
Anakin Skywalker, Jedi. 125.00
AT-AT, *Star Wars*, mail-in, scarce 100.00
AT-ST Driver, Empire. 15.00
A-Wing Pilot, Rebel 10.00

*A-Wing Pilot, Amanaman and Anakin Skywalker coins
(Kenner 1985)*

Luke Skywalker coins, 3 variations (Kenner 1985)

Coins

Barada, Skiff Sentry	10.00
Bib Fortuna, Major Domo, mail-in, very scarce	125.00
Biker Scout, Empire	20.00
Boba Fett, Bounty Hunter	175.00
B-Wing Pilot, Rebel	10.00
Chewbacca, Wookiee	20.00
Chief Chirpa, Ewok Leader, mail-in	40.00
Creatures, *Star Wars*, "at local cantinas"	90.00
Variation "at local cafes"	150.00
C-3PO, Protocol Droid	15.00
Darth Vader, Lord of the Sith	20.00
Droids, *Star Wars*, mail-in, scarce	90.00
Emperor, Galactic Ruler	20.00
Emperor's Royal Guard, Empire, mail-in	75.00
EV-9D9, Torture Droid	10.00
FX-7, Medical Droid, mail-in, very scarce	125.00
Gamorrean Guard, Palace Sentry	30.00
Greedo, Bounty Hunter, mail-in, very scarce	125.00
Han Solo, Carbon Freeze	15.00
Han Solo, Rebel	20.00
Variation, "Hans Solo"	75.00
Han Solo, Rebel Fighter	15.00
Han Solo, Rebel Hero (Hoth gear) mail-in, scarce	75.00
Hoth Stormtrooper, Empire, mail-in, very scarce	150.00
Imperial Commander, Empire, mail-in, scarce	75.00
Imperial Dignitary, Empire	10.00
Imperial Gunner, Empire	12.00
Jawas, Desert Scavengers	15.00
Lando Calrissian, Rebel General (with *Millennium Falcon*)	10.00
Lando Calrissian, Rebel General (with Cloud City) mail-in, scarce	75.00
Logray, Ewok, mail-in	30.00
Luke Skywalker, Rebel Leader, mail-in	25.00
Luke Skywalker, Rebel Leader (on Tauntaun) mail-in, scarce	125.00
Luke Skywalker, Rebel Leader (with landspeeder)	50.00
Luke Skywalker, Rebel Leader (on scout bike)	12.00
Luke Skywalker, Jedi (with X-Wing)	20.00
Luke Skywalker, Jedi Knight (head)	20.00
Luke Skywalker, Jedi Knight (bust, on Dagobah) mail-in, very scarce	125.00
Lumat, Ewok Warrior	10.00
Millennium Falcon, *Star Wars*, mail-in, scarce	120.00
Obi-Wan Kenobi, Jedi Master	20.00
Paploo, Ewok	10.00
Princess Leia, Boushh, mail-in, very scarce	125.00
Princess Leia, Rebel Leader (in Endor outfit)	20.00

Princess Leia, Rebel Leader (head, with R2-D2). 110.00
Romba, Ewok 10.00
R2-D2, Rebel Droid 10.00
Sail Skiff, *Star Wars*, mail-in, very scarce 175.00
    Variation, Does not say "*Star Wars*" 300.00
Star Destroyer Commander, Empire, mail-in, scarce. . . 90.00
Stormtrooper, Empire. 25.00
Teebo, Ewok 20.00
TIE Fighter Pilot, Empire, mail-in 60.00
Too-One Bee, Medical Droid, mail-in, very scarce. . . . 125.00
Tusken Raider, Sand People, mail-in, very scarce . . . 125.00
Warok, Ewok 10.00
Wicket The Ewok. 20.00
Yak Face, Bounty Hunter 125.00
Yoda, The Jedi Master 30.00
Zuckuss, Bounty Hunter, mail-in, very scarce 150.00

Droids Coins, Gold Color (Kenner 1985)
Kea Moll, Freedom Fighter. 5.00
Thall Joben, Speeder Racer. 5.00
Jann Tosh, Adventurer. 5.00
A-Wing Pilot, Rebel 25.00
C-3PO, Protocol Droid 10.00
    Variation, C-3PO, Droids 10.00
Boba Fett, Bounty Hunter. 50.00
Tig Fromm, Techno Villain 5.00
Jord Dusat, Thrill Seeker 5.00
Kez-Iban, Lost Prince. 5.00
Sise Fromm, Gang Leader. 5.00
R2-D2, Droids 10.00
Uncle Gundy, Prospector 5.00

Ewoks Coins, Bronze Color (Kenner 1985)
Dulok, Scout 5.00
King Gorneesh, Dulok 5.00
Dulok Shaman. 5.00
Logray, Ewok Shaman. 5.00

Three Droids & One Ewoks coin (Kenner 1985)

Star Wars Bend-Ems Coins (Just Toys 1994)

Wicket, Ewok Scout. 8.00
Urgah (Lady Gorneesh) Dulok 5.00

Bend-Em coins (JustToys 1994) from 4-packs
Millennium Falcon 5.00
TIE Fighter. 5.00
X-Wing Fighter. 5.00
Star Wars 15th Anniversary Silver Coin (Catch a
Star 1992) limited to 5,000 . . . . 45.00

MILLENNIUM MINTED
COIN COLLECTION

Kenner began to reissue Power of the Force coins in 1998. These coins are gold-colored, so they will not be mistaken for the originals, which were silver. The coins come with figures and are mounted in a stand-up display holder. If they sell, you can expect to see more of them. Coin and figure come in a window box, which has a back window, as well, so you can see the reverse of the coin. The package sells for $10.00, so I have valued the coin at $5.00. Emperor Palpatine and C-3PO are still available in the stores, with the price cut to about $5.00. Will avid exonumia collectors bid the prices up? Who knows? Action figure collectors consider it a shameless gimmick to sell them another copy of a figure that they already own.

Gold-colored Coins (Kenner 1998)
Han Solo Rebel Fighter, with Bespin Han Solo) $5.00
Hoth Stormtrooper, Empire, with Snowtrooper 5.00
Chewbacca Wookiee, with Chewbacca 5.00
Emperor Palpatine. 3.00
Luke Skywalker in Endor Gear. 5.00
Princess Leia in Endor Gear 5.00
C-3PO. 3.00

COMIC BOOKS

Star Wars collectible Number 2 is the comic book adaptation of the movie. It also appeared prior to the movie premiere—just prior. The first six issues of the comic follow the plot of the movie, and the adventures continue on their own until issue #39, when the second movie adaptation begins.

There were no comics from 1987, when the Marvel series ended, until December 1991, when Dark Horse comics started the current explosion with the publication of *Star Wars Dark Empire*. Unlike a television series such as *Star Trek,* which has hundreds of hours of original episodes, there are only about eight hours of original *Star Wars* films. Comics, and books, supply much needed additional material to the *Star Wars* saga, and therefore play a correspondingly greater role than in other series.

CLASSIC STAR WARS
Dark Horse Comics (1992 – 94)

1	$7.00
2 thru 8	@4.00
8 bagged with *Star Wars* Galaxy promo card	12.00
9 thru 19	@3.50
20 final issue	4.00
20 bagged with *Star Wars* Galaxy promo card	10.00
TPB Vol. 1 In Deadly Pursuit, reprint #1–#7	15.99
TPB Vol. 2 The Rebel Storm, reprint #8–#14	16.95
TPB Vol. 3 Escape to Hoth reprint #15–#20	16.95

*Classic Star Wars #20 and Classic Star Wars Devilworlds #1
(Dark Horse Comics 1994 & 1996)*

Classic Star Wars Devilworlds #2 and Classic Star Wars
The Early Adventures #9 (Dark Horse 1996 & 1995)

Comics

CLASSIC STAR WARS:

A NEW HOPE
Dark Horse Comics (1994)

1 Art Adams cover, reprint from Marvel.	$4.25
2 Adam Hughes cover, reprint from Marvel.	3.95
TPB Series reprint	9.95

DEVILWORLDS
Dark Horse Comics (1996)

1 Four Stories, reprint from Marvel UK	$2.50
2 Three Stories, reprint from Marvel UK	2.50

THE EARLY ADVENTURES
Dark Horse Comics (1994 – 95)

1 Gambler's World, newspaper strip reprints	$3.00
2 and 3 Newspaper strip reprints	2.50
3 reprints, bagged with trading card DH2	5.00
4 thru 9, newspaper strip reprints.	@2.50
TPB Series reprint, Al Williamson cover	19.95

THE EMPIRE STRIKES BACK
Dark Horse Comics (1994)

1 and 2 Movie Adaptation, Marvel reprint	@$4.00
TPB Series reprint Al Williamson & Carlos Garzon cover	9.95
TPB Special reprint, Bros. Hildebrandt cover	9.95

HAN SOLO AT STAR'S END
Dark Horse Comics (1997)

1 thru 3 reprint from newspaper strips	@$3.00
TPB Series reprint, Al Williamson cover	6.95

Comics

A LONG TIME AGO
Dark Horse Comics (B&W) (1999)

1 (of 6) reprint Marvel comics $6.00
2 thru 6 . . . . @6.00

RETURN OF THE JEDI
Dark Horse Comics (1994)

1 Movie Adaptation, reprint $4.00
1 bagged with trading card DH3 . . . . 5.00
2 Movie Adaptation, reprint 3.50
TPB Series reprint (1995) 9.95
Special reprint, Bros. Hildebrandt cover 9.95

VANDELHELM MISSION
Dark Horse Comics (1995)

This takes place after the events in the third movie and was written by Archie Goodwin with art by Al Williamson.

1-shot Featuring: Han Solo, Lando and Nien Nunb . . . $3.95

DARK HORSE CLASSICS:
STAR WARS—DARK EMPIRE
Dark Horse Comics (1997)

1 thru 6 Reprints 1991–92 series . . . . @$2.95

DARK HORSE COMICS
Dark Horse Comics (1993–94)

7 Featuring: *Star Wars* $12.00
8 Featuring: *Star Wars* 14.00
9 Featuring: *Star Wars* 8.00
17 thru 19 Featuring: *Star Wars* . . . . @2.75

Classic Star Wars Return of the Jedi #1 &
Dark Horse Comics #7 (Dark Horse 1994 & 1993)

A DECADE OF DARK HORSE
Dark Horse Comics (1996)

Issue #2 of this series featured the *Star Wars* story "This Crumb for Hire," which chronicles the first meeting of Jabba the Hutt and his annoying pet, Salacious Crumb.

2 Allen Nunis cover $2.95

DROIDS
Star/Marvel Comics (1986 – 87)

1 thru 8 . . . . @$3.00

EWOKS
Star/Marvel Comics (1985 – 1987)

1 Based on TV Series $3.00
2 thru 9 . . . . @2.50
10 thru 15 . . . . @1.50

MARVEL MOVIE SHOWCASE FEATURING STAR WARS
Marvel Comics (1982)

1 Reprint, Stars Wars #1-6 . . . . $4.00
2 December, 1982 . . . . 4.00

MARVEL SPECIAL EDITION FEATURING STAR WARS
Marvel Comics (1977 – 78)

1 Reprint of Star Wars #1 thru #3 (1977) $10.00
2 Reprint of Star Wars #4 thru #6 (1978) 8.00
3 Reprint of Star Wars #1 thru #6 (1978) 10.00
Volume 2
2 The Empire Strikes Back (1980) rep. of Marvel
    Super Special #16 . . . . 7.50

*Marvel Special Edition Featuring Star Wars #1 and
Return of the Jedi #4 (Marvel 1977 & 1984)*

Comics

MARVEL SUPER SPECIALS
Marvel Comics (1980 & 1983)

16 The Empire Strikes Back $10.00
27 Return of the Jedi 10.00

RETURN OF THE JEDI
Marvel Comics (1983 – 84)

1 thru 4 . . . . @$3.00

Star Wars #1 and #40 (Marvel 1977 & 1980)

STAR WARS
Marvel Comics (July, 1977)

Although dated July 1977, the first comics actually appeared before the movie opened. The first six issues adapted the movie based on a "rough cut." This has led to considerable wonder about the "missing scenes" where, at the beginning of the movie, Luke goes to see his Tatooine pal, Biggs Darklighter, who tells him that he is going to join the Rebel forces. This scene was cut from the final version of the movie. A later reunion scene between Luke and Biggs, just before they fly off in their X-wing fighters to attack the Death Star, was also cut. It was restored in the 1997 *Special Edition*. Biggs is killed by Darth Vader, but Luke's other wing-mate, Wedge Antilles, survives. In 1998, Biggs was finally immortalized in plastic as an action figure.

The most valuable comic in this series is the 35 cent version of issue Number 1. Only a very few were printed, as a price increase test. The price has increased over 1,000 fold since then. Marvel used its better artists on these comics, at least for the first six years or so, and both comic book and *Star Wars* collectors consider them to be worthy additions to their collections.

Star Wars #100 (Marvel 1985) and
Star Wars King Size Annual #2 (Marvel 1982)

Comics

1 30 Cent, begin: movie adaptation.	$65.00
1a 35 Cent (square Box).	400.00
1b "Reprint"	7.50
2 "Six Against the Galaxy," movie, pt. 2	25.00
2b "Reprint"	4.00
3 "Death Star," movie, pt. 3	25.00
3b "Reprint"	4.00
4 "In Battle With Darth Vader," movie, pt. 4	22.00
4b "Reprint"	4.00
5 "Lo, The Moons of Yavin!," movie, pt. 5	22.00
5b "Reprint"	3.00
6 "Is This The Final Chapter?," end: movie	22.00
6b "Reprint"	3.00
7 "New Planets, New Perils!"	20.00
7b "Reprint"	2.50
8 "Eight for Aduba-3"	20.00
8b "Reprint"	2.50
9 "Showdown on a Wasteland World!"	20.00
9b "Reprint"	2.50
10 "Behemoth From the World Below"	20.00
11 thru 21, each	@18.00
22 thru 38, each	@15.00
39 Begin: *The Empire Strikes Back*	25.00
40 "Battleground Hoth!"	25.00
41 "Imperial Pursuit!"	25.00
42 "To Be A Jedi!"	25.00
43 "Betrayal at Bespin"	25.00
44 "Duel a Dark Lord!," End: *The Empire Strikes Back* .	25.00
45 thru 49, each	@20.00
50 48-page giant size issue	20.00
51 thru 67, each	@15.00
68 thru 99, each	@20.00
100 "First Strike", double-size.	20.00
101 thru 106	@15.00
107 last issue.	50.00
Ann.#1 "The Long Hunt"	10.00
Ann.#2 "Shadeshine"	8.00
Ann.#3 "The Apprentice"	8.00

STAR WARS
Dark Horse Comics (1998 – 2000)

Prelude to Rebellion
1 Featuring: Ki-Adi-Mundi. $2.50
2 thru 6 . . . . @2.50
Outlander
7 thru 12 . . . . @2.50
Emissaries to Malastare
13 thru 16 . . . . @2.50
17 & 18 . . . . @2.95
Twilight
19 pt.1 . . . . 2.95
TPB Prelude to Rebellion 14.95

STAR WARS IN 3-D
Blackthorne Publishing (1987 – 1988)

1 . . . . $3.50
2 thru 7, each 2.50

STAR WARS: A NEW HOPE
THE SPECIAL EDITION
Dark Horse Comics (1997)

1 . . . . $6.00
2 thru 4 . . . . @5.00
TPB *A New Hope*, Tim and Gret Hildebrandt cover . . . 10.00
Special Edition boxed set 30.00

STAR WARS:
A NEW HOPE
Dark Horse Comics (B&W) Manga (1998)

1 (of 4) by Tamaki Hisao, 96pg. $9.95
2 thru 4 . . . . @9.95

*Star Wars A New Hope Sepcial Edition #2 and Star
Wars Pelude to Rebellion #2 (Dark Horse 1997 & 1999)*

Comics

STAR WARS:
THE EMPIRE STRIKES BACK
Dark Horse Comics (B&W) Manga (1998)

1 (of 4) by Toshiki Dudo, 96pg. $9.95
2 thru 4 . . . . @9.95

STAR WARS:
THE RETURN OF THE JEDI
Dark Horse Comics (B&W) Manga (1999)

1 (of 4) by Shin-ichi Hiromoto, 96pg. $9.95
2 thru 4 . . . . @9.95

STAR WARS: BATTLE OF
THE BOUNTY HUNTERS
Dark Horse Comics (1996)

Pop-up comic $17.95

STAR WARS: BOBA FETT
Dark Horse Comics (1995 – 98)

1 Bounty on Bar-Kooda,48pg $9.00
2 When the Fat Lady Swings 7.00
3 Murder Most Foul 7.00
TPB Death, Lies & Treachery, series reprint 12.95
1-shot Twin Engins of Destruction (1997) reprint from
    Star Wars Galaxy Magazine, 32 pages 6.00

STAR WARS: BOBA FETT—
ENEMY OF THE EMPIRE
Dark Horse Comics (1999)

1 (of 4) Vs. The Dark Lord of the Sith. $3.00
2 thru 4 . . . . @3.00

STAR WARS: THE BOUNTY HUNTERS
Dark Horse Comics (1999)
1-shot Aurra Sing $3.00
1-shot Kenix Kil. 3.00
1-shot Scoundrl's Wages. 3.00

STAR WARS: CHEWBACCA
Dark Horse Comics (2000)

1 thru 4 . . . . @$2.95

STAR WARS: CRIMSON EMPIRE
Dark Horse Comics (1997 – 98)

1 . . . . $7.00
2 thru 6 . . . . @4.00

Comics

Comics

Star Wars Crimson Empire II #4 & Star Wars Dark Force Rising #2
(Dark Horse 1998 & 1997)

VOLUME II:

COUNCIL OF BLOOD
Dark Horse Comics (1998)

1	$3.00
2 thru 6	@3.00
TPB Series reprint.	12.95

STAR WARS: DARK EMPIRE
Dark Horse Comics (1991 – 1992)

This was the first *Star Wars* series done by Dark Horse Comics. The story takes place six years after the Battle of Endor and the death of Darth Vader.

1 Destiny of a Jedi	$20.00
1a 2nd Printing	5.00
1b Gold edition	15.00
2 World Destroyer, very low print run	25.00
2a 2nd Printing	5.00
2b Gold edition	15.00
3 Battle for planet Calamari	10.00
3a 2nd printing	4.00
3b Gold edition	10.00
4 Pursued by a bounty hunter	9.00
4a Gold edition	9.00
5 Captured by the Emperor	8.00
5a Gold edition	10.00
6 The Jedi Holocron.	7.00
6a Gold edition	9.00
Gold editions, embossed foil logo, set	75.00
Platinum editions, embossed foil logo, set	135.00
Preview 32pg.	1.00
TPB Dark Empire series reprint, #1–#6	20.00
TPB Dark Empire 2nd ed. (#44-848)	17.95
Lim. Ed. Leather bound, foil-stamped, with slipcase	125.00

RYDER WINDHAM • IAN GIBSON

Star Wars Dark Force Rising #6 & Star Wars Droids
Volume 2 #3 (Dark Horse 1997 & 1995)

STAR WARS: DARK EMPIRE II
Dark Horse Comics (1994 – 1995)

1 2nd chapter.	$7.50
2 thru 6	@5.00
Platinum editions, embossed foil logo, set	50.00
Hero Special ashcan	5.00
TPB Dark Empire II series reprint, plus cover paintings	17.95
Lim. Ed. Leather bound, foil-stamped, with slipcase	100.00

STAR WARS: DARK FORCE RISING
Dark Horse Comics (1997)

1 thru 6	@$6.00
TPB Series Reprint	17.95

STAR WARS: DARK FORCES
Dark Horse Comics (1997 – 98)

A trilogy of graphic novels based on *Star Wars: Dark Forces* interactive games.

HC, Soldier For the Empire by William C. Dietz and Dean Williams	$25.00
HC Rebel Agent, by William C. Dietz & Dean Williams	25.00
HC Jedi Knight, by William C. Dietz & Dave Dorman	25.00
TPB versions of above, each	14.95

STAR WARS: DROIDS
Dark Horse Comics (1994)

These whimsical misadventures of Artoo-Detoo and See-Threepio actually begin in Dark Horse Comics #17 through #19, and this story is included in the series trade paperback. The regular series continues these stories.

1 Featuring C-3PO and R2-D2	$4.00

Comics

```
2 thru 4 . . . . . . . . . . . . . . . . . . . . . . . . . . . . . . . @3.00
5 and 6 . . . . . . . . . . . . . . . . . . . . . . . . . . . . . . . @2.50
```
Spec.#1 Introducing Olag Greck, reprint DHC #17–#19 . . 2.50
TPB The Kalarba Adventures, reprint of #1–#6, the
    Special & story from Star Wars Galaxy mag. 17.95
Lim Ed. Leather bound, foil-stamped, with slipcase. . . 100.00
Regular Series Comics (April 1995 – Dec. 1995)
```
1 Deputized Droids . . . . . . . . . . . . . . . . . . . . . . . . 3.00
2 thru 8 . . . . . . . . . . . . . . . . . . . . . . . . . . . . . @2.50
```
TPB Droids—Rebellion, Reprints #1 through #4 . . . . . . 17.95

STAR WARS: EMPIRE'S END
Dark Horse Comics (1995)

```
1 & 2 Return of Emperor Palpatine . . . . . . . . . . . . @$3.50
TPB Series Reprint . . . . . . . . . . . . . . . . . . . . . . . . 5.95
```

STAR WARS: EPISODE I
THE PHANTOM MENACE
Dark Horse Comics (1999)

```
1 thru 4, each. . . . . . . . . . . . . . . . . . . . . . . . . . @$3.00
1a thru 4a, newsstand editions, photo (c) . . . . . . . . . @3.00
```
½ Wizard Special Magazine Comic 10.00
Graphic Novel The Phantom Menace 12.95
Limited edition hardcover, series reprint 79.95
Spec. Anakin Skywalker, direct or newsstand 3.00
Spec. Obi-Wan Kenobi, direct or newsstand 3.00
Spec. Queen Amidala, direct or newsstand. 3.00
Spec. Qui-Gon Jinn, direct newsstand. 3.00
TPB Star Wars Adventures, reprint 12.95

STAR WARS EPISODE I
Dark Horse Comics (B&W) Manga (2000)

```
1 & 2 . . . . . . . . . . . . . . . . . . . . . . . . . . . . . . . @$9.95
```

Star Wars Episode I: The Phantom Menace #2 & #4
(Dark Horse 1999)

Star Wars Episode I Queen Amidala Special &
Star Wars Heir to the Empire #4 (Dark Horse 1999 & 1996)

Comics

STAR WARS HANDBOOKS
Dark Horse Comics (1998)

1 X-Wing Rogue Squadron	$3.50
2 Crimson Empire	3.00
3 Dark Empire	3.00

STAR WARS:
HEIR TO THE EMPIRE
Dark Horse Comics (1995 – 1996)

Grand Admiral Thrawn is featured in this adaptation of Timothy Zahn's novel.

1 I: Grand Admiral Thrawn	$4.00
2 thru 6	@3.50
TPB Heir to the Empire, from novel by Timothy Zahn	19.95
Lim. Ed. HC. Foil-stamped, 160 pgs, tipped-in art plate with signatures, in slipcase	100.00

STAR WARS: JABBA THE HUTT—
Dark Horse Comics (1995 – 96)

1-shot The Garr Suppoon Hit	$3.00
1-shot The Hunger of Princess Nampi	3.00
1-shot The Dynasty Trap	3.00
1-shot Betrayal	3.00
1-shot The Jabba Tape	3.00
TPB Art of the Deal	9.95

STAR WARS: JEDI ACADEMY
LEVIATHAN
Dark Horse Comics (1998)

1 (of 4) by Kevin J. Anderson	$3.00
2 thru 4	@3.00
TPB series reprint	11.95

Star Wars: Jedi Academy Leviathan #1 & Star Wars The Last Command #3 (Dark Horse 1998)

Comics

STAR WARS: THE LAST COMMAND
Dark Horse Comics (1997 – 1998)

Comic adaptation of Timothy Zahn's *The Last Command*, again featuring Grand Admiral Thrawn.

1	$3.50
2 thru 6	@3.50
TPB Series Reprint	17.95

STAR WARS: MARA JADE— BY THE EMPEROR'S HAND
Dark Horse Comics (1998)

1 (of 6) by Timothy Zahn	$3.50
2 thru 6	@3.00
TPB Series Reprint	15.95

STAR WARS: THE PROTOCOL OFFENSIVE
Dark Horse Comics (1997)

This comic was plotted by Brian Daley, author of *Han Solo at Stars' End,* and written, in part, by Anthony Daniels (C-3PO in the movies). If you guessed that it stars C-3PO, you would be right.

1-shot	$5.00

STAR WARS: RIVER OF CHAOS
Dark Horse Comics (1995)

1 Emperor sends spies	$3.00
2 thru 4	@3.00

STAR WARS:
SHADOWS OF THE EMPIRE
Dark Horse Comics (1996)

This comic series, based on the novel by Steve Perry, takes place between the events in *The Empire Strikes Back* and *Return of the Jedi*. It pits the underworld against the Rebel Alliance against the Empire. This story generated its own group of action figures.

1 The Emperor enlists the criminal underworld	$4.00
2 thru 6	@3.50
TPB Shadows of the Empire	17.95
Lim. Ed. HC Deluxe, signed, with original plate	80.00

STAR WARS: SHADOWS OF
THE EMPIRE—EVOLUTION
Dark Horse Comics (1998)

1 thru 5	@$3.50
TPB Evolution, series reprint	14.95

STAR WARS: SHADOW STALKER
Dark Horse Comics (1997)

This one-shot collects a story which was serialized in Topps' *Star Wars Galaxy* magazine.

1-shot	$3.50

STAR WARS:
SPLINTER OF THE MIND'S EYE
Dark Horse Comics (1995 – 1996)

This series is adapted from the Alan Dean Foster novel, which was originally published in 1978.

Comics

Star Wars Shadows of the Empire #3 and Shadows of the Empire Evolution #1 (Dark Horse 1996 & 1998)

Comics

1	$3.50
2 .thru 4	@3.50
TPB Series reprint	14.95

STAR WARS TALES
Dark Horse Comics (1999)

1 64 pages	$4.95
2 thru 3 64 pages	@4.95

STAR WARS:
TALES FROM MOS EISLEY
Dark Horse Comics (1996)

Tales of the Mos Eisley Spaceport, infamous as a "wretched hive of scum and villainy."

1-shot, from *Star Wars* Galaxy Mag. #2–#4	$3.50

STAR WARS:
TALES OF THE JEDI
Dark Horse Comics (1993 – 1994)

1	$6.00
Gold foil edition	10.00
2	5.00
Gold foil edition	10.00
3	4.00
Gold foil edition	10.00
4	3.50
Gold foil edition	8.00
5	3.50
Gold foil edition	8.00
Gold foil set	40.00
TPB Knights of the Old Republic, series reprint	16.00
TPB 2nd printing	14.95

*Star Wars Shadow Stalker & Star Wars Tales of the Jedi #4
(Dark Horse 1997 & 1994)*

Comics

*Star Wars Tales of the Jedi, The Golden Age of the Sith #5 &
Fall of the Sith Empire #1 (Dark Horse 1996 & 1997)*

STAR WARS: TALES OF THE JEDI:

THE FREEDON NADD UPRISING
Dark Horse Comics (1994)

1	$2.75
2	2.50
TPB Series reprint,	5.95

DARK LORDS OF THE SITH
Dark Horse Comics (1994 – 1995)

1	$3.00
1 Bagged with a trading card DH1	5.00
2 thru 6	@2.50
TPB Series reprint, Hugh Fleming cover.	17.95

THE SITH WAR
Dark Horse Comics (1995 – 96)

1	$3.50
2 thru 6	@2.50
TPB The Sith War, series reprint	17.95

THE GOLDEN AGE OF THE SITH
Dark Horse Comics (1996 – 97)

0 The golden age	$1.00
1 thru 5	@3.50
TPB Series reprint	16.95

THE FALL OF THE SITH EMPIRE
Dark Horse Comics (1997)

1 Naga Sadow prepares his fleet	$3.50
1 variant cover, signed by Kevin J. Anderson	20.00
2 thru 5	@3.50

Star Wars Tales of the Jedi Redemption #1 &
Star Wars Vader's Quest #4 (Dark Horse 1998 & 1999)

TPB Series reprint 15.95

REDEMPTION
Dark Horse Comics (1998)

1 (of 5) by Kevin J. Anderson. $3.50
2 thru 5 . . . . @3.50

STAR WARS: UNION
Dark Horse Comics (2000)

1 thru 4 . . . . @$2.95

STAR WARS: VADER'S QUEST
Dark Horse Comics (1999)

1 (of 4) $3.00
2 thru 4 . . . . @3.00
TPB Star Wars: Vader's Quest, series reprint. 11.95

STAR WARS:
X-WING ROGUE SQUADRON
Dark Horse Comics (1995 – 1998)

This continuing series stars Wedge Antilles, X-wing
pilot who survived both Death Star missions and now leads
the Rogue Squadron. The series is divided into mostly four-
part story arcs, with separate titles, as noted.

The Rebel Opposition
 ½ Wizard limited exclusive $25.00
 1 The Rebel Opposition, Pt.1 . . . . 6.00
 2 thru 4 The Rebel Opposition, Pt.2 thru Pt.4 . . . . . . @3.50
The Phantom Affair
 5 thru 8 The Phantom Affair, Pt.1 thru Pt.4. . . . . @3.50
Battleground Tatooine
 9 thru 12 Battleground Tatooine, Pt.1 thru Pt.4. . . . . . @3.50

Star Wars X-Wing Rogue Squadron #8 & #25
(Dark Horse 1995 & 1997)

Comics

The Warrior Princess
13 thru 16 The Warrior Princess, Pt.1 thru Pt.4 . . . . . . @3.50
Requiem for a Rogue
17 thru 20 Requiem for a Rogue, Pt.1 thru Pt.4 . . . . . @3.50
In the Empire's Service
21 thru 24 In the Empire's Service, Pt.1 thru Pt. 4. . . . @3.50
The Making of Baron Fel
25 The Making of Baron Fel. 5.00
Family Ties
26 thru 30 Family Ties, Pt.1 and Pt. 2. . . . . @3.50
Masquerade
28 thru 31 Masquerade, Pt.1 thru Pt. 4 . . . . @3.50
Mandatory Retirement
32 thru 35 Mandatory Retirement, Pt.1 thru Pt. 4 . . . . . @3.50
Trade Paperbacks
The Phantom Affair, reprint #5–#8 . . . . 12.95
Battleground Tatooine, reprint #9–#12, ... 12.95
The Warrior Princess, reprint #13–#16 . . . . 12.95
Requiem for a Rogue, reprint #17–#20 . . . . 12.95
In The Empire's Service, reprint #21–#24 . . . . 12.95
Blood & Honor, reprint #25–#27 . . . . 12.95
Masquerade, reprint #28–#31 . . . . 12.95

GRAPHIC NOVELS
Dark Horse Comics

Film Adaptations
Star Wars, 104 pages $10.00
The Empire Strikes Back, 104 pages 10.00
Return of the Jedi, 104 pages 10.00

COMIC STRIP REPRINTS

Star Wars, written by Archie Goodwin and drawn by
Al Williamson, black and white comic strip
reprints, hardcovers, three volumes, (Russ
Cochran 1991) boxed set $150.00

CRAFT & ACTIVITY

CRAFT TOYS

In toy industry terminology, Craft and Activity Toys are those that involve painting, coloring, baking, stamping, stickering, etc. There is some collector interest in the early Kenner items, but whether anybody really collects any other activity toys is questionable. Still, there are some interesting, but generally cartoonish, graphics to be found.

Crafts

Coloring
Color N' Clean Machine, 50" roll of scenes to color,
   four crayons & wipe cloth (Craft Master 1980) .. $45.00
Pen and Poster Set (Craft Master 1980). 20.00
Pen and Poster Set (Craft Master 1982). 20.00
Star Wars Mega-Fuzz Coloring Sets (1996) each. 3.00
Star Wars, A New Hope 3-D Crayon by Number
   (Rose Art #01629) 4.00
Star Wars Poster Art coloring set (Craft Master 1978) . 20.00
Star Wars Episode I R2-D2 Art Center (Hasbro
   #63347, 1999). 20.00

Display Making
Star Wars Wonder World display tank, gel, ships,
   tweezers (Kenner 09955, 1995) 15.00

Drawing (Rose Art 1997)
Star Wars Trilogy Light-Up Drawing Desk. 10.00
Star Wars Trilogy Deluxe Light-Up Drawing Desk. 15.00

Figure Making
Millennium Falcon Figure Maker, including two cans
   of air hardening compound & six markers (Ken-
   ner #22161, 1996) 15.00

*Star Wars Episode I Art Scenes Space Battle (Illuminations 1999)
& Qui-Gon Jinn 3-D Figure Painter (Hasbro 1999)*

Droids Kit Figure Maker (Kenner #22185/22183, 1996)   15.00
Slave 1 Figure Maker (Kenner #22175, 1996) 15.00

Painting
Playnts Poster Set, 15½" x 23½" posters and paints,
    5 different posters, 6 paints, 2 brushes, (Kenner
    1977) 35.00
Paint-By-Number, 8" x 10" scene & supplies (Craft
    Master 1980)
        Darth Vader 20.00
        Han & Leia. 20.00
        Luke. 20.00
        Yoda 20.00
Paint-by Number, scenes from Empire 10" x 14"
    scene plus 12 paints, brush (Craft Master 1980)
        The Battle on Hoth. 25.00
        The Chase Through the Asteroids 25.00
Paint-By-Number, scenes from Jedi four different.
    (Craft Master 1983)
        C-3PO/R2-D2. . . . .   20.00
        Jabba the Hutt. 20.00
        Lando and Boushh. 20.00
        Sy Snootles 20.00
Star Wars Acrylic Paint By Number Set (Craft
    House #51451, 1996). 4.00
Darth Vader Dimensional Mask poster set 20.00
Battle on Hoth paint set 15.00
The Empire Strikes Back Glow-in-the-Dark paint sets
        Luke. 10.00
        Leia & Han Solo. 10.00
        Darth Vader 10.00
        Yoda 10.00
Star Wars Paint-by-number, 16" x 20" b&w image
    plus paints (#1411, 1997) 12.00

Painting: Figurines
Figurine Painting Set, 5½" plastic figurine, four dif-
    ferent paints & brush (Craft Master 1980)
        Leia 40.00

Crafts

Star Wars Wonder World (Kenner 1995)

     Luke on Tauntaun 40.00
     Yoda 40.00
     Han Solo 40.00
Figurine Painting Set, plastic figures, paints, and
     brush (Craft Master 1983)
     C-3PO/R2-D2. . . . . 35.00
     Admiral Ackbar. 35.00

Painting: Figurines
Star Wars Episode I 3-D Figure Painters (Hasbro 1999)
     Darth Maul 3-D Figure Painter (#63357) 7.50
     Obi-Wan Kenobi 3-D Figure Painter (#63358). 7.50
     Qui-Gon Jinn 3-D Figure Painter (#63359) 7.50

Painting: Water Colors
Dip Dots *Star Wars* Painting Set, 8½" x 11" scenes,
     water color (Kenner 1977) 40.00
Water Color Paint Set, 8" x 10" Ewok scene, eight
     paints, brush (Fundimensions 1983) three dif-
     ferent, each 20.00
Star Wars Watercolor by Number (Craft House
     #51472, 1996) 3.00

Play Doh Sets
Star Wars Action Play Set (Kenner 1977). 30.00
Star Wars: The Empire Strikes Back Play-Doh Yoda
     Playset (Kenner 1980) 25.00
Star Wars: The Empire Strikes Back Play-Doh Ice
     Planet Playset (Kenner 1980). 15.00
Star Wars: Return of the Jedi Play-Doh Playset
     (Kenner 1983) 15.00
Ewoks Playset (Kenner 1985) 15.00

Presto Magix (American Publishing)
Presto Magix, poster from *The Empire Strikes Back*
     and six different transfer sheets (1980)
     Six different, each 5.00
Presto Magix, poster of *Return of the Jedi* scenes
     and transfer sheets (1983) Four different, each . . . 4.00
Presto Magix, 16" x 24" scene & transfer sheets (1983)
     Three different, each 25.00

Star Wars Figurine Stampers Gift Set (Rose Art 1996)

Crafts

*Empire Strikes Back Rub-Down Transfers (Presto Magic 1980)
and Star Wars Episode I R2-D2 Art Center, box back picture
(Hasbro 1999)*

Return of the Jedi Color Transfers (1983) 24" x 5"
    back-ground scene plus 30 full color transfers ... 15.00

Rug Making
Latch Hook Rug Kit, 6 different. (Lee Wards 1980)
        C-3PO/R2-D2. . . . . 40.00
        Chewbacca 40.00
        Darth Vader 40.00
        R2-D2 . . . . 40.00
        Stormtrooper 40.00
        Yoda 40.00

Stamp Collecting
Stamp Collecting Kit, stamp album, 24 Star War
    seals, 35 stamps (H.E. Harris 1977) 25.00

Stamping (1980s)
1983 rubbers stamps, several different. 7.50
Wicket 3-1 stamp set 5.00
Star Tours stamp set 6.00

Stamping (Rose Art 1996)
C-3PO Figurine Stamper (#01676) carded 4.00
Darth Vader Figurine Stamper (#01676) carded 4.00
R2-D2 Figurine Stamper (#01676) carded 4.00
Stormtrooper Figurine Stamper (#01676) carded 4.00
Yoda Figurine Stamper (#01676) carded 4.00
Star Wars Figurine Stampers Gift Set, including
    Darth Vader, Stormtrooper, Yoda, C-3PO and
    R2-D2 stamps (#01674) boxed. 15.00

Sticking
Wicket the Ewok Transfer Set (Kenner 1985) 12.00
Star Wars Sticker Studio, over 300 stickers (1997) 6.00
Star Wars Sticker Value Pack, 150 stickers (1997) 4.00
Star Wars Push Pin 12 pin set (RoseArt 1997) 4.00
Star Wars Episode I large Collectible Decals (Liquid

Crafts

R2-D2 Suncatcher, baked (Fundimensions 1983)

Blue, 1999)
Characters, six different, each 1.00
Scenes, six different, each 1.00
Star Wars Episode I small Collector Stickers, three
stickers on hanging card (Sandylion 1999)
Six different series, each 0.50

Art Scenes Glow-in-the-Dark Wall Scenes (Illuminations 1999)
Boxes
Characters (#70050) 20.00
Space Battle (#70051) 20.00
Battle Zone (#70045) 13.00
Heroes, Villains & Droids (#70046) 13.00
Bagged four different, each 6.00

Sticking: Magnetic
Star Wars Mix 'N' Match Adventure Playset, magnetic pieces and background (ATA-Boy Inc.) 20.00

Sticking: Static (Priss Prints 1999)
Star Wars Episode I Jumbo Stick-Ups 20.00

Suncatchers (Lee Wards 1980) *Empire Strikes Back* cards
12 different, each 12.00

Suncatchers Makit & Bakit "Stained Glass" (Fun-dimensions
1983) *Return of the Jedi* header cards
Four different, each 10.00

Crafts

ACTIVITY TOYS & EQUIPMENT

While skating, kite flying, and yo-yoing are not really like the artistic activities listed previously, these toys have to be listed somewhere.

Biking
Star Wars Riding Speeder Bike (Kenner 1983) . . . $1,000.00
Queen Amidala Bike, 16" Girls (Dynacraft #51794, 1999) 75.00
Darth Maul Bike (Dynacraft #51311, 1999) 80.00
Jar Jar Bike, 12" (Dynacraft #52163, 1999) 75.00

Boping
Inflatable Bop Bags (Kenner 1977) boxed
Chewbacca, 50" tall (#63050) 60.00
Darth Vader, 50" tall 60.00
Jawa, 36" tall 70.00
Artoo-Detoo, 36" tall 45.00

Kite Flying
Darth Vader Parasail Kite (SpectraStar 1997) 15.00

Skate Boarding
Star Wars Episode I 8" x 31" Double Sided Decal
Darth Maul & Obi Wan Kenobi skateboard 20.00
Star Wars Episode I R2-D2 & C-3PO Skateboard 10.00

Skating
Ice Skates (Brookfield Athletic Shoe 1983)
Darth Vader and Imperial Guard 75.00
Wicket 75.00
Darth and Imperial Guard Roller Skates (Brookfield
Athletic Shoe 1983) 75.00
Wicket Roller Skates (Brookfield Athletic Shoe 1983) . . 75.00
Star Wars Episode I R2-D2 In-Line Youth Adjustable
Skates (Seneca Sports #72006) 20.00

Skating & Biking Helmets & Gear
Star Wars Episode 1 Queen Amidala Multi-Sport
Helmet, Ages 7-14 (Dynacraft #89366) 15.00
Star Wars Episode 1 Darth Maul Multi-Sport Helmet,
Ages 7-14 (Dynacraft #89362) 15.00
Episode 1 Backpack Protective Combo Set 10.00

Yo-Yoing
Star Wars 3D Sculpted Yo Yo (SpectraStar 1995)
Darth Vader (#1624) 5.00
Stormtrooper (#1623) 5.00
Star Wars Episode I Destroyer Droid Yo-Yo
(Tiger 88-201) 7.50

Crafts

DIE-CAST

DIE-CAST FIGURES AND SHIPS

Like ceramics, die-cast figures and ships are their own collecting category. Unlike ceramics, die-cast spaceships are figural. However, they are generally not scaled to fit the characters in the same line nor each other. Typically a die-cast Death Star, Star Destroyer, and X-wing are all about the same size. Die-cast figures and ships which were designed for gaming are listed under "Games." See also "Micro" for Kenner's small die-cast figures designed for plastic playsets.

DIE-CAST SHIPS
Kenner (1978–80)

Kenner issued die-cast ships on header cards and in open boxes. The latter are much more valuable. Several of the boxed ships also came with backgrounds. These say "Special Offer" prominently in red in a yellow oval on the left and right sides of the package.

Ships (Carded)
Darth Vader TIE Fighter (#39160) (removable
    figure of Darth Vader) $50.00
    Loose. 25.00
    Variation, small wings, scarce. 500.00
Imperial TIE Fighter (#38590). 40.00
    Loose. 15.00
Land Speeder (#38570) (Luke and C-3PO in cockpit). 100.00
    Loose. 35.00
Rebel Armored Snowspeeder (#39680) 125.00

Twin-Pod Cloud Car and Slave I die-cast ships (Kenner 1980)

Imperial Cruiser die-cast ship (Kenner 1979)

Loose.	45.00
Slave I (#39670)	90.00
Loose.	35.00
Twin-Pod Cloud Car (#39660)	95.00
Loose.	35.00
X-Wing Fighter (#38680) wings and cockpit open	75.00
Loose.	25.00

Ships (Boxed)

Millennium Falcon (#39210) with swiveling cannon and antennae dish	150.00
Loose.	50.00
Reissue, with background.	500.00
Imperial Cruiser (#39230).	200.00
Loose.	65.00
Reissue, with background.	500.00
Y-Wing Fighter (#39220)	175.00
Loose.	50.00
Reissue, with background.	500.00
TIE Bomber (#39260) test market figure, scarce.	850.00
Loose.	275.00

Metal Figurines (Heritage 1977)

Bantha Set, Bantha with 2 Sand people	45.00
C-3PO	15.00
Chewbacca	20.00
Darth Vader	20.00
Han Solo	15.00
Jawa	15.00
Luke Skywalker	20.00
Obi-Wan Kenobi	20.00
Leia	20.00
R2-D2	20.00
Sand Person, different from Bantha set	15.00
Snitch	15.00
Storm Trooper	20.00

ACTION MASTERS
Kenner (1994–96)

Kenner's Action Masters figures were issued on a header card with an exclusive trading card. A Predator, two Terminators, four Aliens, and several DC Superheroes were also available in the Action Masters series. There was a gold C-3PO available as a free mail-in for six proof of purchase points. I mailed-in but I never received the figure, which is one reason you won't find a picture of it here.

Die-Cast Action Masters Figures, with trading card
Darth Vader (#62671, 1994) $10.00
Luke Skywalker(#62672, 1994) 10.00
C-3PO, gold,(#62673, 1994) 10.00
R2-D2 (#62674, 1994) 10.00
Stormtrooper (#62675, 1994) 10.00
Chewbacca (1994) 10.00
Snowtrooper (1994) 10.00
Special Edition "Gold" C-3PO mail-in figure 25.00
Star Wars Action Masters Collectors Set (4 Pack):
    C-3PO, Princess Leia Organa, R2-D2 and
    Obi-Wan Kenobi, with four trading cards
    (#62634, 1994) 30.00
Star Wars Action Masters Collectors Set (6 Pack):
    with six trading cards (#62640, 1994) 45.00
Star Wars The Power of the Force 6 Pack set: with
    six trading cards (#69782, 1995) 45.00

MICRO MACHINE DIE-CAST
Galoob (1996–98)

The original packaging for these figures was an oval-shaped header card. The packaging was changed in 1997 to a rectangular card with stripes, similar in design to the action fleet packages (see MicroMachines). All of the figures were reissued except the Jawa Sandcrawler. Die-cast figures have

Action Master 6 Pack Collector's Set (Kenner 1994)

Die-Cast

*Jawa Sandcrawler and Executor with Star Destroyer
(Galoob 1996–97)*

interested collectors over the years, and these figures, particularly on the original header cards, might turn out to be a good buy at current prices.

Die-Cast

First Batch (Galoob Asst. #66260, 1996)
X-Wing Starfighter (#66261) $6.00
Millennium Falcon (#66262) 6.00
Imperial Star Destroyer (#66263) 6.00
TIE Fighter (#66264) 6.00
Y-Wing Starfighter (#66265) 6.00
Jawa Sandcrawler (#66266) original card only 7.00

Second Batch (Galoob Asst. #66260, 1997)
Death Star 6.00
Executor with Star Destroyer 6.00
Landspeeder 6.00
Millennium Falcon 6.00
Slave I 6.00
Snowspeeder 6.00
TIE Bomber 6.00
Y-Wing Starfighter 6.00
Reissues, on striped card, 13 different, each 5.00

Episode I Die-cast Vehicles (Galoob Asst. #66520, 1999)
Trade Federation Droid Starfighter (#66522) 5.00
Gian Speeder (#66523) 5.00
Trade Federation Battleship (#66524) 5.00
Royal Starship . . . .
Republic Cruiser(#66526) 5.00
Trade Federation Tanx (#66527) 5.00
Sebula's Podracer(#66528) 5.00

Episode I Pod Racers (Galoob 1999)
Pod Racer Packs, four different, each 5.00

PEWTER FIGURES
Rawcliffe (1993–95)

Star Wars Characters
Admiral Ackbar (#RF969) $15.60
C-3PO 15.60
Chewbacca (#RF963) 22.00
Lando Calrissian 15.60
Princess Leia (#RF958) 14.00

Luke Skywalker (#RF959) 14.00
Obi-Wan Kenobi (#RF961) 22.00
R2-D2 (#RF957) 14.00
Han Solo (#RF960) 14.00
Ewok-Wicket 10.00
Yoda (#RF955) 10.00

Characters, Darkside
Bib Fortuna (#RF970) 15.60
Boba Fett (#RF966) 15.60
Emperor Palpatine (#RF968) 15.60
Gamorrean Guard (#RF971) 15.60
Stormtrooper (#RF965) 15.60
Darth Vader (#RF962) 24.00

PEWTER VEHICLES
Rawcliffe (1993–95)

Star Wars Vehicles
A-Wing (#RF953) $32.00
B-Wing (#RF954) 32.00
Millennium Falcon 30.00
Outrider 36.00
Snow Speeder (#RF972) 30.00
X-Wing, 3" tall (#RF975) 36.00
Y-Wing (#RF973) 36.00

Vehicles Darkside
Sail Barge 34.00
Star Destroyer (#RF964) 60.00
Slave I 28.00
TIE Fighter (#RF974) 32.00
Shuttle *Tydirium* (#RF967) 36.00
TIE Bomber 36.00

Vehicles Special Limited Edition, with base
Death Star 160.00
Millennium Falcon (#RF951, 1993) 140.00
TIE Interceptor 76.00
Vader's Custom TIE Fighter (#RF950, 1993) 108.00
X-Wing (#RF952, 1993) 76.00
Star Wars Rancor Statuette (#42735, 1997) 60.00
Star Wars Sandtrooper on Dewback cold-cast resin
    statuette (#42687, 1997) 60.00

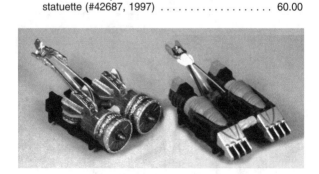

Star Wars Episode I Pod Racers, loose, Pack 3 (Galoob 1999)

Die-Cast

DOLLS & FIGURES

Between 1979 and 1980, Kenner produced a dozen Large Size Action Figures, (i.e. dolls) in window boxes with a flap. All the figures were made to the same 12" scale, but R2-D2 and the Jawa were small characters and so their dolls are about 8" tall, while Chewbacca, Darth Vader and IG-88 were about 15" tall. These are highly prized collectibles, both in and out of box (loose). The Radio Control R2-D2, listed under ELECTRONICS, was made to the same scale as the listed figures.

DOLLS
Kenner (1979–80)

Large Figures, *Star Wars* logo (1979)

Princess Leia Organa (#38070) 11½" tall	$225.00
Loose, in Alderaanian cape, royal belt, long socks & shoes with comb, brush & booklet	125.00
Luke Skywalker (#38080) 11¾" tall	375.00
Loose, in Tattooine desert costume with light saber, grappling hook, boots and utility belt	200.00
Chewbacca (#38600) 15" tall	175.00
Loose, with ammunition belt with removable cartridges and crossbow laser rifle	85.00
Darth Vader (#38610) 15" tall	225.00
Loose, with lightsaber and removable cloth cape	100.00
See-Threepio (C-3PO) (#38620) 12" tall	150.00
Loose, issued without equipment	50.00
Artoo-Detoo (R2-D2) (#38630) 7½" tall	140.00
Loose, with removable Death Star Plans	50.00
Han Solo (#39170) 11¾" tall	550.00
Loose, with shirts, pants, vest, boots, laser	

See-Threepio (C-3PO) Doll, in box and out of box (Kenner 1979)

Stormtrooper Doll, in box, and Boba Fett, out of box (Kenner 1979)

pistol, holster and belt, and Rebel Alliance Medal of Honor.	250.00
Stormtrooper (#39180) 12" tall	300.00
Loose, with laser rifle	130.00
Ben (Obi-Wan) Kenobi (#39340) 12" tall	350.00
Loose, in hooded cloak and boots, with lightsaber	175.00
Jawa (#39350) 8" tall	175.00
Loose, with laser rifle, ammunition belt and hooded cloak	75.00
Boba Fett (#39140) 13" tall	500.00
In *The Empire Strikes Back* box	600.00
Loose, with cape, Wookiee scalps, utility belts, laser pistol and rocket backpack	200.00

Large Figure, *The Empire Strikes Back* logo (1980)

IG-88 (Bounty Hunter) (#39960) 15" tall	750.00
Loose, with rifle, pistol and cartridge belt with four cartridges	300.00

STAR WARS:
COLLECTOR SERIES—12" DOLLS
Kenner (1996–2000)

Kenner began issuing Collector Series dolls in 1996. The first series of dolls had a dark blue background card inside the package. In December, light blue cards appeared. Obi-Wan Kenobi was scarce and almost impossible to find in stores from the very first. He was just as difficult to locate later with the light blue backing card. Chewbacca is pictured on the back of the boxes, but he was not included in the series and did not actually arrive until the fourth series. Instead of Chewbacca, the second series had two Tusken Raiders—one with a blaster and one with a more authentic Gaderffii Stick. Lando Calrissian from this batch did not sell out as quickly as the other dolls, and could still be found in many stores well into 1999.

Luke Skywalker and Chewbacca Dolls (Kenner 1996 & 1997)

Dolls

12" Dolls (Aug. 1996) in window box with flap cover
Darth Vader (#27726)
  On original dark blue package card, black light-
    saber handle $30.00
  Reissue, on light blue package card, black light-
    saber handle 25.00
  Reissue, black and silver lightsaber handle 22.00
Han Solo (#27725)
  On original dark blue package card 35.00
  Reissue, on light blue package card, painted or
    unpainted belt pouch 25.00
Luke Skywalker (#27724)
  On original dark blue package card, binoculars
    on belt, black lightsaber handle 60.00
  Reissue, binoculars on card 40.00
  Reissue, on light blue package card 25.00
  Reissue, black and silver lightsaber handle 22.00
Obi-Wan Kenobi (#27719)
  On original dark blue package card, black light-
    saber handle and silver belt buckle 65.00
  Reissue, on light blue package card, black or
    black and silver lightsaber handle and silver
    buckle 45.00
  Reissue, gold buckle 55.00

Second Batch (Asst. #27754, Jan. 1997)
Lando Calrissian (#27755) 15.00
Luke Skywalker in Bespin Fatigues (#27757) 40.00
Tusken Raider (with Rifle) (#27758, 1997) 40.00
Tusken Raider (with Gaderffii Stick) (#27758, 1997) . . . 40.00

Third Batch (Asst. #27690, July 1997)
Boba Fett (#27693) 75.00
Luke Skywalker in X-wing Gear (#27692) 40.00

Stormtrooper (#27689)...................... 40.00
Princess Leia (#27691) 45.00

Chewbacca, was pictured on the first series packages, but he did not appear until the fourth batch. The package back depicts the three figures in the first assortment (plus Chewbacca) and is unlike the other figures in this assortment, which picture six figures. When Chewbacca did arrive, he was very short-packed in the assortment, and only 12" tall, which is not to scale.

Fourth Batch (Asst. #27862, Sept. 1997)
Admiral Ackbar (#27866)...................... 40.00
C-3PO (#27865) 30.00
Chewbacca (#27756)........................... 90.00
Chewbacca (#27756) 1996 box................. 500.00
TIE Fighter Pilot (#27864) 35.00

In 1998, the packaging no longer included a front box flap. Gone, too, is the character bio information. However, the quality of the figures continued to impress collectors. The smaller figures seem to hang around on store shelves for a little longer than the taller ones. Nevertheless, the only one of the entire series that has lingered long enough to see a red tag is Lando Calrissian.

Fifth Batch, Star Wars Trilogy (Asst. #27741, Feb. 1998)
      green background window box, no flap
Jawa, 6" (#27744) with light-up eyes 15.00
R2-D2, 6" (#27742) with retractable leg 15.00
Yoda, 6" (#27743) 40.00

Sixth Batch, A New Hope (Asst. #27903, April
      1998) in green background window box, no flap
Greedo (#27904)............................. 25.00

Grand Moff Tarkin and Princess Leia Dolls (Kenner 1998–99)

Grand Moff Tarkin with "Interrogation Droid" (#27905). . 30.00
Luke Skywalker in Ceremonial Gear (#27907) 20.00
Sandtrooper with Imperial Droid (#27906) 20.00

Seventh Batch, The Empire Strikes Back (Asst. #27915,
    April 1998) in green background window box, no flap
AT-AT Driver (#27918) 25.00
Han Solo in Hoth Gear (#27916) 30.00
Luke Skywalker in Hoth Gear (#27917) 25.00
Snowtrooper (#27919) 20.00

Eighth Batch, Return of the Jedi (Asst. #28025, Nov. 1998)
Barquin D'an (#28026) 25.00
Chewbacca in Chains (#28027) 50.00
Emperor Palpatine (#28029) 18.00
Luke Skywalker in Jedi Gear (#28028) 20.00

Ninth Batch (Asst. #57111, 1999)
Luke Skywalker with "Dianoga Tentacle," in Storm-
    trooper Gear (#57113) 25.00
Obi-Wan Kenobi with "Glow-in-the-dark Lightsaber,"
    Training Droid and Blast Shield Helmet (#57112) . . 25.00
Ponda Baba with "Removable Arm," and "Blaster"
    (#57114) 20.00

Tenth Batch (Asst. #57135), 1999)
Chewbacca, "over 13" tall" (#53136) 20.00
Han Solo with "Magnetic Detonators" (#57138) 30.00
Princess Leia (Jabba's Prisoner) with Chain (#57137) . . 25.00
Note: Loose figure sell for about 40% of above prices

COLLECTOR SERIES—EXCLUSIVES

While all the collectors were looking for Chewbacca,
some of them were lucky enough to find one or more of the
1997 store exclusives. Many of these had store shelf-lives of
less than one day. The first to appear was the Han and Luke

*FAO Schwarz Special: Wedge Antilles & Biggs Darlighter
Dolls (Kenner 1998)*

Stormtrooper two-pack at Kay-Bee stores. Target stores got an exclusive Luke Skywalker and Wampa, while Toys "R" Us had Han Solo mounted on a Tauntaun. During the one day that these figures were available at retail, they sold for about $50.00 each. It was more like $150.00 within a week. The demand for each figure is different, depending on which stores are nearby. In any give area, exclusive figures from out-of-town stores are usually more in demand, because few, if any, local collectors have one.

In 1998, Kenner sent additional shipments of some of the exclusive dolls and re-issued others as part of its regular Collector Series. The dolls in the additional shipments are identical to the originals and the re-issues differ only slightly from the originals. Many collectors are annoyed that Kenner even considered reissuing the figures that they were lucky enough to acquire, but feel that it's not such a bad idea for Kenner to produce a few more of the ones they haven't found yet—just enough for them to get one and no more!

12" Exclusive Dolls
FAO Schwarz 12" Exclusive Dolls
Grand Moff Tarkin & Imperial Gunner with Interrog- ator Droid (#27923, 1997) $125.00
Jedi Knight Luke Skywalker & Bib Fortuna (#27924, 1997). 135.00
Princess Leia Organa and R2-D2 as Jabba's Prisoners (Princess Leia collection) (#61777, 1998) in window box with flap. 80.00
Wedge Antilles and Biggs Darklighter (#57106, 1998) in window box with flap 75.00

Direct Market (Comic Shops) 12" Exclusive Dolls
Sandtrooper (#27928, 1997) 50.00

JC Penney 12" Exclusive Dolls
Greedo (#27976, 1997) 50.00

Kay-Bee Special: Luke Skywalker, Princess Leia and Han Solo Dolls (Kenner 1998)

Electronic Boba Fett and Electronic Jar Jar Binks (out of box)
(Kenner 1998 & 1999)

Electronic Power F/X Obi-Wan Kenobi vs. Darth
    Vader, battery powered (#27661, 1997) 60.00
Luke Skywalker in Hoth Gear, Han Solo in Hoth
    Gear, Snowtrooper and AT-AT Driver (#57109,
    1998) 4-pack in window box 75.00

Kay-Bee 12" Exclusive Dolls
Han Solo & Luke Skywalker in Stormtrooper Gear
    (KB Limited Edition of 20,000) (#27867, July
    1997) in window box with flap cover 125.00
Luke Skywalker in Tatooine Gear, Princess Leia in
    Boushh Disguise and Han Solo in Bespin Gear
    (#57101, 1998). 75.00

Service Merchandise 12" Exclusive Dolls
AT-AT Driver (#27977, Oct. 1997) 60.00
Princess Leia in Hoth Gear, with "Firing Rebel Blas-
    ter (#57110, 1998) in window box 35.00

Target 12" Exclusive Dolls
Luke Skywalker vs. Wampa (27947, 1997) 75.00
Han Solo in Carbonite (#30018, 1998) 50.00
Electronic Emperor and Royal Guard 50.00

Toys "R" Us 12" Exclusive Dolls
Han Solo & Tauntaun (#27834, Aug. 1997) 75.00
Electronic C-3PO & R2-D2 (#57108, 1998) 45.00

WalMart 12" Exclusive Dolls
Cantina Band (1997)
        Doikk Na'ts with Fizzz 45.00
        Figrin D'an with Kloo Horn 50.00
        Ickabel with Fanfar. 45.00
        Nalan with Bandfill 45.00
        Tech with Ommni Box. 45.00
        Tedn with Fanfar 45.00
R2-D2 with "Detachable Utility Arms" (#27801, 1998) . . 15.00
R5-D4 (#27802, 1998) 15.00

Dolls

Wicket the Ewok (#27800, 1998). 15.00

Book Stores 12" Masterpiece Book & Doll
Anakin Skywalker, Masterpiece 12" doll & book in
    trapazoidal box with flap, limited edition
    (Kenner #02158) 75.00

Electronic Dolls (Kenner 1998)
Electronic Darth Vader, 14" (#27729) 40.00
Electronic Boba Fett (#57100) Kaybee Exclusive. 40.00

EPISODE I DOLLS

12" Dolls (Hasbro 1999)
Jar Jar Binks (#57130). $20.00
Qui-Gon Jinn with "Lightsaber" (#57131)
    "Trade Fedration" error box 30.00
    "Trade Federation" corrected 25.00
Darth Maul with "Lightsaber" (#57132) 30.00

Second Wave
Anakin Skywalker, 6" (#26229). 12.00
R2-A6, 6" (#26230) 12.00
Pit Droid, 6" (#26228). 12.00

Third Wave
Obi-Wan Kenobi with "Lightsaber" (#26232) 25.00
Watto with "Datapad" (#26233). 20.00
Battle Droid with "Blaster Rifle" (#26234) 20.00

Electronic Talking Dolls
Electronic Talking Jar Jar Binks (#84166) [.0100] 30.00
Electronic Talking Darth Maul (#84162) [.0000] 30.00
Electronic Talking Qui-Gon Jinn (#) 30.00

FASHION DOLLS
Star Wars Portrait Edition Doll (Hasbro 1999)
Princess Leia in Ceremonial Gown (#61772) num-
    ber 1 in series $40.00

Ultimate Hair Queen Amidala and
Queen Amidala in Red Senate Gown (Hasbro 1999)

Episode I Portrait Edition Dolls (Hasbro 1999)
Queen Amidala in Black Travel Gown, 1999 Portrait
    Edition (#61773) number 2 in series 40.00
Queen Amidala in Red Senate Gown, 1999 Portrait
    Edition (#61774) number 3 in series 40.00

Queen Amidala Collection 12" Dolls (Hasbro 1999)
Hidden Majesty Queen Amidala (#61776) 25.00
Royal Elegance Queen Amidala (#61779) 25.00
Ultimate Hair Queen Amidala (#61778) 25.00

Obi Wan Kenobi and Luke Skywalker Bend-Ems
(Just Toys 1993–95)

OTHER FIGURES

BEND-EMS—VINYL—PVC

    This category includes most of the figural collectibles
other than Action Figures, Ceramics, Die-Cast, Dolls and
Model Kits.

BEND-EMS
Just Toys (1993–96)

    The Just Toys *Star Wars Galaxy* Bend-Ems were origi-
nally shipped in August 1993 and, by early 1994, they were
fairly hot items. Each figure was accompanied by a Topps
Star Wars Galaxy variant trading card. In mid-1994, they lost
the trading card, but before 1995 came around, they had the
trading cards back. The 28 variant *Star Wars Galaxy* cards,
plus three mail-ins, are listed in the TRADING CARD section.

    The popularity of Bend-Ems declined as the action fig-
ures appeared. The sculpting on these figures is quite good
and there are a lot less of them in collectors' hands than the
new Kenner action figures. In the long run, these figures may
turn out to be a reasonable investment. Sources which list or

offer to sell trading cards and sources which list or offer to sell Bend-Ems do not seem to be acquainted with each other, because sometimes the cards are reported to be selling for more than the figures with the cards.

Bend-Ems (1993–95) with matching *Star Wars Galaxy* card

Admiral Ackbar (#2549, 1995)	$10.00
Bib Fortuna (#12552, 1995)	10.00
Boba Fett (1995)	30.00
C-3PO (#12362) 8-back header card	8.00
Chewbacca (#12416) 8-back header card	8.00
Darth Vader (#12361) 8-back header card	8.00
The Emperor (#12455, 1994)	10.00
Emperor's Royal Guard (#12551, 1995)	10.00
Gamorrean Guard (#12548, 1995)	10.00
Han Solo (#12453, 1994)	10.00
Lando Calrissian (#12550, 1995)	10.00
Luke Skywalker (#12417) 8-back header card	8.00
Luke Skywalker in X-wing gear (1995)	25.00
Obi Wan Kenobi (#12454, 1994)	10.00
Princess Leia (#12418) 8-back header card	10.00
R2-D2 (#12363) 8-back header card	8.00
Stormtrooper (#12364) 8-back header card	8.00
Tusken Raider (#12553, 1995)	10.00
Wicket, the Ewok (#12452, 1994)	10.00
Yoda, the Jedi Master (#12415) 8-back header card	15.00
Reissues with random, non-matching Trading Card	6.00
Reissues with no Trading Card, each	3.50
Loose, any figure, each	2.00

Multi-packs

K-Mart exclusive 8-pack includes Leia, Darth Vader, Wicket, Emperor, R2-D2 C3-PO, Stormtrooper, and Luke (#12433) 35.00

4 Piece Gift Set: Stormtrooper, R2-D2, C-3PO, Darth Vader (#12492, 1993) no cards 15.00

4 Piece Gift Set: The Emperor, R2-D2, Luke Sky-

Dolls

Star Wars Bend-Ems 4 Piece Gift Set (Just Toys 1993)

walker and Darth Vader plus four trading cards
(#12493, 1993). 20.00
4 Piece Gift Set: Ben (Obi-Wan) Kenobi, Princess
Leia, Han Solo and C-3PO plus four trading
cards (#12494, 1993). 20.00
4 Piece Gift Set: Imperial Stormtrooper, Wicket, an
Ewok, Yoda and Chewbacca plus four trading
cards (#12498, 1993). 20.00
Darth Vader bust Collector Case (Just Toys
#15018, 1994) 15.00
Deluxe Collector Set, all 20 figures in Darth Vader
bust case (#15021, 1995). 75.00
4 Piece Gift Set: Jabba's Palace, with cards and
coin (#12558, 1995) not seen. 20.00
4 Piece Gift Set: Cantina, with cards and coin
(#12557, 1995) not seen 20.00
10 Piece Gift Set (I) R2-D2, Stormtrooper, Darth
Vader, Admiral Ackbar, Chewbacca, Han, Leia,
Luke, Bib Fortuna and Emperor's Royal
Guard, plus trading cards and brass colored
coin (#12360, 1995). 40.00
10 Piece Gift Set (II) Yoda, Ewok, Tusken Raider,
Emperor Palpatine, C-3PO, Lando, Boba Fett,
Obi-Wan, Luke in X-wing uniform and Gamorrean Guard, plus trading cards and brass
colored coin (#12320, 1995). 40.00

Dolls

Star Wars Classic Collector Series PVC Set (Applause 1995)

PVC FIGURES
Applause (1995–98)

Applause started producing its current series of PVC
figures in 1995, with its Classic Collector set of six figures.
The figures have also been available individually at comic
shops and party stores. The figures all come on a circular
molded stand which has a date on the bottom. One cost effec-
tive way to acquire figures was been the Read-Along Play
Pack from Walt Disney Records. They include a storybook,
an audiocassette, and three PVC figures for about $10.00,

which is only $1.00 more than the retail cost of the figures alone. There are three of these, one for each movie.

Boxed Set

Star Wars Classic Collectors Series (six figures):
Luke Skywalker, Darth Vader, Han Solo,
C-3PO, R2-D2 and Chewbacca with Bespin
Display Platform (Applause #46038, 1995) $20.00

3½" PVC Figures (Applause)
Admiral Ackbar (#42946, 1998) 3.00
Boba Fett (#46239, 1996) 4.00
Bossk (#42947, 1998) 3.00
C-3PO (#46108, 1995). 3.00
Chewbacca (#46107, 1995) 4.00
Darth Vader (#46104, 1995). 5.00
Emperor Palpatine (#46214, 1996). 3.00
Greedo (#42677, 1997) 3.00
Han Solo (#46106, 1995). 3.00
Lando Calrissian (#42675, 1997) 3.00
Luke Skywalker (#46105, 1995). 3.00
Obi-Wan Kenobi as ghostly Jedi (#42676, 1997) 4.00
Obi-Wan Kenobi (#42965, 1998) 3.00
Princess Leia (#46216, 1996) 3.00
R2-D2 (#46109, 1995). 3.00
Snowtrooper (#42948, 1998) 3.00
Stormtrooper (#46218, 1996). 3.00
TIE-Fighter pilot (#42708, 1997). 3.00
Tusken Raider (#42949, 1998) 3.00
Wedge Antilles (#42707, 1997) 4.00
Yoda (#42678, 1997) 3.00
Store Assortment Box, 10¾" x 15¼" x 10" listing all
        16 figures from 1995–97 (#42674) empty 5.00
Han Solo, Chewbacca, Boba Fett, Darth Vader and
        Luke Skywalker (#42989) Gift Box 20.00

Jumbo Dioramas (Jan. 1997)
Han Solo and Jabba the Hutt, 4½" x 6¼" x 4" (#42691) 10.00
R2-D2 and C-3PO, 4¾" x 3½" x 2½" (#42690) 10.00

Read-Along Play Packs (Walt Disney Records 1997)
Star Wars, A New Hope Cassette and 3 PVCs
        (Stormtrooper, R2-D2, C-3PO) 10.00
Star Wars, The Empire Strikes Back Cassette and

Three figures from Episode I PVC Gift Set (Applause 1999)

Dolls

3 PVCs (Han Solo, Chewbacca, Boba Fett) 10.00
Star Wars, Return of the Jedi Cassette and three
    PVCs (Luke Skywalker, Emperor, Princess Leia) . 10.00

Episode I PVC Figures (Applause 1999)
Figurine Gift Set, four figures, including exclusive
    OOM-9 (#43036) 10.00
Figurine Gift Set, four figures (#61580) 10.00
PVC Figures, eight different, each 3.00

Naboo Starship Dangler (Applause 1999)

PVC SHIPS
Applause (1995–99)

Star Wars Danglers, on a wire hanger, with suction-
    cup, in clear acetate box, six different, each $4.00
Set of six 20.00
Store Display Box (#46037) empty 3.00

Episode I Danglers (Asst. #43034, Applause 1999)
    Six different, each 4.00

VINYL FIGURES
Suncoast Vinyl Dolls (1993)

Darth Vader $20.00
Luke Jedi Knight 20.00
Luke X-Wing Pilot 20.00
Han Solo 20.00
Chewbacca 20.00
R2-D2 . . . . 20.00
C3-PO 20.00
Leia in white gown 20.00

VINYL FIGURES
Applause (1995–99)

Most of the vinyl figures produced by Applause were
sold loose, with only a folded wrist tag or card to identify the
figure and contain the UPC code for scanning. The figures are
generally available in comic shops and specialty stores like
Spencer Gifts, but not in toy stores. They are not articulated,
although sometimes the arms or waist allows some motion,

Dolls

but this does not detract from their collectibility. In early 1998, Spencer Gifts was selling much of their stock for about $10.00, making them an attractive purchase. Applause also issued boxed figures of Darth Vader and Luke Skywalker in X-wing gear, plus a series of boxed resin figurines and dioramas. These are reasonably priced when compared to expensive statues and fine replicas sold by other manufacturers.

9"–11" Vinyl Figures (1995–98)
Boba Fett (#46238, 1996) $15.00
C-3PO, 9½" (#42955, 1998). 15.00
Chewbacca, with C-3PO, 11" (#46043, 1995). 15.00
Darth Vader, limited to 20,000 pieces (#46039, 1995). . 20.00
Darth Vader, 2nd edition, removable helmet, 11"
   (#46234, 1996). 17.00
Dash Rendar, 10½" (#46243, 1996) 17.00
Emperor Palpatine 10½" (#46240, 1996) 16.00
Greedo, 10" (#42670, 1997). 15.00
Han Solo as Stormtrooper, 10" (#46042, 1995). 15.00
Lando Calrissian, skiff guard, 10" (#42671, 1997). 15.00
Luke Skywalker with Yoda, 9¼" (#46040, 1995) 15.00
Luke in Jedi Training, 9" (#42945, 1998) 15.00
Obi-Wan Kenobi, 10" (#42672, 1997). 15.00
Princess Leia with R2-D2, 8½" (#46041, 1995). 15.00
Princess Leia in poncho (1996) 15.00
Princess Leia Slave Girl (1998) 20.00
Prince Xizor, 11" (#46244, 1996) 17.00
R2-D2 with sensor scope, 5½" (#42673, 1997). 15.00
TIE Fighter Pilot, 10" (#42688, 1997) 15.00
Tusken Raider, 11" (#46241, 1996) 15.00
Wedge Antilles, 11" (#42689, 1997) 17.00

Boxed Figures
Darth Vader, 12" (#61096) 25.00
Luke Skywalker, in X-wing Pilot Gear, 9" (#61091) 20.00

Episode I Collectible Figures (Applause 1999) 13"
   with lightsabers that light up, boxed.
Qui-Gon Jinn (#43023). 30.00

Dash Rendar and Princess Leia (Slave Girl) Vinyl Figures
(Applause 1996 & 1998)

Dolls

*Watto and Anakin Skywalker Kid's Collectible Figures
(Applause 1999)*

Darth Maul (#43021) 30.00
Obi-Wan Kenobi (#43022) 30.00

Episode I Character Collectibles (Applause 1999)
Qui-Gon Jinn, 10½" with Glow-in-the-Dark Light-
   sabers (#43029) 15.00
Obi-Wan Kenobi, 10½" with Glow-in-the-Dark Light-
   sabers (#43031) 15.00
Darth Maul, 10½" with Glow-in-the-Dark Lightsabers
   (#43028) 20.00
Queen Amidala, 9" head turns (#43030) 17.00

Episode I Kid's Collectible Figures (Applause 1999)
Anakin Skywalker, 6½" (#43024) 10.00
Jar Jar Binks, 7½" (#43026) 10.00
Watto, 7" (#43027) 10.00
Darth Maul, 7" (#43025) 10.00

DIORAMAS AND FIGURINES
Applause (1995–99)

Resin Figurines (Applause 1995–98)
Darth Vader Limited Edition Resin Figurine, limited
   to 5,000 pieces (#46048,1995) light-up base . . . $50.00
Luke Skywalker Limited Edition Resin Figurine,
   limited to 5,000 (#46049, 1995) light-up base 50.00
Bounty Hunters Resin Diorama, includes Boba Fett
   Bossk and Zuckuss, limited to 5,000 pieces
   (#46196, 1996) 60.00
Jabba and Leia, with Salacious Crumb, limited to
   5,000 pieces (#46197, 1996) 60.00
Shadows of the Empire, includes Emperor
   Palpatine, Darth Vader and Prince Xizor,
   limited to 5,000 pieces (#46199, 1996) 60.00
Leia's Rescue Statuette, includes Luke, Leia, Han
   and Chewbacca (#42669, 1997) 70.00
Han Solo Release From Carbonite Statue, with
   built-in light source, limited to 2,500 copies
   (#61064, 1997) Diamond Previews exclusive . . . 110.00

Dolls

Wampa Attack Statuette (Applause 1998)

Wampa Attack Statuette (1998). 75.00
Luke Skywalker in Bacta Tank Sculpture (1998) 125.00

Episode I Dioramas & Sculptures (Applause 1999)
Duel of the Fates Diorama, Qui-Gon Jinn, Obi-Wan
    Kenobi vs. Darth Maul Cold Cast Resin, 6" x 7"
    (#43113) with certificate 00
The Guardians of Peace Lighted Sculpture, Qui-
    Gon Jinn & Obi-Wan Kenobi, Cold Cast Resin,
    9" x 7" limited edition of 3,000 (#43119) 00
Queen Amidala Miniature Figurine, Cold Cast
    Resin, limited to 7,500 pieces (#43117) 00
Qui-Gon Jinn Miniature Figurine, Cold Cast Resin,
    limited to 7,500 pieces (#43118). 00
Darth Maul Miniature Figurine, Cold Cast Resin, lim-
    ited to 7,500 pieces (#43115) 00
Obi-Wan Kenobi Miniature Figurine, Cold Cast
    Resin, limited to 7,500 pieces (#43116) 00

FIGURAL BANKS

Plastic (Adam Joseph 1983)
Darth Vader, 9" tall. $25.00
Emperor's Royal Guard, 9" tall. 25.00
Gamorrean Guard, 9" tall, rare, ... 50.00
R2-D2, 6" tall. 30.00
Princess Kneesa, 6" tall, playing tambourine 15.00
Wicket, 6" tall, playing drum. 15.00

Metal
Darth Vader Bust Metal Bank, 6" high (Leonard
    Silver Mfg. 1981) 65.00
Darth Vader Metal Bank, tin litho box with combin-
    ation dials (Metal Box Co. 1980). 50.00
Yoda Metal Bank, tin litho box with combination
    dials (Metal Box Co. 1980) 50.00
The Empire Strikes Back Metal Bank, tin octagonal
    bank with character photos (Metal Box Co. 1980). 40.00

Dolls

Episode I Figural Banks (Applause 1999)
Darth Maul on Sith Speeder Bank, 7" (#43032) 15.00
Jar Jar Binks Bank, 8" (#43033). 15.00

KOOSH
Hasbro (1999)

Koosh Assortment, all (#09060) Four different, each . . . 5.00

PLUSH FIGURES

Star Wars, Plush
Chewbacca (Regal) $60.00
Chewbacca, 20" tall (Kenner 1977) 35.00
R2-D2, 10" tall (Kenner 1977) 50.00
Ewoks (Kenner 1983)
      18" Zephee 40.00
      14" Wicket 30.00
      14" Princess Kneesa 30.00
      14" Paploo. 40.00
      14" Latara 40.00
      8" Woklings, six different, each. 15.00
Ewok, 12", light brown with green cowl (Disney). 15.00
Ewok, 8", dark brown with pink cowl (Disney). 12.00

Episode I, Small Plush (Applause 1999)
Jar Jar Binks, with bead eyes and removable vest
    and sash, 12" x 3½" plus 5½" ears (#43072) 10.00
Watto, with bead eyes and removable vest and
    sash, 10" x 7" (#43073). 10.00

Episode I, Medium Plush (Applause 1999)
R2-D2, 12" (#43071). 15.00
Watto, 14" (#43070) 15.00
Jar Jar Binks, 14" (#43069). 15.00

Dolls

Jar Jar Binks Bank and
Jar Jar Binks Small Plush (Applause 1999)

PUPPETS

Classic Star Wars Puppets
Yoda Hand Puppet, plastic, 8½" tall (Kenner 1981). . . $40.00
Chewbacca Hand Puppet (Regal) 50.00

Episode I Puppets (Applause 1999)
Yoda Latex Latex Puppet, 12" (#42964) 20.00
Jar Jar Binks Latex Puppet, 12" (#43035). 20.00

STAR WARS BUDDIES
Kenner (1997–99)

These Beanie Baby knock-offs are either cute and imaginative or a curse, depending on your view of the real thing. Episode I buddies are currently languishing on the shelves.

Buddies (Bean Bag)
Chewbacca, original black bandolier strap $15.00
Chewbacca, new brown bandolier strap 8.00
Others, 15 different, each. 8.00

Episode I Buddies (Asst. #26242, 1999)
     eight different, each 5.00

OTHER FIGURES

Complete Galaxy Figure Assortment (April 1998)
Death Star with Darth Vader $10.00
Planet Endor with Ewok and Glider 10.00
Planet Dagobah with Yoda & Flying Predator 10.00

Episode I Battle Bags (Hasbro Asst. #63349, 1999)
Sea Creatures (#63351). 4.00
Sea Creatures (#63352). 4.00
Swamp Creatures (#63353) 4.00
Swamp Creatures (#63354) 4.00

Episode I (Hasbro 1999)
Jabba Glob, Jabba the Hutt figure with jar of Jabba
     Glob Play Gel to ooze out of his mouth and six
     frogs to eat (#63355). 10.00

& Max Rebo Buddies figure (Kenner 1997)
and Jabba Glob (Hasbro 1999)

ELECTRONIC

ELECTRONIC AND COMPUTER

This section covers electronic and computer games and toys, plus related items. Other types of games are covered in the GAMES section. The electronic toys generally produce recorded sound effects, music or short sound bites from the movies. Actual sound tracks, audio performances and *Star Wars* music are listed in the RECORDINGS Section.

The earliest electronic games and toys were made by Kenner. They still make radio and remote controlled toys.

Currently, the predominant manufacturer of *Star Wars* electronic hand-held games and other items is Tiger Electronics, Inc. By 1997, they had produced a large number of such games. There were no new ones for 1998, and Toys "R" Us has discounted some of their existing stock, so this may be the time to buy. In 1999, they produced many new games based on the new movie and this may create interest in the earlier games, but has not dones so yet. Their Stormtrooper Laser Target Game contains a 13½" Stormtrooper figure which has drawn some interest from doll and figure collectors. The original remote controlled R2-D2 is also sometimes considered a figure for collecting purposes.

Radio-Controlled/Remote Controlled
Radio Controlled R2-D2, 8", *Star Wars* logo
    (Kenner #38430, 1979). $150.00
    Loose. 65.00
Radio Controlled Imperial Speeder Bike with figure
    (Kenner #27846, 1997) 25.00

Radio Controlled R2-D2 (Kenner 1979)

Radio Controlled Imperial Speeder Bike (Kenner 1997)

Electronic Remote Control R2-D2 (Kenner #27736,
      Sept. 1997) 20.00
Radio Control Speeder Bike with Luke Skywalker 33.00

Classic Electronic Games
Electronic Battle Command Game, 9½" x 7" box,
      Star Wars logo (Kenner #40370, 1977). 75.00
Electronic Laser Battle Game, 20" x 6½" box, *Star
      Wars* logo (Kenner #40090, 1977) 100.00
X-Wing Aces Target Electronic Game, plug-in, *Star
      Wars* logo (Kenner 1978) very rare 1,000.00
Destroy Death Star Electronic Game, 17" x 25" box
      (Palitoy 1978). 150.00

Electronic Games (Micro Games of America 1995)
Star Wars Shakin' Pinball (MGA 207) (#22623, 1995) . 17.00
Star Wars Electronic Game (MGA 220) (#02033, 1995) 10.00
The Empire Strikes Back Electronic Game
      (MGA 222) (#02034, 1995). 10.00
Return of the Jedi Electronic Game (MGA 224)
      (#02035, 1995). 10.00
Star Wars Intimidator (INT-200) (1995). 10.00

Electronic Games and Toys (Tiger Electronics)
Star Wars Millennium Falcon Challenge R-Zone
      Headgear (#71-196, 1997) 15.00
Star Wars Jedi Adventure R-Zone Xtreme Pocket
      Game (#71-331, 1997). 30.00
R-Zone Cartridges :
      Millennium Falcon Challenge (#71-316) 10.00
      Jedi Adventure (#71-317). 10.00
      Rebel Forces (#71-319) 10.00
      Imperial Assault (#71-321) 10.00
Star Wars Imperial Assault 3-D Figure Hand Held
      Game "Joystick Games" (#88-001, 1997) 20.00
Millennium Falcon Challenge Electronic LCD Game
      (#88-005, 1997) 20.00
Millennium Falcon Sounds of the Force Electronic
      Memory Game (#88-089, 1997) 30.00
Boba Fett Room Alarm with Laser Target Game,
      13½" figure in window box, with Han Solo
      Laser Blaster (#88-080, 1997) 25.00
Stormtrooper Room Alarm with Laser Target Game,
      13½" figure in window box, with Han Solo

Star Wars Electronic Game and Star Wars Intimidator (MGA 1995)

Laser Blaster (#88-081, 1997) 25.00
Star Wars Rebel Forces Laser Game (#79-212, 1997) . 20.00
Star Wars Electronic Galactic Battle game (#88-088, 1997) 25.00
Star Wars Death Star Escape Game (#88-090) 25.00
Star Wars Quiz Whiz (*Star Wars Trilogy* Episode IV) Electronic Question & Answer Game (#88-091) 25.00

Star Wars Episode I Electronic Games (1999)
Episode 1 Galactic Battle Strategy Game (Tiger #88-507) 40.00
Escape From Naboo Skill and Action Game (Tiger #88-505) 25.00
Naboo Fighter Game, with Anakin Skywalker figure (Hasbro #40969) 20.00
Electronic Naboo Defense Game (Tiger #88-504) 25.00
Lightsaber Duel Game (Tiger #88-502) 25.00

Video Board Game
Star Wars Interactive Video Board Game (Parker Bros. #40392, 1996). 32.00

Computer Games/Software
The Software Toolworks *Star Wars* Chess game (Software Toolworks 1992) 15.00
The Lucas Archives, Vol. I, CD-ROM (also includes non-*Star Wars* disks) (Lucas Arts, 1995). 30.00
The Lucas Archives, Vol. II, CD-ROM *Star Wars* Collection (Lucas Arts, 1996) 60.00
TIE Fighter Wars, CD-ROM (Lucas Arts, 1995) 55.00
X-wing vs. TIE Fighter, CD-ROM (Lucas Arts, 1997). . . 60.00
Shadows of the Empire, CD-ROM (Lucas Arts, 1997). . 50.00
Rebel Assault, CD-ROM (Lucas Arts #30418, 1993). . . 30.00
Yoda Stories, CD-ROM (Lucas Arts #31118, 1997). . . . 20.00
Rebel Assault II, CD-ROM (Lucas Arts #30918, 1995) . . 60.00
Dark Forces, CD-ROM (Lucas Arts #30618, 1994) 30.00

Electronic

Electronic Game Cartridges
Star Wars SNES Cartridge (JVC NES 1993) 50.00
Super *Star Wars* SNES Cartridge (JVC NES 1993) . . . 60.00
The Empire Strikes Back Nintendo Cartridge (JVC
    NES #91014, 1992) 40.00
Star Wars Gameboy Cartridge (Capcom 1993). 30.00
The Empire Strikes Back Gameboy Cartridge
    (Capcom #12014, 1993). 30.00

Radios and Cassette Players
Luke Skywalker AM Headset Radio, battery
    powered (Kenner #38420, 1979) 40.00
Millennium Falcon Cassette Player (Micro Games
    of America #SW-24M, 1995) 30.00
R2-D2 Data Droid Cassette Player (Tiger Elec-
    tronics #88-083) 10" high 27.00
R2-D2 Personal Cassette Player (Tiger Electronics
    #88-087, 1997). 17.00

Darth Vader AM/FM Clock Radio (Micro Games of
    America #SW-3124, 1995) 32.00
Darth Vader FM Bike Radio (Micro Games of
    America #SW-3180, 1995) 37.00
C-3PO AM/FM Radio (Micro Games of America
    #SW-3190, 1995). 27.00
Darth Vader AM/FM Clock Radio, with molded head
    on top, LCD display (#SW-3124) 25.00

"Talking" Toys
Star Wars Electronic Talking Bank with 8" C-3PO
    and 5" R2-D2, (Thinkway #13902, 1995). 22.00
Star Wars Electronic Talking Bank with Darth Vader
    (Thinkway #13903, 1996). 22.00
R2-D2 Repeating Robot (Micro Games of America
    #SW-3194, 1995). 32.00
Darth Vader Power Talker Voice Changing Mask
    #SW-3815 (Micro Games of America #22586,

*Darth Vader Electronic Talking Bank (Thinkway 1996)
& Stormtrooper Room Alarm (Tiger Electronics 1997)*

*Star Wars A-Wing Calculator and Millennium Falcon Squawk Box
(Tiger Electronics 1997)*

1995)................................... 20.00
R2-D2 Ditto Droid game (Tiger Electronics
    #88-031, 1997)......................... 10.00
Darth Vader Voice Changer (Tiger Electronics #88-
    041, 1997) 15.00

Star Wars Episode I Wake-Up Systems (Thinkway 1999)
Anakin's Podracer Wake-Up System (#13703) 40.00
Jar Jar Binks Wake-Up System (#13704)........... 40.00
Naboo Starfighter with Anakin Skywalker and R2-D2
    Wake-Up System (#)..................... 40.00

Star Wars Episode I Talking Banks (Thinkway 1999)
Darth Maul Interactive Talking Bank (#13709) 30.00
Obi-Wan Kenobi Interactive Talking Bank (#13708) 30.00
Qui-Gon Jinn Interactive Talking Bank (#13707) 30.00

Electronic Keychains (Tiger Electronics 1997)
    12 different, each....................... 7.00

Electronic Pens (Tiger Electronics 1997
Luke Skywalker Way Cool Sounds FX Pen (#88-051) .. 8.00
Darth Vader Way Cool Sounds FX Pen (#88-052) 8.00
C-3PO Way Cool Sounds FX Pen (#88-054) 8.00
Star Wars Lightsaber FX Recording Pen (#88-055) ... 25.00

Squawk Boxes (Tiger Electronics 1997)
C-3PO Squawk Box (#88-071)................. 15.00
Darth Vader Squawk Box (#88-072)............. 15.00
Millennium Falcon Squawk Box (#88-073) 15.00

Other Electronic Toys (Tiger Electronics 1997)
A-Wing Calculator (#88-085) 13.00
Star Wars Lightsaber Image Projector (#88-086) 15.00
Star Wars Lazer Tag, Rebel Infantry Deluxe Pack
    (#88-094)............................ 45.00

Star Wars Episode I Electronic Toys (Tiger Electronics 1999)
Queen Amidala Compact Phone (#88-315) 25.00
Darth Maul Compact Phone (#88-316) 25.00

Electronic

Destroyer Droid Room Alarm (#88-303). 30.00
Darth Maul Binoculars with Listening Device (#88-284) . 20.00
Picture Plus Image Camera (#88-304) 25.00

Electronic Toys
Electronic X-wing Flight Simulator, 30" x 10" x 17",
    (Kenner #27847, Aug. 1997) green box 23.00
Millennium Falcon Flight Simulator (Kenner 1998) 23.00
Dancing Jar Jar Binks (Thinkway #13712, 1999). 30.00

Audioclips
Star Wars Audioclips for IBM-PC 20.00
The Empire Strikes Back Audioclips for IBM-PC 20.00
Return of the Jedi Audioclips for IBM-PC 20.00

Clocks
R2-D2 and C-3PO Talking Alarm Clock, 9" tall
    (Bradley Time 1980). 90.00
R2-D2 and C-3PO Clock Radio (Bradley Time 1984) . 100.00
R2-D2 and C-3PO 3-D Sceni-Clock, 8" tall (Bradley
    Time). 75.00
Ewok Teaching Clock, shaped like Ewok village
    with Wicket on face of clock (Kenner Preschool). . 75.00
Star Wars Wall Clock, pictures R2-D2 & C-3PO
    (Welby Elgin 1981). 65.00
The Empire Strikes Back Wall Clock, square, Darth,
    Stormtroopers & logo (Welby Elgin 1981) 65.00
Droid wall clock (Bradley). 25.00
The Empire Strikes Back wall clock (Bradley). 25.00
Portable clock/radio (Bradley 1984) 15.00
Star Wars Special Edition Clock, Drew Struzan art,
    9" x 11" battery powered (1997) 40.00
The Empire Strikes Back Special Edition Clock,
    Drew Struzan art, 9" x 11" battery powered (1997) . 40.00
Return of the Jedi Special Edition Clock, Drew
    Struzan art, 9" x 11" battery powered (1997). 40.00

Electronic Household Products
Luke Skywalker's Lightsaber Universal (TV) Re-
    mote Control (Kash 'N' Gold 2366, 1997) boxed. . 35.00
R2-D2 figural telephone, 12" high, 9¼" wide, 6"

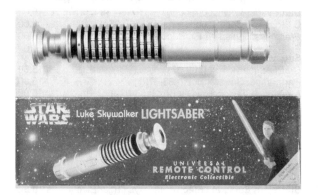

Luke Skywalker Lightsaber Remote Control (Kash 'N' Gold 1997)

Anakin Skywalker Mousepad (Handstands 1999)

Electronic

deep, battery powered with handset in leg, droid movements and sound effects (Kash 'N' Gold #2363, 1997) boxed.................... 80.00

Mousepads 8½" x 11½" (MousTrak 1995)
Darth Vader Mouse Pad (#SW-1)................ 12.00
Yoda Mouse Pad (#SW-2) 12.00
Millennium Falcon Mouse Pad (#SW-3) 12.00
Luke & Leia, *Return of the Jedi* Mouse Pad (#SW-4) .. 12.00
Rebel Assault Game Art Mouse Pad (#SW-5) 12.00

Star Wars Mousemats (Handstands 1998)
    Four or more different, each 8.00
Star Wars Episode I Mousemats (Handstands 1999)
    Eight or more different, each 8.00

Giga Pets (Tiger Electronics 1997)
Yoda Giga Pet, Electronic Virtual Pet (#70-135) 7.50
Rancor Giga Pet, Electronic Virtual Pet (#70-136) 10.00
R2-D2 Giga Pet, Electronic Virtual Pet (#70-137) 7.50

Preschool
Ewok Talking Phone, 9" tall (Kenner Preschool 1984).. 70.00
Sit n' Spin (Kenner Preschool 1984)................ 60.00

Computer Mice (1998)
Darth Vader, C-3PO or Stormtrooper, each.......... 10.00

Star Wars Episode I Wrist Rests
Jedi vs. Sith 10.00
Podrace 10.00

Episode I, CD Wallet (Pentech 1999)
Star Wars Episode One collage 10.00

FOOD

BREAKFAST FOOD, FAST FOOD, JUNK FOOD AND PIZZA

Over the years, *Star Wars* has had promotions with each of the four major food groups—Fast, Junk, Breakfast and Pizza—not to mention a Pet Food promotion in Australia. These promotions generate a variety of collectibles, from food containers, to toys, to mail-in premiums.

BREAKFAST FOOD

Every toy collector should start off with a hearty breakfast. General Mills, who owned Kenner at the time, started promotions off with various *Star Wars* Cheerios boxes beginning in 1978. This was probably the high point of *Star Wars* food products, nutrition-wise, until the 1997 Taco Bell promotion. From then on the offers were on cereals like Boo Berry, Count Chocula and Lucky Charms. *Star Wars* moved to Kellogg's in 1984 and C-3PO got his own cereal. Finally, in 1996 Froot Loops had its highly successful Han Solo action figure offer. Toocan Sam and R2-D2—perfect together. The boxes are just as collectible as the premiums.

Listed prices are for complete and clean boxes. A complete box has all four top flaps, all four sides (no missing coupons) and all four bottom flaps. A box that has the top and bottom flaps opened is a "collapsed" box (but still complete). A "Flat" is a mint (usually a file copy) unused cereal box. A flat commands up to 40% more than the listed price.

If you liked a little toast with your cereal, you should have bought Wonder Bread. They offered a series of *Star Wars* trading cards in 1977. Look for them in the TRADING CARDS section.

General Mills Cereal Boxes

Cheerios, with *Star Wars* tumbler offer	$35.00
Cheerios, 1978, *Star Wars* Poster in Pack, Space Scenes	30.00
Boo Berry, with trading card premium	25.00
Franken Berry, with trading card premium	25.00
Cocoa Puffs, with trading card premium	25.00
Chocolate Crazy Cow, with trading card premium	25.00
Strawberry Crazy Cow, with trading card premium	25.00
Trading Cards, 18 different, see Trading Cards section.	
Frankenberry, with sticker premium	25.00
Count Chocula with sticker premium	25.00
Trix, with sticker premium	25.00

*Froot Loops Cereal Box, front, and back with Han Solo offer
(Kellogg's 1996)*

Cocoa Puffs, with sticker premium 25.00
Lucky Charms, with sticker premium 25.00
Stickers, 16 different, each. 2.00
Lucky Charms, with spaceship hang glider premium. . . 25.00

Kellogg's Cereal Boxes
C-3PO Cereal (1984) with sticker trading card offer . . . 20.00
C-3PO Cereal (1984) with Mask on Back, six
    different masks of C-3PO, Chewbacca, Darth
    Vader, Luke Skywalker Stormtrooper or Yoda,
    each. 30.00
    Set, eight different C-3PO Mask boxes 200.00
C-3PO Cereal (1984) with Rebel Rocket in pack
    plus stickers 20.00
    Set, eight different Boxes + Stickers 200.00

Other Cereal Boxes
Froot Loops (1996) with Han Solo in Stormtrooper
    outfit mail-in offer 10.00
Apple Jacks (1996) with Dark Horse comic book
    mail-in offer 2.00
Corn Pops (1996) with *Star Wars* video offer 2.00
Raisin Bran (1996) with *Star Wars* video offer 2.00

Star Wars glasses (Burger King/Coke 1977)

Food

Return of the Jedi glasses (Burger King/Coke 1983)

FAST FOOD

The 1970s and 1980s promotions of choice with fast food restaurants were glasses and plastic cups. The most famous of these promotions were the Burger King/Coke four-glass sets sold for each of the three movies. Coke also produced a number of collector plastic cups which were distributed in various fast food chains, both national and regional.

Glassware (Burger King/Coca-Cola 1977–83)
Star Wars Promotional Glasses (four diff. glasses:
    Luke, Han Solo, Darth and R2-D2/C-3PO, each . $15.00
    Set of four (1977) 60.00
The Empire Strikes Back Promotional Glasses (four
    diff. glasses: Luke, Lando, R2-D2/C-3PO and
    Darth) each 12.00
    set of four (1980) 50.00
Return of the Jedi Promotional Glasses (four diff.:
    Sand barge fight scene, Jabba's palace, Ewok
    village, & Luke/Darth fighting, each 10.00
    set of four (1983) 40.00
    Plastic cups, Mass. only, each 12.50
    Set of four 50.00

Plastic Coca-Cola Cups 1970s–80s
Star Wars numbered 20-cup set, each 10.00
    Set of 20 . . . . 175.00
Star Wars numbered eight-cup set
    Large, "7–11" or "Coke" each 5.00
    Set of eight Large cups 30.00
    Small, "Coke" each. 5.00
    Set of eight Small cups. 25.00
Star Wars unnumbered 1979 eight-cup set, each 5.00
    Set of eight "Coke" cups. 30.00
Return of the Jedi 12-cup set, each 5.00
    Set of 12 "7-11" cups, large or small 50.00

The Empire Strikes Back movie theater plastic cup
    (Coke1980) depending on size, each 7.00
Return of the Jedi movie theater plastic cup (Coke
    1983) depending on size, each. 6.00
Star Wars Trilogy Special Edition movie theater
    plastic cup, featuring picture of AT-AT (Pepsi 1997) . 2.00

Food

Star Wars Fast Food toys (Taco Bell 1997)

Taco Bell ran a promotion in late 1996 and early 1997 in conjunction with the release of the *Star Wars Trilogy Special Edition* films. There were a lot of neat toys to collect, along with boxes plus a wrapper and bag. The best part for me is that I get paid to show you pictures of them in this book, enjoy the tacos, and deduct the cost of the meals and toys, all while telling my wife that its not just an excuse to eat at fast food restaurants. This worked for the pizza, Pepsi, and junk food just as well. Now if only a beer company would run *Star Wars* promotion. . . .

The toys each came in a plastic bag, with a two page booklet encouraging you to "collect all seven!" They cost about a buck each, but the taco wrapper, bag or box was free.

Fast Food (Taco Bell 1996–97)
Taco Bell taco wrapper picturing C-3PO $1.00
Taco Bell taco bag picturing R2-D2 or C-3PO. 1.00
Star Wars food box, with movie scene 2.00
The Empire Strikes Back food box, with movie scene. . . 2.00
Return of the Jedi food box, with movie scene 2.00

Fast Food Toys (Taco Bell 1996–97)
Millennium Falcon Gyro 3.00
R2-D2 Playset 2.50

Food

Star Wars Trilogy box and R2-D2 Bag (Taco Bell 1997)

Magic Cube, Yoda/Darth Vader 2.50
Floating Cloud City 2.50
Puzzle Cube 2.50
Balancing Boba Fett. 2.00
Exploding Death Star Spinner 2.50

Under 3 years old
Yoda figure 5.00

EPISODE I FAST FOOD

Star Wars Episode I The Phantom Menace was so big it took three restaurant chains to distribute its fast food toys— Pizza Hut, KFC, and Taco Bell. I gained at least 10 pounds just collecting them, and that was before I started in on the potato chips bags and pepsi cans. All of the restaurant's fast food toys were made by Applause and are listed on their website. All of the toys came in pictorial boxes which could be put together to form a poster scene. In addition, each restaurant had four figural plastic drink toppers for sale. KFC also had two flying disks, i.e. frisbees which doubled as chicken bucket toppers. In addition, you could collect paper drink cups with movie pictures and plastic soda cups at the movies.

Pizza Hut (Coruscant)
Yoda's Jedi Destiny (#66515) $2.00
Lott Dodd Walking Throne (#66516) 2.00
Planet Coruscant (#66517) 2.00
Sith Holoprojector (#66518) 2.00
Jar Jar Binks Squishy (#66519) under three 2.00
Darth Maul's Sith Infiltrator (#66520) 2.00
Queen Amidala's Royal Starship (#66521) 2.00
R2-D2 (#66522) 2.00
Boxes for above, each 1.00

Yoda and Queen Amidala cup toppers (Pizza Hut & KFC 1999)

Drink Toppers with plastic cup and long straw

Jar Jar Binks	4.00
Mace Windu	4.00
Nute Gunray	4.00
Yoda	4.00

KFC (Naboo)

Queen Amidala's Hidden Identity (#66506)	2.00
Jar Jar Binks Squirter (#66507)	2.00
Swimming Jar Jar Binks (#66508)	2.00
Gungin Sub Squirter (#66509)	2.00
Opee Sea Creature Chaser (#66510)	2.00
Naboo Ground Battle (#66511)	2.00
Anakin Skywalker's Naboo Fighter (#66512)	2.00
Trade Federation Droid Fighter (#66513)	2.00
Planet Naboo (#66514)	2.00
Boss Nass Squirter (#66535)	2.00
Boxes for above, each	1.00

Drink Toppers with plastic cup and long straw

Queen Amidala	4.00
R2-D2	4.00
Boss Nass	4.00
Captain Tarpals	4.00

Flying Disks

Battle Droid	5.00
Jar Jar Binks	5.00

Chicken Buckets

each	1.50

Taco Bell (Tatooine)

Joking Jar Jar Binks (#66488)	2.00
Anakin's Podracer (#66489)	2.00
Sebulba's Podracer (#66490)	2.00
Hovering Watto (#66491)	2.00
Walking Sebulba (#66492)	2.00

Food

Tatooine Fast Food Boxes (Taco Bell 1999)

Lott Dodd Walking Throne, Jar Jar Binks Squishy, and Anakin's Pod Racer (Pizza Hut, KFC and Taco Bell 1999)

Darth Maul's Sith Speeder (#66493) 2.00
Levitating Queen Amidala's Royal Starship (#66494). . . . 2.00
Planet Tatooine (#66495) 2.00
Anakin Bust Viewer (under 3) (#66496). 2.00
Sith Probe Droid Viewer (#66497) 2.00
Anakin Skywalker Transforming Bank (#66498) 2.00
Boxes for above, each 1.00

Drink Toppers with plastic cup and long straw
Anakin Skywalker 4.00
Darth Maul 4.00
Watto 4.00
Sebulba 4.00

Store Signage
Pizza Hut Toy Display containing all eight8 toys 150.00
KFC Toy Display containing all ten toys. 150.00
Taco Bell Toy Display containing all ten toys. 150.00

CUPS

Cups, plastic, large, movie theater
Darth Maul. $2.00
Qui-Gon Jinn 2.00
Anakin SKywalker. 2.00
Watto 2.00

Cups, medium or large
    Paper, various, three different restaurants, each . . . 1.00
    Plastic, several different, each. 2.00

JUNK FOOD

Pepsi had a number of promotional plastic bottles and 12-pack and 24-pack cartons available for the *Star Wars Trilogy Special Edition* movies. The cartons had an offer for three posters for $9.99 plus the order form on the back of the carton. The UPC symbol from two bags of Lay's Potato Chips plus $1.99 got you the Spirit of Obi-Wan action figure. It's a 3¾" blue-green semi-translucent plastic figure of Obi-Wan and it came in a plastic bag in a plain white mailing box with "SKU #69736" on it. The figure has no discernable action and belongs in this section, but it's from Kenner so everybody lists it as a mail-in action figure. That's where you'll find it in this book, too.

The collectible value of the Pepsi cartons, or the Lay's Potato Chip bags listed below, are about 90% less if they are not complete. Empty is okay, but cutouts are not, meaning that you can't have a mint bag or box and send away for the mail-in premium too.

Pepsi has issued various coasters and travel cups in the last few years, and put out 24 different soda cans in conjunction with *Episode I The Phantom Menace*. Pepsico generated a lot of initial interest with promo cans, available as internal give-aways. They were sealed empty, so they are easy to distinguish from the regular cans.

SODA (or Pop, if you are a mid-westener)
***Star Wars Trilogy Special Edition* Soda Boxes** (1996)
  12 or 24-pack, empty box, several different, each $2.00
***Star Wars Episode I* Soda Boxes** (1999)
  12 or 24-pack, empty box, several different, each 2.00

***Star Wars Trilogy Special Edition* Soda Bottles** (1996)
Darth Vader Pepsi 20 oz or 2-liter bottle 1.00
C-3PO Diet Pepsi 20 oz or 2-liter bottle. 1.00

Star Wars Episode I (Can or plastic bottle)
Pepsi: 1. Anakin Skywalker; 2. Sebulba; 3. Qui-Gon
    Jinn; 4. Watto; 5. Jabba The Hutt; 6. Senator
    Palpatine; 7. R2-D2; or 8. Darth Sidious, each 1.00
Mountain Dew: 9. Darth Maul; 10. Jar Jar; 11. Mace
    Windu; 12. Obi-Wan Kenobi; 13. Captain Pan-
    aka; 14. Rune Haako; 15. Ric Olie; or 16. Des-
    troyer Droid, each 1.00
Diet Pepsi: 17. Queen Amidala; 18. Padme;
    19. Shmi Skywalker; 20. Battle Droid, each 1.00
Pepsi One: 21. Chancellor Valorum; 22. C-3PO;
    23. Nute Gunray; or 24. Boss Nass, each 1.00
Gold Yoda Chase Can 20.00
Seven-Up 19. Nute Gunray 5.00
Episode I Promo cans, sealed in white box, each 10.00

Star Wars Pepsi Promo Cans #1 & #2 with box (Pepsico 1999)

Food

Star Wars Trilogy Pepsi Travel Bottles (Pepsico 1997)

Other Star Wars Trilogy Pepsi Products (1997)
Travel Bottles, four different, each.................. 8.00
Coasters, four different, each 5.00
Cups, four different, each 6.00

CHIPS
Lay's Potato Chip bag with "Spirit of Obi-Wan" figure
    offer, various sizes .... 1.00 to 2.00
Doritos bag with 3-D Motion card premium........... 1.00

Star Wars Episode I
5½ oz. Lays Potato Chip bags, several different, each .. 1.00
14½ oz. Doritos Chip bags, several different, each..... 1.50

Candy
Topps Candy Boxes (1980–83)
The Empire Strikes Back figural head candy con-
    tainers (Topps 1980) box with 18 containers..... 40.00
      Containers, each........................ 2.50
      Set, including Stormtrooper, Boba Fett, Chew-
        bacca, C-3PO and Darth Vader 12.50
      Box, empty.............................. 5.00
The Empire Strikes Back figural head candy con-
    tainers (Topps 1981) box with 18 containers,
    New Yoda series 40.00
      containers, each........................ 2.50
      Set of six, Tauntaun, Bossk, Yoda, 2-1B 12.50
      Box, empty.............................. 5.00
Return of the Jedi figural head candy containers
    (Topps 1983) box with 18 containers 50.00
      containers, six different, each............... 2.50
      Set of six, Admiral Ackbar, Darth Vader, Ewok,
        Jabba The Hutt, Sy Snootles and Wicket 15.00
      Box, empty.............................. 5.00

Queen Amidala and Jar Jar Binks Potato Chips Bags (Lays 1999)

Hersheys Products, 6-pack cartons (1980s) photos on back
Boxes with large C-3PO or Chewbacca photos 15.00
Boxes with smaller Luke on Tauntaun, Boba Fett or
    Darth Vader photos 10.00

Star Wars Trilogy Candy Container collection and
    card set, 4 head figural candy containers and
    10-card set, on header card (Topps 1997) 25.00

Star Wars Episode I Candy Dispensers (Cap Candy 1999)
Jar Jar Binks Pez Handler (Mos Espa Scene) (#4645) . 25.00
R2-D2 Candy Handler, M & M Minis (#46862) 15.00
Naboo Fighter Dispenser, Skittles (#4666) 20.00

Pez Dispensers (Asst #8633, 1997) bagged or carded
    Nine or more different, each 2.00

PIZZA

In late 1996 and early 1997, Pizza Hut sold its take-out
pizzas in coloring boxes with *Star Wars* pictures promoting
the *Star Wars Special Edition* movies. The boxes are 12½"
square. Too bad they didn't change their company logo to
read "Pizza Hutt" for the promotion and use a picture of their
"founder," Jabba the Hutt, on the boxes.

Pizza Hut *Star Wars* coloring boxes (1996)
        C-3PO and *Millennium Falcon* $1.00
        R2-D2 and X-wing fighters 1.00
        Stormtrooper and AT-AT 1.00
        Darth Vader and Star Destroyer 1.00

Episode I Pizza Hut coloring boxes
Pizza Hut Star Wars Episode I boxes (1999)
        Jar Jar Binks 1.00
        R2-D2 personal pan pizza box 50

Food

GAMES & PUZZLES

GAMES

Kenner made the first *Star Wars* games, as well as a variety of jigsaw puzzles, bop bags, vans, and of course, action figures. Many of these were advertised in their various mini-catalogs that came in the boxes for the vehicles. Parker Bros. started making the games in about 1983, and continues to do so today. Kenner is now part of Hasbro, as is Parker Bros.

Original Kenner Games (1977–82)
Adventures of R2-D2, board game (Kenner 1977) . . . $25.00
Destroy Death Star game (Kenner 1979) 30.00
Escape From Death Star board game (Kenner 1979). . 25.00
Hoth Ice Planet Adventure Game (Kenner 1980) logo . 25.00
Yoda, The Jedi Master board game (Kenner 1981). . . . 25.00

Parker Bros. Games (1982–98)
Star Wars (Parker Brothers 1982) box pictures
    Luke in X-Wing gear. 30.00
Wicket the Ewok (Parker Brothers 1983) 20.00
The Ewoks Save the Trees! (Parker Brothers 1983) . . . 20.00
Battle at Sarlacc's Pit (Parker Brothers 1983). 30.00
Return of the Jedi Card Game (Parker Brothers 1983) . 10.00
Star Wars Death Star Assault Game (Parker Bros.
    #40390, 1995) 13.00
Star Wars Monopoly Classic Trilogy Edition (Parker
    Bros #40809, 1997). 35.00
Star Wars Classic Trilogy Trivial Pursuit (#40825) 35.00
Ewok Card Games (Parker Brothers 1984) several
    different, each 15.00
Star Wars Escape the Death Star Action Figure
    Game with two figures (Parker Bros. #40905) 15.00

Wicket the Ewok board game (Parker Bros.1983)

Star Wars Episode I *Battle For Naboo 3-D Action Game*
(Hasbro 1999)

Other Games
Star Wars Card Trick (Nick Trost 1978) 10.00
Top Trumps New Spacecraft (Waddington). 15.00
Yoda, the Jedi Master magic answer fortune telling
    toy (Kenner 1981) 50.00

Star Wars Episode I Games (1999)
Naboo Fighter Target Game (Hasbro-Milton Bradley
    #40971) 20.00
Lightsaber Duel (Hasbro-Milton Bradley #40991). 20.00
Jar Jar Binks 3-D Adventure Game (Hasbro #40997) . . 15.00
Simon Space Battle Game (Hasbro (#40983) 35.00
Star Wars Episode 1 Monopoly (Parker Bros #41018). . . 40.00
Clash of the Lightsaber's Card Game with two pew-
    ter figures (Milton Bradley #40993) 13.00
Battle For Naboo 3-D Action Game with 20 Heroes
    and Villains (Hasbro #40979). 20.00
See also Electronic & Computer

PUZZLES

    The earliest puzzles came in blue or purple-bordered
boxes. Later, they were switched to black borders. Several are
advertised in Kenner's mini-catalogs. They are among the
earliest Kenner products, since it is fairly easy to put a *Star
Wars* picture on an existing jigsaw pattern and add a box. You
have to sculpt an action figure before it can go into production. Kenner jigsaw puzzles are not titled. The box contained
the movie logo, the puzzle's picture and the number of pieces.

140-Piece Puzzles 14" x 18" (add $5.00 for blue box)
Sand person atop Bantha. $10.00
C-3PO and R2-D2. . . . .   10.00
Han Solo and Chewbacca 10.00
Jawas capture R2-D2. . . . .   10.00
Luke and Han in trash compactor. 10.00
Sand person 10.00
Stormtroopers 10.00

Games

500-Piece Puzzles 15" x 18" (add $5.00 for blue box)
Ben Kenobi and Darth Vader dueling 12.00
Cantina Band. 12.00
Luke and Leia 12.00
Luke on Tatooine 12.00
Jawas selling Droids 12.00
Space battle. 12.00
Victory celebration 12.00
X-Wing Fighter in hanger 12.00
1,000-Piece Puzzles 21½" x 27½"
Crew aboard the *Millennium Falcon* 15.00
Movie art poster, Hildebrandt Bros. art 15.00
1,500-Piece Puzzles 27" x 33"
Millennium Falcon in space 20.00
Stormtrooper in corridor 20.00

Craft-Master (1983) *Return of the Jedi* logo
Jig-Saw Puzzles
Battle of Endor, 170 pieces 12.00
B-Wings, 170 pieces 12.00
Ewok leaders, 170 pieces 12.00
Jabba's friends, 70 pieces 10.00
Jabba's throne room, 70 pieces 10.00
Death Star, 70 pieces. 10.00
Wicket and Friends, three different, each 5.00

Frame Tray Puzzles
Darth Vader Frame Tray. 5.00
Gamorrean Guard Frame Tray. 5.00
Jedi Characters Frame Tray. 5.00

Wicket The Ewok Frame Tray puzzles
Ewoks on hang gliders Frame Tray 5.00
Ewok Village Frame Tray 5.00
Leia and Wicket Frame Tray 5.00
R2-D2 and Wicket Frame Tray. 5.00
Wicket Frame Tray. 5.00
Match Blocks Puzzles
Ewoks Match Block Puzzle 10.00
Luke and Jabba Match Block Puzzle 10.00

Stormtroopers 140-piece jigsaw puzzle (General Mills 1977)

Games

Mos Espa Podrace Glow-in-the Dark Puzzle (Hasbro 1999)

Jigsaw Puzzles (Milton Bradley 1995–98)
Star Wars Puzz 3D *Millennium Falcon*, 857 pieces.... 25.00
Star Wars Puzz 3D Imperial Star Destroyer, 823 pieces 35.00
Star Wars Darth Vader 3-D Sculpture, 144 layers..... 35.00
Star Wars, *A New Hope*, 550 piece 12.50
Star Wars, *The Empire Strikes Back*, 550 piece 12.50
Star Wars, *Return of the Jedi*, 550 piece 12.50

Jigsaw Puzzles (RoseArt 1997)
Star Wars: A New Hope 500-piece................ 12.00
Star Wars: *The Empire Strikes Back* 500-piece 12.00
Star Wars: *Return of the Jedi* 500-piece............ 12.00
Star Wars: A New Hope Poster Illustration Puzzle 7.50
The Empire Strikes Back 1,500 piece jigsaw puzzle,
   28¾" x 36" (Springbok/Hallmark 1997) 17.00

Episode I Jigsaw Puzzles (Hasbro 1999)
R2-D2, Puzz 3D, 708 pieces, battery power 25.00
Jar Jar Binks 3-D Sculpture, 9" tall, 133 layers....... 30.00
Yoda Shaped Puzzle, 100-piece................... 4.00
Darth Maul Shaped Puzzle, 100-piece 4.00
R2-D2 Shaped Puzzle, 100-piece 4.00
Jar Jar Binks Shaped Puzzle, 100-piece) 4.00
Mos Espa Podrace Puzzle, Glow-in-the-Dark, 200-piece 5.00
Movie Teaser Poster Puzzle, 300 piece............. 7.50
50-Piece Mini-Puzzles
Queen Amidala 3.00
Pod Race 3.00
Obi-Wan Kenobi, Darth Maul and Qui-Gon Jinn....... 3.00
Droids....................................... 3.00
Other Puzzle
Darth Maul Rubik's Cube Puzzle (#30020) 15.00

ROLE PLAY GAMES

West End Games began producing role playing games
in the *Star Wars* universe in 1987. This was in the middle of
the dark age, when there were no more action figures produced and no new *Star Wars* novels or comics. During this

period, they were the only company keeping the *Star Wars* saga alive with anything like new *Star Wars* storylines.

Role playing games have their own section in most book stores. As such, their books and boxed sets are generally available. Politicians no longer consider them satanic rituals or communist plots. They even have to compete with CCGs (Customizable Card Games) for the game fanatics' attention. Lastly, their fanatics accumulate game modules, rule books, and other items in order to (gasp!) play the games, not collect them. New and revised editions of rule books are much more useful than original editions. The consequences of this are that most of these items, even in near mint condition, are worth little more than their original price!

Boxed Games (9" x 11½" boxes)
Star Warriors Role-Playing Board Game (1987) $35.00
Assault on Hoth, two person board game (1988) 35.00
Battle for Endor, board game (1989) 30.00
Escape From the Death Star, (1990) 30.00
     Reprints (1992) 20.00

Basic Game and Sourcebooks (8½" x 11" hardcovers)
Star Wars, The Role-Playing Game, basic rules
    book, (1987) 25.00
    2nd Ed.: (1993) 25.00
    2nd Ed.: Revised and Expanded (1996) 30.00
Star Wars Sourcebook, 144 pages (1988) 20.00
    2nd Edition (1994) 22.00
Star Wars Movie Trilogy Sourcebook (1993) 25.00
Imperial Sourcebook (1989) 20.00
    TPB reissue (1991) 18.00
    2nd Edition (1994) 22.00
Rebel Alliance Sourcebook, (1991) 20.00
    TPB reissue (1991) 18.00
    2nd Edition (1994) 22.00
Heir to the Empire Sourcebook (1992) 18.00
Dark Force Rising Sourcebook (1993) 18.00

Games

Dark Force Rising Sourcebook & Adventure Journal
(West End 1990s)

*Craken's Rebel Operatives and Rule of Engagement
(West End 1990s)*

Dark Empire Sourcebook (1993) 25.00
The Movie Trilogy Sourcebook (1997) 28.00
Han Solo and the Corporate Sector Sourcebook (1993) 20.00
Shadows of the Empire Sourcebook (1996) 20.00
The Jedi Academy Sourcebook (1996). 22.00
Thrawn Trilogy Sourcebook (1996). 25.00
Truce at Bakura Sourcebook (1996). 22.00
Star Wars Introductory Adventure Game (1997) 20.00
Star Wars X-Wing Rogue Squadron Sourcebook,
    based on novels (1998) TPB 25.00
Star Wars Hideouts and Strongholds Sourcebook
    (1998) 22.00

Adventure Modules (1988–91)
    15 or more different, each 10.00

Classic Adventures reprints, updated to 2nd edition rules
    Volumes One to Four (1995–96) each 20.00

Softcovers (1991-98)
    Many different, each. . . . . 10 to 15.00

Galaxy Guide Books (8½" x 11" Trade Paperbacks)
Galaxy Guides 1 to 12 (1989–95) each 13.00
    2nd Editions, (1995–96) each. 12.00

One-Player Games
Scoundrel's Luck, (40102, 1990) 13.00
Jedi's Honor, (40103, 1990) hardcover. 13.00

Other Guide Books (8½" x 11" Trade Paperbacks)
    Many different (1991–95) each . . . . 13 to 18.00
    Hardcovers, combined editions, each 25.00

Supplements
    Several different, each . . . . 12 to 15.00
Mos Eisley boxed set (40212, 1997) hardcover 35.00

Games

*Mos Eisley Cantina and The Rancor Pit Adventure Sets
(West End 1990s)*

GAMING MINIATURES
West End Games (1988–97)

     West End Games produced 25mm lead miniature fig-
ures to accompany its games starting in 1988. They have produced a lot of them, but they are not heavily collected by non-
gamers. They were, however, popular with modelers, who
paint and display them. There are 14 boxed sets, usually containing 10 figures, which were produced from 1988 to 1991.
All of the figures came with statistics for use with West End's
role playing games. Bob Charrette and Julie Guthrie were
credited as sculptors on the first ten packs, while Jonathan
Woods sculpted the last four. In 1993, West End Games began
producing three-figure blister packs of figures. They have
made over fifty different packs to date, plus several sets of
ships.

Miniatures: Figures (1988–92) (25mm figures, 4" x 8" boxes)
    10 figure packs, each . . . . $20 to 25.00
    8 figure packs, each . . . . 18 to 22.00

25mm pewter, 3-figure blister packs
Heroes 1 (40401, 1993) Luke, R2-D2 & C-3PO 9.00
Heroes 2 (40402, 1993) Han, Chewbacca and Leia 9.00
    51 different packs (1993–96) each 5.00
Jabba the Hutt (40444, 1996) one figure 6.00
Imperial Troop 12-pack (50455, 1997) 20.00
Rebel Troop 12-pack (50456, 1997) 20.00

Ships/Vehicles
    Eight different, each . . . . 7 to 10.00

Miniatures Battles (Boxed)
Star Wars Miniatures Battle (1995) 35.00
Star Wars Miniatures Rules, 2nd Ed. (1994) 18.00
Star Wars Miniatures Battle, Starter Set (1995) 35.00

Vehicles Starter Set (1996) 35.00
The DarkStryder Campaign, books, cards (1995) 30.00
Darkstryder Deluxe Campaign Pack, boxed set 39.00
Darkstryder: Endgame (1996) 18.00
Lords of the Expanse, books, guides, maps (1997) . . . 30.00

CUSTOMIZABLE CARD GAMES

Customizable Card Games (CCGs) were one of the 1990s hottest items. There were many players around and lots of new product. Many of the playing cards are quite valuable. The primary reasons for this are scarcity and play value in the game. Scarcity is always a factor in value, but the other factor is usually some kind of intrinsic desirability or charisma in the item. The simple truth is that game cards are not exactly great art, and even if they were great art, too much of the card is taken up by the game text for one to appreciate the art.

As long as the game is played, scarce cards will be valuable. When the world moves on to the next game, they may not be quite so valuable. But then, as Dennis Miller says, that's just my opinion, I could be wrong.

Decipher has the license for *Star Wars* (and *Star Trek*) CCGs. They have produced a lot of games in the last few years and have no plans to quit.

PREMIERE SET

This initial card set is based on characters and events from the first *Star Wars* movie. It was introduced in December 1995, and was long awaited by Customizable Card Game fanatics.

STAR WARS LIMITED

Complete Set: 324 cards $600.00
Starter Box: 10 starter decks 110.00

Two Premiere Set Light Side Cards (Decipher 1995)

Games

Starter Deck: 60 cards 11.00
Booster Box: 36 packs 140.00
Booster Pack: 15 cards 4.00
Common Card. 0.15–0.40
Uncommon Card. 1.00–2.50

STAR WARS UNLIMITED
Decipher Inc. (1996–98)

Complete Set: 324 cards $400.00
Starter Box: Five starter decks 85.00
Starter Deck: 120 cards 15.00
Starter Deck: 90 cards 9.50
Booster Box. 75.00
Booster Pack: 15 cards 3.00
Starter Display, 12 decks and display 114.00
Booster Display, 36 packs and display 108.00
Rare and Uncommon cards are worth about 75% of
    the same card in the "Limited Series."

A NEW HOPE
Decipher (1996)

Complete Set: 162 cards $200.00
Booster Box: 36 pack. 95.00
Booster Pack: 15 cards 3.00
Star Wars: A New Hope Booster Display, 36 packs
    and display. 110.00

EXPANSION SETS

THE EMPIRE STRIKES BACK: HOTH
Decipher (1996)

Complete Set: 162 cards $200.00
Booster Box: 36 packs. 80.00
Booster Pack: 15 cards 3.00
The Empire Strikes Back: Hoth Limited CCG
    Booster Display 36 packs and display. 108.00

DAGOBAH
Decipher (1997)

Complete Set: 180 cards $200.00
Booster Box: 60 packs. 140.00
Booster Pack: Nine cards (inc. One rare) 2.50
Star Wars Dagobah Booster Display, 60 packs and
    display 150.00

CLOUD CITY
Decipher (1997)

Complete Set: 180 cards $175.00
Booster Box: 60 packs. 125.00
Booster Pack: Nine cards (inc. One rare) 2.50
Star Wars Cloud City Booster Display, 60 packs and
    display 150.00

Games

Two cards from the Hoth Expansion Set (Decipher 1996)

JABBA'S PALACE
Decipher (1998)

Complete Set: 180 cards $160.00
Booster Box: 60 packs 125.00
Booster Pack: Nine cards (inc. One rare) 2.50
Jabba's Palace Booster Display, 60 packs & display . . 150.00

STAR WARS SPECIAL EDITION
Decipher (1998)

Complete Set: 324 cards $275.00
Starter Deck: 60 cards 11.00
Starter Box: 110.00
Booster Box: 30 packs 60.00
Booster Pack: Nine cards (inc. One rare) 2.50

YOUNG JEDI: ENDOR
Decipher (1999)

Complete Set: 180 cards $150.00
Booster Box: 30 packs 60.00
Booster Pack: Nine cards (inc. One rare) 3.00
Foil Set: 18 cards 275.00

EPISODE I:
THE MENACE OF DARTH MAUL
Decipher (1999)

Complete Set: 140 cards $95.00
Starter Deck: 60 cards 10.00
Booster Box: 30 packs 80.00
Booster Pack: Nine cards (inc. One rare) 3.00
Foil Set: 18 cards 100.00

Games

Jabba's Palace box (Decipher 1998)

STAR WARS TWO-PLAYER
CUSTOMIZABLE CARD GAME
Parker Brothers (1996)

The Premiere two-player game was introduced in February 1996, and is distributed by Parker Brothers. That means that it found its way into toy stores. The box includes a Light Side and a Dark Side deck, each comprised of 60 common cards, plus a 15-card expansion pack.

Star Wars Two-Players Customizable Card Game,
  licensed from Decipher (#40360, 1996) $20.00

THE EMPIRE STRIKES BACK
INTRODUCTORY TWO-PLAYER GAME

The Empire Strikes Back two-player game was introduced in March 1997 and is also distributed by Parker Brothers. It's the second of a series of three, but I wouldn't bet against others based on the new movies. There are seven unique cards in the set.

Box Set:. $20.00

FIRST ANTHOLOGY SET

First Anthology Set in a 15" x 13" x 6" box $32.00

STAR WARS EPISODE I

Star Wars Episode 1 Customizable Card Game
  (Decipher #10550) $20.00

HOUSEHOLD

This household section covers *Star Wars* items for use in the Bathroom, Bedroom, Kitchen, and other rooms in a house, as well as holiday and party items.

BATHROOM

Bathroom products include soaps, grooming products and towels. Some of the combs are designed to be carried in your pocket and some of the towels are designed for the beach, but they are still listed here. Many collectors have one or more of these items in their collections, but they do not seem to be looking for more of them so as to have, for example, every *Star Wars* towel. They just treat what they have as part of their "other *Star Wars* stuff."

Bubble Bath
Bubble Bath Character Containers, 4½" x 9½" tall
   (Omni 1981–83), 8 different, each $15.00
Bubble Bath Refueling Station, 6½" tall bottle
   decorated with ships and SW logo (Omni 1981) . . . 5.00
Bubble Bath (Addis 1983) 8 different, each. 15.00
R2-D2 & C-3PO Bubble Bath Gift Set (Addis 1985) . . . 30.00
Ewoks Bubble Bath Gift Set (Addis 1985). 25.00

Star Wars Episode I Bubble Bath (Minnetonka Brands 1999)
Jar Jar Binks Galactic Bubble Bath bottle, 16oz 3.00

Personal Grooming
Comb and Keeper (Adam Joseph Industries 1983)
     Cantina Band (*Return of the Jedi* header card). . . 15.00
     Land Speeder (*Return of the Jedi* header card) . . 15.00

Landspeeder Comb and Keeper (Adam Joseph 1983) & C-3PO Galactic Shampoo (Minnetonka Brands 1998)

Kneesaa (Wicket the Ewok header card) 10.00
Pop-Up Comb, with flip-up mirror (Adam Joseph 1983)
    R2-D2 and C-3PO *Star Wars* logo 15.00
    Darth Vader *Return of the Jedi* logo 15.00
    Leia Pop-Up Comb, *Return of the Jedi* logo 15.00
Ewok Personal Care Kit, including. comb & mirror
    (Adam Joseph 1983) 25.00

Return of the Jedi Toothbrushes, in box, on header card
Princess Leia Toothbrush (Oral-B 1985) 15.00
Darth Vader Toothbrush (Oral-B 1985) 10.00
Luke Skywalker Toothbrush (Oral-B 1985) 10.00
Ewoks Toothbrush (Oral-B 1985) 12.00
Jedi Master Three-pack, shrink wrapped (Oral-B 1985) 30.00
Electric Toothbrush, battery powered (Kenner 1978). . . 40.00
The Empire Strikes Back Electric Toothbrush,
    battery powered (Kenner 1980) 30.00
Wicket Electric Toothbrush (1984) 25.00

Star Wars & Episode I Toothbrushes (Colgate 1999)
    several different styles, each 1.50
    Styles with figural holder, each 2.00

Episode I Galactic Bubble Mint Toothpaste (Colgate 1999)
    several different 5.6 oz tubes, each 3.00
Combo packs of toothbrush & toothpaste, each. 5.00

Shampoo
Shampoo Character Containers (Omni 1981-83)
    8 different, each 15.00
Shampoo Refueling Station, 6½" (Omni 1981) 5.00
Princess Leia Beauty Bag (Omni 1981) 40.00
Luke Skywalker Belt Kit (Omni 1981) 40.00

Star Wars & Episode I Galactic Shampoo,
with bust figure topper (Minnetonka Brands 1999)
    Three different, each 3.00

Soaps
C-3PO Soap, 4" (Cliro 1977) 10.00

Star Wars and Episode I Toothbrushes (Colgate 1999)

R2-D2 Soap, 4" (Cliro 1977). 10.00
Character Soaps (Omni 1981-83) boxed
    10 different, each 10.00
Star Wars Soap Collections (Omni 1981) each. 30.00

Soap (Minnetonka Brands 1999)
Galactic Glycerin Soap, 3.5 oz, with Jar Jar Binks
    Head inside (#53050). 2.00

Star Wars & Episode I Towels
    Beach or Bath Towels from 1980s or 1990s, each   15.00
    Hand Towels from 1980s or 1990s, each 5.00

BEDROOM

    Star Wars bedding was popular from 1978 to 1984, and
a variety of sheets, pillowcases, blankets, bedspreads, and
curtains were made. Most collectors are happy if they still
have the ones they slept on as kids, but don't seem to be particularly interested in acquiring the same items in original
condition. There is little that you can do with a sheet if you
don't sleep on it, and if you do sleep on it, it would loose its
value as a collectible. For this reason, sheets and similar
items, in original packaging, are worth, at most, about the
same as a new *Star Wars* sheet in its packaging, with possibly
a small premium for the original ones from the 1970s. Your
old sheets may be worth something to you, but probably not
to anyone else. *Star Wars* sleep products made a comeback in
1997, and new ones are available.

Bedding (1978–79)
Star Wars sheets (1978–79). $25.00
Star Wars blanket (1978–79) 35.00
Star Wars pillowcase (1978–79). 7.50
All Other Bedding (1980–99)
Sheets, twin 20.00
Sheets, full 25.00
Pillowcase 7.00
Curtains 25.00

Household

Star Wars Beach Towel (1978)

Blanket 30.00
Pillow 15.00
Comforter, twin 50.00
Comforter, full 60.00

Sleeping Bags
Star Wars sleeping bag (1978) 25.00
Sleeping bag (1980 or 1990s) each 20.00

Nightlights
Return of the Jedi & Wicket Night Lights (Adam Joseph 1983)
    Seven different, each 5.00

Episode I Containers (Applause 1999)
Darth Maul head container, 11" (#43058) 30.00
R2-D2 figural container, 10" (#42967) 25.00

Episode I Treasure Keepers (Applause 1999)
    Four different, each 5.00

KITCHEN

    Star Wars kitchen items include the usual plates, bowls
and mugs, plus paper cups and tissues. See also CERAMICS.

Child's Dinnerware
Star Wars china set (Sigma) $25.00
Return of the Jedi dinnerware set (Deka 1983) 20.00
Wicket the Ewok Three piece set (Deka 1983) 10.00
Bowls (Deka 1980) 10.00
Cups (Deka 1980) 7.00

Cake Baking items
R2-D2 cake decorating kit (Wilton 1980) 15.00
Darth Vader cake decorating kit (Wilton 1980) 15.00
C-3PO cake pan (Wilton 1980) 10.00
Boba Fett cake pan (Wilton 1980) 25.00
Darth Vader cake pan (Wilton 1980) 15.00

Darth Maul Head Container (Applause 1999)
Princess Leia Dixie Cups and Box (1978)

Star Wars Episode I Child's Dinnerware Set (Zak Designs 1999)

R2-D2 & C-3PO figural CakeTops (Wilton #3607, 1979) 10.00
Darth Vader and Stormtrooper figural CakeTops
(Wilton #3643, 1979) 10.00
R2-D2 and C-3PO figural PutOns (Wilton 1980) 8.00
Chewbacca Cake Candle 3½" (Wilton 1980) 5.00
Darth Vader Cake Candle 3½" (Wilton 1980) 5.00
R2-D2 Cake Candle 3½" (Wilton 1980) 5.00

Kids Mugs, 6oz vinyl (Applause)
Star Wars, four different (1997) each 5.00
Episode I, four different (1999) each 5.00

Paper Cups and Tissues
Puffs facial tissue boxes (Puffs 1981) picturing:
    AT-ATs on Hoth 10.00
    Darth Vader and Luke battle over Bespin 10.00
    R2-D2 in Dagobah swamp 10.00

Star Wars Dixie Cups (1978–83) 5 oz. cups, packs
of 100 in assorted styles, in picture boxes:
    Star Wars (1978) each 10.00
    The Empire Strikes Back (1980) each 8.00
    Return of the Jedi (1983) each 6.00

***Star Wars* Film Cups** (Dixie Cup 1984) in boxes picturing:
    C-3PO and R2-D2 .... 10.00
    Princess Leia, Han Solo and Stormtroopers 12.00
    Darth Vader 10.00

Episode I Commuter Mugs (Applause 1999)
Darth Maul Commuter Mug, 15 oz (#43097) 10.00
Jar Jar Binks Commuter Mug, 15 oz (#43099) 10.00

OTHER ROOMS

Most *Star Wars* furniture, rugs, and wastebaskets were initially designed for kids' bedrooms or playrooms, but now that those kids have grown up, or at least gotten older, and

Household

Return of the Jedi Wastepaper Basket (Chein 1983)
& Jar Jar Bandages Pack (Curad 1999)

have their own houses and apartments, *Star Wars* items can be
found all over the house.

Cork Bulletin Boards (Manton Cork 1979)
    Star Wars or Characters, different sizes. . . $10 to 15.00

Drapery
Vehicle Diagram Rod Pocket Drape, 84" x 84" (1997). . 45.00
Vehicle Diagram Rod Pocket Drape, 84" x 63" (1997). . 35.00
Vehicle Diagram Rod Valance 84" x 15" (1997) 20.00
Character Study Rod Pocket Drape, 84" x 84" (1997). . 45.00
Character Study Rod Pocket Drape, 84" x 63" (1997). . 35.00
Character Study Rod Valance 84" x 15" (1997) 20.00

Episode I Drapery (1999)
Drapes (Westpoint Stevens #80438) 20.00
Valance (Westpoint Stevens #80440) 15.00

Furniture (Am. Toy and Furniture Co. 1983)
Return of the Jedi Bookcase 150.00
Ewok and Droid Toy Chest. 175.00
Darth Vader Coat Rack, 47" tall. 100.00
Desk and Chair, 32" high, movie scenes. 175.00
Return of the Jedi Nightstand. 150.00
Picnic Table, 36" long, movie scenes 175.00
Return of the Jedi Table and Chair Set. 175.00
R2-D2 Toy Chest, 28" tall, wooden base on wheels . . 150.00

Star Wars Inflatable Chairs (Intex 1999)
Queen Amidala, vinyl, 32" x 31½" x 38" (#68524) 13.00
Jar Jar Binks, vinyl, 32" x 31½" x 37" (#68523) 13.00
Darth Mall, vinyl, 42" x 36" x 48" (#685255). 18.00
C-3PO Junior Chair, 22½" x 22" x 30" (#68522) 10.00

Switcheroos
The Empire Strikes Back Switcheroos, "light switch
    cover for kids rooms" (Kenner 1980)
        Three different, each 25.00

Rugs
Star Wars Wool Hook Rug, 45" x 69" picturing
    C-3PO and R2-D2 (1997). 200.00

Household

Tins
Star Wars Special Edition Popcorn Tin (with three
    types of popcorn) 8 lbs. (1997) 35.00

Wastepaper Baskets (Chein Industries 1983)
Return of the Jedi wastepaper basket 25.00
Ewoks wastepaper basket 20.00

Episode I Playhouse (Ero 1999)
Star Wars Episode One Playhouse (#11535) 25.00

Millennium Falcon Island/River Raft (Intex 1999)

OUTDOORS

Gym Set
Star Wars Gym Set (Gym-Dandy 1983) $1,200.00

Star Wars & Episode I Pool Toys (Intex 1999)
Millennium Falcon Island/River Raft, 66" x 52" (#58283) 15.00
Jar Jar Ride-In, 2-person, 58½" x 27" (#58533) 10.00
Trade Federation Droid Starfighter Pool Ride-On,
    56" x 37" (#58170) 12.00
Naboo Starfighter Pool Ride-On, 74" x 41" (#58525) . . . 10.00
Landspeeder Boat/Lounge (#58380) 12.00
Anakin's Podracer Pool Lounge, 82" x 37" (#58810) . . . 15.00
Jar Jar's World Aquarium Pool (#58479) 20.00
Trade Federation Droid Control Ship Spray Pool,
    73" diameter x 13" high (#56470) 20.00

Star Wars Bandages (Curad 1998–99)
C-3PO 30-pack 2.00
Jar Jar Binks 30-pack 2.00

HOLIDAY AND PARTY

    Hallmark has made collectible Christmas ornaments for
many years. In 1996, Hallmark discovered the marketing
hype for the *Star Wars Trilogy Special Edition* movies and
produced . . . a grand total of one ornament! Five more ornaments followed in 1997, and four more in 1998 and 1999,

Household

Darth Vader Christmas Ornament (Hallmark 1997)

plus two for *Star Wars Episode I*. The best way to buy them
has been to wait until just after Christmas, when they go on
sale or 50% or more off.

Star Wars Christmas Ornaments (Hallmark 1996–99)
Millennium Falcon ornament (#7474, 1996) $60.00
Darth Vader hanging ornament (#17531, 1997) 25.00
Yoda hanging ornament (#16355, 1997). 30.00
C-3PO and R2-D2 set of ornaments (#14265, 1997) . . 20.00
Luke Skywalker hanging ornament (#5484, 1997) 25.00
Vehicles of *Star Wars*, three miniatures (#4024, 1997) . 40.00
X-wing Starfighter, light-up (#7596, 1998) 23.95
Boba Fett hanging ornament (#4053, 1998) 14.95
Princess Leia hanging ornament (#4026, 1998). 13.95
Ewoks, three miniatures (#4223, 1998) 16.95
Han Solo (#14007, 1999) 14.00
Chewbacca (#14009, 1999) 15.00
Darth Vader's TIE Fighter (#17399, 1999) 24.00
Max Rebo Band, set of three (#14597, 1999) 20.00

Star Wars Episode I Christmas Ornaments (Hallmark 1999)
Queen Amidala (#14187) 15.00
Naboo Starfighter (#17613). 19.00

Party Supplies (1980–99)
Napkins, invitations, other party supplies 2.00–5.00

MASKS & COSTUMES

MASKS, HELMETS AND COSTUMES

Mask and Costume collecting extends far beyond *Star Wars*. Just about every famous or infamous person and fictional character has appeared on some type of Halloween costume over the years. Classic monsters, superheroes, and science fiction characters have always been popular, and *Star Wars* provides a host of interesting mask and costume possibilities. Both masks and costumes appeared in 1977, months before there were any *Star Wars* action figures.

MASKS AND HELMETS

Don Post Studios has always made the high-end masks—those designed for adults and for display, rather than for a child's Halloween costume. Lately, they have added hands and collector helmets to their line-up. They also produce deluxe replica helmets, which are listed under STATUES.

Masks (Don Post Studios 1977–98)
C-3PO latex mask (Don Post 1977) $100.00
    reissue (1978) 75.00
    reissue (late 1980s) 50.00
    reissue, 12" gold tone heavy vinyl (1994) 40.00
Cantina Band Member rubber mask (Don Post 1980). . 75.00
    reissue (1990s) 60.00
    reissue, 13" latex (#82005, 1994) 40.00
Chewbacca rubber mask (Don Post 1977) 250.00
    reissue (1978) 100.00

Don Post Masks advertisement (Don Post 1983)

       reissue (1990) 75.00
       reissue, 11" multicolored hair (#82003, 1990s) . . . 60.00
Darth Vader Collector Helmet, plastic (1977) 200.00
       reissue (1978–82) 75.00
       reissue (1983) 50.00
       reissue (#82001, 1994) 60.00
Stormtrooper Collector Helmet, plastic (1977). 90.00
       reissue (1978) 75.00
       reissue (#82002, late 1980s) 60.00
Tusken Raider rubber mask (Don Post late 1970s). . . . 90.00
       reissue (late 1980s) 70.00
       reissue, 11" latex (#82016, 1995) 32.00
Ugnaught mask (Don Post 1980s) 75.00
Yoda rubber mask (Don Post 1980s) 60.00
       reissue (1990s) 50.00
       reissue, 10" latex with hair (#82007, 1994) 40.00
Admiral Ackbar rubber mask (Don Post 1983) 75.00
       reissue (1990s) 60.00
       reissue, 13" latex (#82011, 1994) 40.00
Gamorrean Guard rubber mask (Don Post 1983) 75.00
       reissue, 11" (#82017, 1995) 32.00
Klaatu rubber mask (Don Post 1983) 75.00
       reissue (1990s) 60.00
       reissue, 12" latex with hood (#82018, 1995) 40.00
Nien Nunb rubber mask, 11" (#82015, 1996) 32.00
Weequay rubber mask (Don Post 1983). 90.00
Wicket W. Warrick rubber mask (Don Post 1983) 90.00
       reissue (1990) 75.00
       reissue, 10" hair and hood (#82012, 1994) 40.00
Emperor Palpatine rubber mask. 80.00
       reissue, 11" latex with cloth hood (1994) 40.00
Greedo, 11" latex (#82027, 1997). 40.00
Prince Xizor, 12" latex and hair (#82021, 1994) 40.00

Hands

Prince Xizor's Hands, 9" latex (#82041, 1994) 30.00
Cantina Band Member's Hands, 10" latex (1994) 23.00
Greedo Hands (#82045) 30.00
Admiral Ackbar Hands, 15" latex (#82044, 1994) 30.00

Collector Helmets (Don Post 1996–98)
Boba Fett, 10" plastic with smoked viewplate and

Wicket W. Warrick and Klaatu masks (Don Post 1990s)

Masks

Boba Fett and Stormtrooper Helmets (Don Post 1990s)

moveable antenna (#82019, 1996)	60.00
Darth Vader, 13" plastic faceplate and overhelmet, with tinted eyepieces (#82001)	40.00
Emperor's Royal Guard, 18" crimson plastic with smoked visor (#82020, 1996)	60.00
Stormtrooper, 11" white plastic with simulated breathing filters and com-link (#82002)	60.00
TIE Fighter, 11" (#82025, 1997)	70.00
Scout Trooper Helmet, 11" (#82024, 1997)	70.00
X-wing Fighter, 13" (#82026, 1997)	70.00

Episode I Masks (Don Post 1999)

Queen Amidala Theed (#82205)	50.00
Jar Jar Binks (#82206)	40.00
Darth Maul (#82208)	40.00
Sebula (#82212)	40.00
Watto (#82213)	40.00
Ki-Adi-Mundi (#82214)	50.00
Even Piell (#82216)	50.00
Nute Gunray Deluxe (#82219)	90.00
Rune Haako Deluxe (#82220)	70.00
Jar Jar Binks Deluxe (#82302)	120.00
Sebula Deluxe (#82303)	70.00

Episode I Collector Helmets (Don Post 1999)

Anakin's Podracer Helmet (#82200)	55.00
Naboo Starfighter Helmet (#82210)	50.00

Classic Action Helmets (Don Post 1997)

Darth Vader Classic Action Helmet, 15" (#82108)	180.00
Stormtrooper Classic Action Helmet, 13" (#82107)	150.00
TIE Fighter Classic Action Helmet, 15" (#82105)	150.00

RIDDELL MINI-HELMET
Collectible Mini-Helmets, 45% of scale with display base

Darth Vader Mini-Helmet, three pieces	95.00
X-wing (Pilot) Mini-Helmet, moveable pieces	85.00
C-3PO Mini-Helmet, battery powered eyes	80.00
Stormtrooper Mini-Helmet, with die-cast metal parts	85.00
Boba Fett Mini-Helmet, die-cast metal parts	85.00

Masks

COSTUMES

      Ben Cooper was the most famous maker of collectible Halloween costumes in the 1970s and 1980s. All of the firms product was made for kids. This means that it was made, and sold, inexpensively, and was not initially designed as a collectible. This also means that old costumes in prime condition are hard to find.

      Rubies currently makes Halloween costumes for the same market. Their current crop of classic *Star Wars* items may never receive much collector attention, since it must compete with the Ben Cooper originals and with the Don Post Studios higher quality.

Costume and Mask, boxed (Ben Cooper)
Darth Vader (#740, 1977–85)
    Star Wars. $35.00
    The Empire Strikes Back 20.00
    Return of the Jedi. 20.00
Luke Skywalker (#741, 1977–85)
    Star Wars. 35.00
    The Empire Strikes Back 20.00
    Return of the Jedi. 20.00
C-3PO (#742, 1977–85)
    Star Wars. 35.00
    The Empire Strikes Back 20.00
    Return of the Jedi. 20.00
Luke Skywalker, X-Wing
    Star Wars. 35.00
    The Empire Strikes Back 20.00
    Return of the Jedi. 20.00

Masks

Darth Maul Deluxe Makeup Kit (Rubies 1999)

Boba Fett: *T-shirt (Liquid Blue 1998); Pez Dispenser (Pez 1997); Flying Toy (Taco Bell 1997); Twin Engines of Destruction comic book (Dark Horse 1997); vinyl figure (Applause 1997); and Slave I spaceship (Kenner 1981)*

Jabba the Hutt: *Jabba Ceramic Bank (Sigma 1982); Jabba the Hutt Action Playset with added figures (Kenner 1983); and Jabba the Hutt Buddies figure (Kenner 1998)*

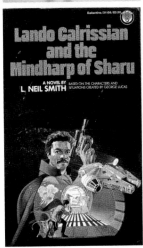

Lando Calrissian: *Action figure, no teeth (Kenner 1980); in Skiff Guard Disguise, action figure (Kenner 1983); in General's Gear, action figure and Freeze Frame Action Slide (Kenner 1998); and Paperback books (Ballantine Del Rey 1983)*

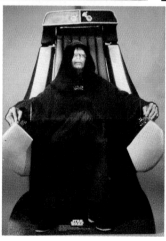

Senator/Emperor Palpatine and his Royal Guard: *Bust (Legends in Three Dimension 1997); vinyl figure (Applause 1997); action figure (Hasbro 1999); plastic bank (Adam Joseph 1983); and standees (Advance Graphics 1996)*

Biggs Darklighter & Wedge Antilles: *Biggs, page from Star Wars #1 (Marvel 1977) and action figure (Kenner 1998); Wedge vinyl figure (Applause 1996) and X-Wing rogue Squadron #11 (Dark Horse 1996); and close-up of 12" dolls (Kenner 1998)*

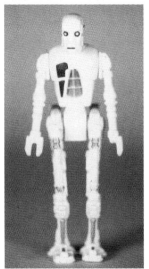
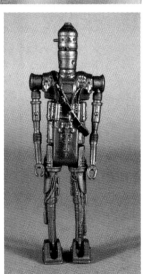

Droids: *Pit Droid, 12" scale figure (Hasbro 1999); Destroyer Droid Room Alarm (Tiger 1999); 8D8 (Kenner 1998); IG-88 Droid, 12" figure (Kenner 1980); R2-B1 AstroMech Droid (Hasbro 2000); and R2-A6 Droid, 12" scale figure (Hasbro 1999)*

Cantina Aliens: *Cantina Adventure Set (Kenner 1979); Cantina Showdown, cinema scene (Kenner 1997); Lak Sivrak (Kenner 1998); Greedo (Kenner 1980); and Creature Cantina Action Playset (Kenner 1979)*

Entertainers: *Max Rebo Band Keepsake Ornaments (Hallmark 1999); Doink Nats, Cantina Band 12" Doll (Kenner 1998); Max Rebo customizable card game card (Decipher 1997); Max Rebo Band (Kenner 1985); and Jabba's Dancers (Kenner 1998)*

Qui-Gon Jinn: *Qui-Gon Ginn, Jedi Duel action figure (Hasbro 1999); Doritos Smokey Red BBQ Chips bag (Lays 1999); 12" Doll (Hasbro 1999); fast food paper drink cup (1999); Opee and Qui-Gon Jinn (Hasbro 1999)*

Obi-Wan Kenobi, Episode I: *12" Doll (Hasbro 1999); Mountain Dew Stand-up and soda can (Pepsico 1999); Lays Potato Chip Bag (Lays 1999); and 3-D Figure Painter (Hasbro 1999)*

Jar Jar Binks: *Collectible sticker (Liquid Blue 1999); Inflatable Chair (Intex 1999); Wake-up system (Thinkway 1999);Aura Glow Scene (Illuminations 1999); Keychain and Pin (Applause 1999); and 100-piece puzzle (Hasbro 1999)*

Queen Amidala: *Padme Naberrie action figure (Hasbro 1999);*
Bandages (Curad 1999); Christmas ornament (Hallmark 1999);
Queen Amidala, Coruscant action figure (Hasbro 1999); Hidden
Elegance doll (Hasbro 1999); and Folder (Impact 1999)

Anakin Skywalker: *Naboo Pilot action figure (Hasbro 1999); Drink Topper (Taco Bell 1999); Toothpaste (Colgate 1999); lip balm and holder (Minnetonka Brands 1999); coloring book (Random House 1999); action figure as adult (Kenner 1983)*

Darth Maul: *Lunch Bag (1999); Pen and collector box (Pentech 1999); wallet (Pyramid 1999); and Darth Maul Rubik's Cube (Hasbro 1999)*

Mace Windu & Jedi: *Stand-up (Pepsico 1999); Ki-Adi-Mundi action figure (Hasbro 1999); Mountain Dew can (1999); cover of Lee's AFN&TR #88 (1999); Tales of the Jedi: Redemption #5 and The Golden Age of the Sith #1 (Dark Horse Comics 1998 & 1996)*

Galactic Dysfunctional Family: *Shmi Skywalker; Anakin Skywalker, youth and adult; Darth Vader; Queen Amidala/Padme; Luke Skywalker; Princess Leia; Han Solo;* **Who was Anakin's father?:** *Qui-Gon Jinn, Darth Sidious, Senator Palpatine or Yoda?*

R2-D2 (#744, 1977–85)

Star Wars. 35.00
The Empire Strikes Back 20.00
Return of the Jedi. 20.00

Princess Leia (#745, 1977–85)

Star Wars. 35.00
The Empire Strikes Back 20.00
Return of the Jedi. 20.00

Chewbacca (#746, 1977–85)

Star Wars. 35.00
The Empire Strikes Back 20.00
Return of the Jedi. 20.00

Stormtrooper (#747, 1977–85)

Star Wars. 35.00
The Empire Strikes Back 20.00
Return of the Jedi. 20.00

Boba Fett (#748, 1977–85)

Star Wars. 35.00
The Empire Strikes Back 20.00
Return of the Jedi. 20.00

Yoda Costume (#749, 1980–85)

The Empire Strikes Back 30.00
Return of the Jedi. 30.00

Wicket, *Return of the Jedi* (#735, 1983–85) 25.00
Admiral Ackbar, *Return of the Jedi* (#736, 1983–85). . . 25.00
Gamorrean Guard, *Return of the Jedi* (#737, 1983–85) 25.00
Klaatu, *Return of the Jedi* (#738, 1983–85) 25.00

Costumes and Masks (1995–97)

Darth Vader polyester jumpsuit, bootcovers, cape
   and PVC mask (JC Penney 1997) 25.00
Chewbacca costume, includes jumpsuit, mask and
   sash (#15242, 1996) 95.00
Chewbacca rubber mask (#C2867) 20.00

Masks

Darth Maul Adult Mask (Rubies 1999)

Darth Vader costume, includes jumpsuit, chest-
piece, cape, and mask (#15236, 1996)......... 75.00
Stormtrooper costume, includes jumpsuit, chest-
piece, and mask (#15243, 1996) 70.00
C-3PO Costume (#15237, 1997) 70.00
Yoda Costume (#15400, 1997)................. 50.00

Halloween Costumes (1997) Party City Catalog.
Costumes come in small, medium, or large child's sizes:
Darth Vader deluxe child costume, with silk-screen-
ed jumpsuit, cape and 3/4 mask (#26) 13.00
Super Deluxe Darth Vader child costume, with jump-
suit, boot tops, chestpiece, cape & mask (#27)... 30.00
Super Deluxe Princess Leia child costume, with
dress, belt, and wig (#80) 30.00
Stormtrooper deluxe child costume, with silkscreen-
ed jumpsuit and 3/4 mask (#105) 13.00
C-3PO deluxe child costume, with silkscreened
jumpsuit and 3/4 mask (#14) 13.00
Darth Vader adult costume with silkscreened jump
suit, cape, and two-piece PVC mask (#231) 40.00

Star Wars Costumes (Rubies 1996–98)
Darth Vader mask (#2865)..................... 25.00
C-3PO hard mask (#2866) 30.00
Chewbacca mask (#2867) 25.00
Stormtrooper latex mask (#2868) 25.00
Yoda mask (#2869) 30.00
Darth Vader Costume Kit, cape, chest armor, mask,
and lightsaber (#17016, 1996), boxed......... 15.00
Darth Vader mask (#2993).................... 25.00
Chewbacca mask (#2994) 30.00
C-3PO mask (#2995)......................... 25.00
Princess Leia wig........................... 20.00

Episode I Costumes (Rubies 1999)
Darth Maul Costume Kit, with Hooded Cloak, Belt,
PVC Mask & Glo Lightsaber (#17033) on card.... 18.00
Obi-Wan Kenobi Costume Kit (#17039) on card 18.00
Obi-Wan Kenobi Costume Kit (#17041) boxed........ 18.00
Qui-Gon Jinn Costume Kit (#17042) boxed 18.00

Episode I Adult Masks (Rubies 1999)
Darth Maul, Jar Jar Binks, etc., each 25.00

Episode I Costumes, sizes 3-4, 5-7 & 8-10
Darth Maul 35.00
Anakin Skywalker 35.00

Episode I Costumes, sizes 4-6, 8-10, 12-14
Jar Jar Binks, one-piece costume & mask........... 60.00
Anakin Skywalker, costume & helmet 60.00
Queen Amidala, costume & headpiece 60.00
Qui-Gon Jinn, one-piece costume................. 60.00
Obi Wan Kenobi, one-piece costume.............. 60.00

Make-Up Kit
Queen Amidala Makeup Kit (Rubies #19661) 5.00
Darth Maul Deluxe Makeup Kit (Rubies #19658) 10.00

Masks

STAR WARS MICRO COLLECTION
Kenner (1982)

Kenner's Micro Collection consists of plastic playsets and plastic vehicles for use with 1" die-cast figures. The nine playsets could be bought individually or grouped into three "Worlds": Hoth Ice Planet, Bespin Cloud City and Death Star. With nine playsets and three worlds, you might think that there would be three playsets per world, but you would be wrong. There were two Death Star playsets, three Bespin playsets, and four Hoth playsets. The Hoth Generator Attack set was omitted from the Hoth World group.

There were two ships in the original Micro Line: The X-Wing Fighter and the TIE Fighter. Each had a pilot and a crash feature so that it suffered battle damage at the push of a button along with battle damage stickers. Two exclusive ships were offered in 1983—the *Millennium Falcon* was a Sears exclusive, while the Rebel Armored Snowspeeder was a JC Penney exclusive.

There was also two mail-in "Build Your Armies" sets of six figures, and one mail-in set of four figures offered. All of the die-cast figures have product numbers on the base or body. They are given below to aid in identification of loose figures. Die-cast ships are not listed here. They are in the DIE-CAST section.

Action Playsets
Bespin Control Room (#69920) with two Luke figures
and two Darth Vader figures (#256-001–004) . . . $30.00

Micro

Bespin World Action Playset (Kenner 1982)

Bespin Freeze Chamber (#69930) includes eight
   figures (#460-009–017) 75.00
Bespin Gantry (#69910) includes two Luke figures
   and two Darth Vader figures (#258-001–004) 30.00
Bespin World: Bespin Control Room, Bespin
   Freeze Chamber, and Bespin Gantry sets,
   includes 16 figures (#69940, 1982). 150.00
Death Star Compactor (#93300) includes eight fig-
   ures (#517-014–021) 60.00
Death Star Escape (#69990) includes six figures
   (#583-018–023) 60.00
Death Star World: Death Star Compactor and Death
   Star Escape sets (#93310) includes 14 figures . . 125.00
Hoth Generator Attack (#93420) includes six figures
   (#668-001–006) 25.00
Hoth Ion Cannon (#69970) includes eight figures
   (#692-001–008) 35.00
Hoth Turret Defense (#69960) includes six figures
   (#463-010–015) 25.00
Hoth Wampa Cave (#69950) includes a Wampa
   and four figures (#269-001–004 & #269-009-A) . . 25.00
Hoth World: Hoth Generator Attack, Hoth Ion
   Cannon, and Hoth Wampa Cave sets, 19 figures 100.00

Vehicles
Imperial TIE Fighter, with pilot figure (#270-010). 75.00
X-Wing Fighter (#69670) with pilot figure (#270-014) . . 65.00
Millennium Falcon (#70140) includes six figures
   (#733-001–006) Sears exclusive 400.00
Rebel Armored Snowspeeder, with working
   harpoon (#70150) includes pilot and Harpoon-
   er figures (#261-015–016) JC Penney exclusive . 200.00

Mail-In Figures
Build Your Armies: three Rebel Soldiers (#088-001–
   003) and three Snowtroopers (#088-005–007) . . . 25.00

Hoth Turret Defense Action Playset (Kenner 1982)

Micro

MICROMACHINES
Galoob (1993–99)

The Galoob *Star Wars* MicroMachines collection debuted in 1994, as part of their "Space" segment. At the time, *Star Wars* was the hottest collectible going, but very few new items had started to appear. The JustToys *Star Wars* Bend-Ems were out, but the action figures from Kenner were not. The first batch of MicroMachines contained a three figure set for each of the three movies. The earliest ones have a 1993 Lucasfilm Ltd. copyright, an individual movie logo in the front, and only list the first three series on the back (3-back). These were reissued when the next three items were released, with a generic "*Star Wars*" logo on the front, a 1994 copyright, and list all six series on the back (6-back). All were issued on rectangular header cards as part of MicroMachines "Space" series.

In April 1996, they were replaced by the *Star Wars* Vehicle Collection, which also said "Space" on its original packages, but had different figures in the numbered collections and different UPC codes. Packaging was then changed to omit "Space" and just say "*Star Wars*." Packaging was changed again in 1997 to a striped design, similar to the stripes on the Action Fleet packages.

All of the MicroMachines have small parts and small figures, so, even if they survive battles between the Galactic Empire and the Rebel Forces, most of them are destined to an ignominious defeat at the hands of mom's vacuum cleaner. This will make completing any loose set very difficult. The larger X-Ray fleet, and the even larger Action Fleet ships, are covered below. See also DIE-CAST for Galoob's Micro-Machine Die-Cast ships.

Micro

The Empire Strikes Back MicroMachine Vehicles #2 (Galoob 1993)

The Empire Strikes Back MicroMachines Vehicles #5 (Galoob 1994)

SPACE SERIES VEHICLES (1993–95)
First Batch (Asst. #65860, 1993) on 3-back header card
#1 *Star Wars*: *Millennium Falcon*; Imperial Star-
    Destroyer; X-wing Starfighter (#65886) $15.00
    Reissue as *Star Wars: A New Hope*, 1994
        copyright, generic logo, 6-back 7.00
#2 *The Empire Strikes Back*: TIE Starfighter;
    Imperial AT-AT; Snowspeeder (#65887) 15.00
    Reissue, 1994, generic logo, 6-back 7.00
#3 *Return of the Jedi*: Imperial AT-ST (Chicken
    Walker); Jabba's Desert Sail Barge; B-wing
    Starfighter (#65888) 15.00
    Reissue, 1994, generic logo, 6-back 7.00
#4 *Star Wars: A New Hope*: Y-wing Starfighter;
    Jawa Sandcrawler; Rebel Blockade Runner
    (#65897) 8.00
#5 *The Empire Strikes Back*: Imperial TIE
    Bomber, Boba Fett's *Slave I*; Bespin Twin-Pod
    Cloud Car (#65898) 8.00
#6 *Return of the Jedi*: Speeder Bike with Rebel
    Pilot; Imperial Shuttle *Tyderium*; A-wing
    Starfighter (#65899) 8.00

VEHICLE COLLECTION (Asst. #65860, 1996–98)
I   TIE Interceptor, Imperial Star Destroyer, Rebel
     Blockade Runner (#66111) 7.00
II   Landspeeder, *Millennium Falcon*, Jawa Sand-
     crawler (#66112) 7.00
III Darth Vader's TIE Fighter, Y-wing Starfighter,
     X-wing Starfighter (#66113) 7.00
IV   Imperial Probot, Imperial AT-AT, Snowspeeder
     (#66114) 7.00
V   Rebel Transport, TIE Bomber, Imperial AT-ST
     (#66115) 7.00
VI   Escort Frigate, Boba Fett's *Slave I*, Bespin
     Twin-Pod Cloud Car (#66116) 7.00
VII Mon Calamari Star Cruiser, Jabba's Desert
     Sail Barge, Speeder Bike with Rebel Pilot (#66117) 7.00

Micro

VIII Speeder Bike with Imperial Pilot, Imperial Shuttle *Tydirium*, TIE Starfighter (#66118) 7.00

IX Super Star Destroyer *Executor*, B-wing Starfighter, A-wing Starfighter (#66119) 7.00

X Incom T-16 Skyhopper, Lars Family Landspeeder, Death Star II (#66137) 7.00

XI Bespin Cloud City, Mon Calamari Rebel Cruiser, Escape Pod (#66138) 6.00

XII Battle-Damaged: A-wing Starfighter, TIE Starfighter, Y-wing Starfighter (#65154) 6.00

XIII Battle-Damaged X-wings: Red, Green & Blue Squadrons (#65155) 6.00

XIV Imperial Landing Craft, Death Star, S-Swoop (#65123) 6.00

XV *Outrider*, Tibanna Gas Refinery, V-35 Landspeeder (#65124) 6.00

SPECIAL EDITION VEHICLES (1995) Pewter finish, boxed

Star Wars: A New Hope, eight ships (#65851) 20.00
The Empire Strikes Back, eight ships (#65852) 20.00
Return of the Jedi, eight ships (#65853) 20.00

SHADOWS OF THE EMPIRE VEHICLES (1996)

I Stinger, IG-2000, Guri, Asp, and Darth Vader (#66194) 7.00

II Virago, Swoop with Rider, Prince Xizor, and Emperor Palpatine (#66195) 7.00

III Outrider, Hound's Tooth, Dash Rendar, LE-BO2D9, and Luke Skywalker (#66196) 7.00

COLLECTOR SETS

Star Wars Collector's Gift Set, 14 vehicles, 12 figures, bronze finish, with special Death Star Battle Station 2 (#64624, 1995) 30.00

Master Collector's Edition, 19 *Star Wars* vehicles inc. exclusive Super Star Destroyer *Executor* (#64061) 20.00

Micro

Tusken Raiders Figure Collection VIII (Galoob 1997)

FIGURE COLLECTIONS (1996–98) nine figures per pack

I	Imperial Stormtroopers (#66081)	7.00
II	Ewoks (#66082)	7.00
III	Rebel Pilots (#66083)	7.00
IV	Imperial Pilots (#66084)	7.00
V	Jawas (#66096)	7.00
VI	Imperial Officers (#66097)	7.00
VII	Echo Base Troops (#66098)	7.00
VIII	Tusken Raiders (#66109)	7.00
IX	Rebel Fleet Troops (#66108)	7.00
X	Imperial Naval Troopers (#66099)	7.00
XI	Classic Characters (#66158)	7.00
XI	Classic Characters, new poses (#67111)	7.00
XII	Endor Rebel Strike Team (#67112)	7.00
XIII	Imperial Scout Troopers (#67113)	7.00
XIV	Bounty Hunters (#67114)	7.00

DROIDS COLLECTION (1997)
Droids, 16 articulated droids (#66090) 17.00

EPIC COLLECTIONS (1997) three figures and three vehicles
in a box which looks like a paperback book.
Heir to the Empire (#66281) 3.50
Jedi Search (#66282) 3.50
The Truce at Bakura (#66283) 3.50

PLAYSETS (1994–98)
The Death Star playset, includes X-wing Starfighter
    and five figures (#65871, 1994) 11.00
Ice Planet Hoth playset, includes Imperial AT-AT
    and five figures (#65872, 1994) 11.00
Endor playset, includes Imperial AT-ST and five
    figures (#65873, 1994) 11.00
Planet Tatooine playset, includes cargo skiff and
    five figures (#65858, 1996) 11.00
Planet Dagobah playset, includes X-wing Star-
    fighter and five figures (#65859, 1996) 11.00
Cloud City playset, includes Twin-pod Cloud Car
    and four figures (#65995, 1998) 11.00
Rebel Transport playset, includes X-wing Starfighter
    and 3 figures (#65995, 1998) 11.00

Slave I Transforming Action Playset (Galoob 1998)

Micro

TRANSFORMING ACTION SETS (1996)
First Batch Helmet/Head shaped, boxed
C-3PO becomes Mos Eisley Cantina (#65811) 15.00
Darth Vader becomes Bespin Imperial outpost (#65812) 15.00
R2-D2 becomes Jabba's Desert Palace (#65813) 15.00
Stormtrooper becomes Death Star (#65814) 15.00
Chewbacca becomes Endor's forest moon (#65815) . . 15.00
Boba Fett becomes Bespin's Cloud City (#65816) 15.00
Luke Skywalker becomes ice planet Hoth (#65817) . . . 15.00
Royal Guard becomes the Death Star II (#65695) 15.00
TIE Fighter Pilot becomes Imperial Academy (#65694) . 15.00

Second Batch (1998)
Yoda becomes swamp planet Dagobah (#68063) 15.00
Jabba becomes Mos Eisley Spaceport (#68064) 15.00
Slave I becomes planet Tatooine (#67095) 15.00
Star Destroyer becomes Space Fortress (#67094) 15.00

MINI-ACTION TRANSFORMING PLAYSETS
Three heads on a header card; each head opens to reveal a
  micro figure inside the head.
Mini-Action Transforming Playsets (Asst. #68020, 1997)
I   Boba Fett, Admiral Ackbar and Gamorrean
      Guard (#68021) 6.00
II   Nien Nunb, Greedo and Tusken Raider (#68022) . . . 6.00
III Jawa, Yoda, Princess Leia (Boushh Disguise)
      (#68023) 6.00
IV   Bib Fortuna, Figrin D'an, Scout Trooper (#68024) . . 6.00

Mini-Action Boxed Set (1996) with Widevision promo card
Mini-Action seven-head set, includes Gamorrean
  Guard, Nien Nunb, Darth Vader, Jawa, Greedo,
  Admiral Ackbar and Princess Leia (#68038) 15.00

ADVENTURE GEAR/PLAYSET (Asst. #68030, 1996) boxed
Weapon or Gear, which opens into a playset.
Vader's Lightsaber opens into Death Star Trench,
  includes vehicle and three figures (#68031) 12.00

Mini-Action Transforming Playset # IV (Galoob 1997)

Micro

*Target Exclusive Imperial ForcesGift Set, Second Edition
(Galoob 1995)*

Luke's Binoculars open into Yavin Rebel Base,
    includes vehicle and three figures (#68031) 12.00

DOUBLE TAKES
Death Star, transforms into planet Tatooine and
    Mos Eisley spaceport, includes *Millennium
    Falcon* and four figures (#75118, 1997) 40.00

EXCLUSIVE SETS
Star Wars Fan Club Star Destroyer vehicle, with
    Darth Vader, boxed 25.00
Star Wars Fan Club *Millennium Falcon* vehicle, with
    Han Solo, boxed 30.00
Star Wars Toy Fair 3-pack, *Millennium Falcon*,
    Slave I, and Death Star, window box 25.00
Rebel Forces Gift Set, four vehicles and four figures
    (#65836, 1994) Target exclusive 12.00
Imperial Forces Gift Set, five vehicles and three fig-
    ures (#65837, 1994) Target exclusive 12.00
Galaxy Battle Collector's Set, three ships and three
    figures each from the Rebel Alliance and the
    evil Empire (#64602, 1994) K-Mart exclusive 9.00
11 Piece Collector's Gift Set, seven from the Rebel
    Alliance and four from the evil Empire (#65847,
    1994) Kay-Bee exclusive 16.00
Master Collector's Edition 19 vehicle set, 6 vehicles
    from *Star Wars: A New Hope*, seven vehicles
    from *The Empire Strikes Back* and six vehicles
    from *Return of the Jedi* (#64601, 1994) Toys
    "R" Us exclusive 30.00
Star Wars Special Rebel Forces Gift Set, Second
    Edition, four figures and four ships (#65856,

Micro

MICROMACHINE X-RAY FLEET
Galoob (1996–97)

X-Ray Fleet vehicles are the same size as Galoob's die-cast vehicles and considerably bigger than the regular MicroMachine size, but still a lot smaller than their Action Fleet ships. For me, it's a very attractive size, because I can appreciate the details without a magnifying glass.

Star Wars MicroMachine X-Ray Fleet III (Galoob 1996)

Micro

The outer hull of each X-Ray Fleet ship is clear plastic, allowing the collector to view the inner portions of each vehicle. This only works if the inside portions correspond to the known insides of the ship, as seen in the movies. Some of the X-Ray Fleet correspond fairly well to the movie version, notably the Imperial AT-AT and AT-ST, but most are not so successful.

The *Star Wars* Trilogy Gift Set includes only one X-Ray Fleet ship, the Shuttle *Tyderium*. The other nine ships are the same size as the X-Ray Fleet (and Die-Cast ships) but are painted. This set was originally a JC Penney exclusive, but leftover sets found their way to KayBee Toys and sold for $15.00. That's where I got mine.

X-Ray Two Packs (1996) "Space" packaging

I	Darth Vader's TIE Fighter & A-wing Starfighter (#67071)	$7.00
II	X-wing Starfighter & Imperial AT-AT (#67072)	7.00
III	*Millennium Falcon* & Jawa Sandcrawler (#67073)	7.00
IV	Boba Fett's *Slave I* & Y-wing Starfighter (#67074)	7.00
V	TIE Bomber and B-wing Starfighter	7.00
VI	TIE Fighter and Landspeeder	7.00
VII	Imperial AT-ST and Snowspeeder	7.00

Large Boxed Set

Star Wars Trilogy Gift Set, 10 larger, X-Ray vehicle-sized, ships with display stands (#67079, 1996) .. 35.00

Action Fleet Luke's X-wing Starfighter (Galoob 1996)

MICROMACHINE ACTION FLEET
Galoob (1996–98)

VEHICLES

Action Fleet vehicles are larger than Galoob's X-Ray fleet and die-cast vehicles, but still smaller than Kenner's

Ice Planet Hoth Action Fleet Playset (Galoob 1997)

action figure vehicles. It has proven to be a popular size with both kids and collectors.

The first 2,500 pieces, from the production run of each of the first batch vehicles, were numbered with a special blue collector's sticker, The Rebel Snowspeeder was short packed in the assortment.

In 1997, Galoob introduced Series Alpha, which included both an original concept design vehicle and the familiar final design vehicle, along with two figures. This is one of the only ways to collect design prototypes, but some see it as just a gimmick to get them to buy another copy of the a vehicle that they already own.

First Batch (Spring 1996) ship, with two figures
Luke's X-wing Starfighter (#67031)	$12.00
With numbered collector sticker	20.00
Darth Vader's TIE Fighter (#67032)	12.00
With numbered collector sticker	20.00
Imperial AT-AT (#67033)	12.00
With numbered collector sticker	20.00
A-wing Starfighter (#67034)	12.00
With numbered collector sticker	20.00
Imperial Shuttle *Tydirium* (#67035)	12.00
With numbered collector sticker	20.00
Rebel Snow Speeder (#67036)	15.00
With numbered collector sticker	20.00

Second Batch (Fall 1996)
Jawa Sandcrawler (#67039)	10.00
Y-wing Starfighter (#67040)	10.00
Slave I (#67041)	10.00
TIE Interceptor (#67058)	10.00

Third Batch (Asst. #67030, Spring 1997)
Rancor (#66989)	10.00
Virago (#66990)	10.00
X-wing Starfighter (#66991)	10.00
Y-wing Starfighter (#66992)	10.00

Micro

A-wing Starfighter (#66993) 10.00
TIE Fighter(#66995) 10.00
TIE Bomber (#67059) 10.00

Fourth Batch (Asst. #67030, Fall 1997)
Bespin Twin-Pod Cloud Car (#66996) 10.00
B-wing Starfighter (#66994) 10.00
X-wing Starfighter (#67023) 10.00
Y-wing Starfighter (#67024) 10.00
Rebel Snowspeeder (#67025) 10.00

Fifth Batch (Spring 1998)
Millennium Falcon 10.00
Rebel Blockade Runner 10.00
Incom T-16 Skyhopper 10.00
Imperial Landing Craft 10.00

Sixth Batch (Fall 1998)
Jabba's Sail Barge 10.00
TIE Defender 10.00
E-wing Starfighter 10.00

TWO-PACKS, Kay Bee exclusive (1995)
Luke's Landspeeder, with Luke Skywalker and Obi
    Wan Kenobi and Imperial AT-ST with Imperial
    Driver and Stormtrooper (#67077) 20.00

SERIES ALPHA (1997–98)
Concept Design Prototype and Final Design
1.   X-wing Starfighter (#73421) 15.00
2.   Imperial AT-AT (#7342) 15.00
3.   Imperial Shuttle (#73422) 15.00
4.   Rebel Snowspeeder (#73423) 15.00

Second Batch (Spring 1998)
Twin-Pod Cloud Car 15.00
Y-wing Starfighter 15.00
B-wing Starfighter 15.00

Micro

Action Fleet KayBee Exclusive Two-Pack (Galoob 1995)

*Action Fleet Battle Packs #4 (Imperial Hunters
& #11 Cantina Encounter (Galoob 1996 & 1997)*

CLASSIC DUELS (1997–98)
Toys "R" Us special (Galoob 1997) two ships, four figures
Millennium Falcon vs. TIE Interceptor (#68302) 20.00
X-wing Starfighter vs. TIE Fighter (#68301) 20.00

FLIGHT CONTROLLERS (1997–98)
First Batch (Spring 1997)
Rebel Flight Controller, with Luke's X-wing Star-
    fighter and two figures (#73417). 20.00
Imperial Flight Controller, Darth Vader's TIE Fighter
    and two figures (#73418) 20.00

Second Batch (Spring 1998)
Rebel Flight Controller with Y-wing Starfighter and
    two figures. 20.00
Imperial Flight Controller with TIE-Interceptor and
    two figures. 20.00

BATTLE PACKS (1996–98)
#1	Rebel Alliance (#68011, 1996)	8.00
#2	Galactic Empire (#68012, 1996)	8.00
#3	Aliens and Creatures (#68013, 1996)	8.00
#4	Imperial Hunters (#68014, 1996)	8.00
#5	*Shadows of the Empire* (#68015, 1996)	8.00
#6	Dune Sea (#68016, 1997)	8.00
#7	Droid Escape (#68017, 1997)	8.00
#8	Desert Palace (#68018, 1997)	8.00
#9	Endor Adventure (#68019, 1997)	8.00
#10	Mos Eisley Spaceport (#68020, 1997)	8.00
#11	Cantina Encounter (#68021, 1997)	8.00
#12	Cantina Smugglers and Spies (#68090, 1998)	8.00
#13	Hoth Attack (#68091, 1998)	8.00
#14	Death Star Escape (#68092, 1998)	8.00
#15	Endor Victory (#68093, 1998)	8.00
#16	Lars Family Homestead (1998)	8.00
#17	Imperial Troops (1998)	8.00
#18	Rebel Troops (1998)	8.00

Micro

PLAYSETS
Asst. #67090 in box with slant side
Ice Planet Hoth, includes six figures (#67091) 30.00
The Death Star, includes six figures (#69092) 30.00
Yavin Rebel Base, includes six figures (#69090) 30.00

STAR WARS EPISODE I
MICRO MACHINES
Galoob (1999)

Episode I Vehicle/Figure Collections (1999)
Collection I (#66501) $5.00
Collection II (#66502). 5.00
Collection III (#66503). 5.00
Collection IV (#66504) 5.00
Collection V (#66505) Gungans 5.00
Collection VI (#66506) Battle Droids. 5.00
Collection VII (#66507). 5.00
Collection VIII (#66508) 5.00
Collection IX (#66509) 5.00
Collection X (#66510) 5.00

Episode I Platform Action Sets (1999)
Podrace Arena (#66541). 10.00
Naboo Temple Ruins (#68542) 10.00
Galactic Senate (#66543) 10.00

Episode I Turbo Podracers (1999) Action Fleet
Ody Mandrell's Podracer (#68149) 13.00
Gasgano's Podracer (#68148). 13.00

Episode I Action Fleet Playsets (1999)
Podracer Hanger Bay with Pit Droid and Pit Mech-
    anic (#68156). 15.00
Mos Espa Market with Anakin Skywalker and C-
    3PO (#68157) 15.00

Star Wars Episode I Podrace Arena (Galoob 1999)

Star Wars Episode I Action Fleet Naboo Starfighter (Galoob 1999)

Gian Speeder/Theed Palace 20.00
Trade Federation MTT/Naboo Battlefield (#66560 . . . . . 20.00
Naboo Hanger–Final Conflict (#68177). 15.00

Episode I Action Fleet (1999)
Naboo Starfighter, featuring Anakin Skywalker (#65131) 10.00
Trade Federation MTT, featuring Battle Droid (#68132) . 10.00
Sebulba's Pod Racer, featuring Sebula (#68133) 10.00
Republic Cruiser, featuring Qui-Gon Jinn (#68134) 10.00
Trade Federation Droid Fighter, featuring Daultay
    Dofine (#68135) 10.00
Gungan Sub, featuring Qui-Gon Jinn (#68136) 10.00
Flash Speeder, featuring Naboo Royal Guard (#68137). 10.00
Trade Federation Landing Ship, featuring Battle
    Droid (#68138) 10.00
Anakin's Podracer, featuring Anakin Skywalker (#68139)10.00
Mars Guo's Podracer, featuring Mars Guo (#68140) . . . 10.00

Episode I Action Fleet Mini Scenes (Asst #68120, 1999)
1. STAP Invasion (#68121) 5.00
2. Destroyer Droid Ambush (#68122) 5.00
3. Gungan Assault (#68123) 5.00
4. Sith Pursuit (#68124) 5.00

Episode I Inside Action Sets (Asst. #79003, 1999)
Gungan Sub/OTOH Gunga (#69554) 13.00
Darth Maul/Theed Generator 13.00
Jar Jar Binks/Naboo (#66551). 13.00
Battle Droid/Trade Federation Droid Control Ship
    (#66552) 13.00

Episode I Misc.(Galoob 1999)
Electronic BoontaEve Challenge Track Set (#66570). . . 40.00
Podracer Launchers (#66547) 12.00

Micro

MODEL KITS

MPC was Kenner's model kit company. Early kits have their logo. When The Ertl Company bought MPC in about 1990, the logo was changed to MPC/Ertl. Still later, the logo was changed to AMT/Ertl, which is what it is today. The original models have been reissued, and this availability has brought down the collectors' price of the originals. The most notable exception is the original *Millennium Falcon*, with lights, since the reissues are unlighted.

Star Wars Characters
The Authentic C-3PO (See-Threepio) 10" tall, 1/7
    scale (MPC #1913, 1977) 7½" x 10" *SW* box . . . $25.00
    Reissue, 6" x 10" box. 20.00
C-3PO (MPC #1935, 1984) *RotJ* box 15.00
The Authentic R2-D2 (Artoo-Detoo) 6" tall, 1/10
    scale (MPC #1912, 1977) *SW* box 25.00
    Reissue, 6" x 10" box. 20.00
R2-D2 (MPC #1934, 1984) *RotJ* box 15.00
Darth Vader, 11½" tall, 1/7 scale, black full figure,
    with glow-in-the-dark lightsaber (MPC #1916,
    1979) *SW* box 45.00
Darth Vader Bust Action Model Kit, snap-togeth-
    er, 1/2 scale (MPC #1921, 1978) illuminated
    eyes and raspy breathing sound, *SW* box. 60.00

Star Wars Space Ships
The Authentic Darth Vader TIE Fighter, 7½" wide,
    1/48 scale, with Darth Vader pilot figure (MPC
    #1915, 1977) 14" x 10" *SW* box 35.00
    Reissue, 14" x 8" *SW* box 25.00
The Authentic Luke Skywalker X-Wing Fighter,
    12" long, 10" wingspan, 1/48 scale (MPC
    #1914, 1977) 14" x 10" *SW* box 35.00

R2-D2 (original wide box) Model Kit (MPC 1977) and Darth Vader Glow-in-the-dark Commemorative Model Kit (MPC 1980s)

Luke Skywalker X-Wing Fighter (narrow box) (MPC 1980s)

Reissue, 14" x 8" *SW* box 25.00
Han Solo's *Millennium Falcon*, 18" long, 1/72 scale,
with lights (MPC #1925, 1979) *SW* box 120.00

The Empire Strikes Back Ships (MPC)
Star Destroyer, 15" long (#1926, 1980). 45.00
Luke Skywalker's Snowspeeder, (#1917, 1980) 40.00
AT-AT (#1918, 1980) 40.00
Millennium Falcon, no lights (#1933, 1982). 40.00
X-Wing Fighter, 12½" (#1930, 1982) 25.00
Boba Fett's *Slave I* (MPC #1919, 1982) 35.00

Return of the Jedi Ships (MPC 1983)
AT-AT(#1929) 25.00
Shuttle *Tyderium*, 20" wingspan (#1920) 30.00
Speeder Bike Vehicle, 12" long (#1927) 22.00

Snap Kits (MPC 1983)
AT-ST, 6" high, scout walker (#1976) *RotJ* box 30.00
A-Wing Fighter (#1973) *RotJ* box............... 15.00
B-Wing Fighter (#1974) *RotJ* box............... 15.00
TIE Interceptor (#1972) *RotJ* box 20.00
X-Wing Fighter (#1971) *RotJ* box 15.00
Y-Wing (#1975) *RotJ* box..................... 15.00

Dioramas (MPC)
Rebel Base, snap together (#1924,1981) *ESB* box.... 45.00
Battle on Ice Planet Hoth, snap together kit,
   11¾" x 17¾" (#1922, 1981) *ESB* box 35.00
Encounter with Yoda on Dagobah, snap together kit,
   5¾" x 10" (#1923, 1981) *ESB* box 35.00
Jabba the Hutt Throne Room (#1928, 1983) *RotJ* box . 40.00

Mirr-A-Kits (MPC 1984)
AT-ST (#1105) *RotJ* box...................... 15.00
Shuttle *Tyderium* (#1103) *RotJ* box.............. 15.00
Speeder Bike (#1106) *RotJ* box 15.00
TIE Interceptor (#1102) *RotJ* box 15.00
X-Wing (#1101) *RotJ* box..................... 15.00
Y-Wing (#1104) *RotJ* box 15.00

Structors Action Walking models, wind-up motor
AT-AT (MPC/Structors #1902, 1984) 30.00

Models

AT-AT (AMT/Ertl #6036, 1998). 10.00
AT-ST, 4½" high (MPC/Structors #1903, 1984) 25.00
    Scout AT-ST (AMT/Ertl #6029, 1998) 10.00
C-3PO (MPC/Structors #1901, 1984) 25.00

Vans: (MPC) Snap together, with glow-in-the-dark decals
Artoo-Detoo Van, 1/32 scale (#3211, 1979) 30.00
Darth Vader Van, 1/32 scale (#3209, 1979) 35.00
Luke Skywalker Van, 1/32 scale (#3210, 1979) 35.00

MPC/ERTL and AMT/ERTL (1990–99)
Figures (AMT/Ertl)
Darth Vader, stands 12" tall, glow in the dark light
    saber (MPC/Ertl #8154, 1992) 14" x 8¼" *SW* box . 15.00
    Reissue: AMT/Ertl 12.50
Darth Vader(#8784, 1996) 25.00
Luke Skywalker (#8783, 1995). 25.00
Han Solo (#8785, 1995). 25.00
Prince Xizor (#8256, 1996) *SotE* box 25.00
Emperor Palpatine (#8258, 1996) *SotE* box 25.00

Action Scenes
Rebel Base Action Scene (MPC/Ertl and AMT/Ertl
    #8735, 1993) 18¾" x 12¾" *ESB* box. 15.00
Jabba's Throne Room Model (#8262, 1996). 13.50
Encounter with Yoda Model (#8263, 1996) 13.50
Battle on Hoth Action Scene, with 11½" x 17½" vacu-
    formed base (#8743, 1995) 13.50

Flight Displays (AMT/Ertl)
TIE Fighter Flight Display (#8275, 1996) 20.00
Speeder Bike Flight Display (#6352, 1997). 20.00
X-Wing Flight Display (#8788, 1995) 19.50

Limited Editions (AMT/Ertl)
X-Wing Limited Edition (#8769, 1995) 31.50
TIE Interceptor Limited Edition (#8770, 1995) 31.50
B-Wing Limited Edition (#8780, 1995) 25.00

Ships (MPC/Ertl & AMT/Ertl 1990–92)
Shuttle *Tyderium* (#8733) 18¾" x 12¾" *RotJ* box 15.00
Speeder Bike (#8928)14" x 8" *RotJ* box 10.00
Luke Skywalker's Snowspeeder (#8914) *ESB* box 15.00

Speeder Bike (MPC 1980s)

Star Destroyer (#8915) 20" x 10" *ESB* box 15.00
Darth Vader TIE Fighter (#8916) 14" x 10¼" *SW* box . . 12.00
Millennium Falcon (#8917) 19¾" x 14½" *RotJ* box 20.00
X-Wing Fighter (#8918) 14" x 8" *RotJ* box 12.00
AT-AT (#8919) 14" x 8" *RotJ* box. 15.00

Ships (AMT/Ertl 1995–98)
Shadows of the Empire Virago (#8377, 1997). 15.00
TIE Fighter Plus Pack (#8432, 1997) 16.00
Slave I (#8768, 1995). 13.50
Fiber Optic Star Destroyer (#8782,1995) *ESB* box 50.00
Millennium Falcon Cutaway (#8789, 1996) 27.00

Snap Kits (AMT/Ertl) *Return of the Jedi* box
AT-ST, snap together (#8734, 1992) 10" x 7" 9.00
TIE Interceptor, snap together (#8931, 1990) 10" x 7" . 10.00
X-Wing Fighter, snap together (#8932, 1990) 10" x 7". . 11.00
A-Wing Fighter, snap together (#8933, 1990) 10" x 7" . 10.00
Y-Wing Fighter, snap together (#8934, 1990) 10.00
Return of the Jedi 3-piece Gift Set: B-Wing Fighter,
    X-Wing Fighter, TIE Interceptor, (MPC/Ertl and
    AMT/Ertl #8912, 1992) 14¼" x 10" box. 20.00

VINYL MODEL KITS

Pre-Painted Models (Polydata 1995)
Luke Skywalker, 1/6 scale $35.00
Obi Wan Kenobi, 1/6 scale) 35.00
Tusken Raider, 1/6 scale 35.00
Princess Leia, 1/6 scale 35.00
Chewbacca, 1/6 scale 35.00
Lando Calrissian, 1/6 scale 35.00
Boba Fett, 13" tall, 9,000 copies (1997) 35.00

Vinyl Models (Screamin')
Luke Skywalker, 1/4 scale (#3010, 1996) 65.00
Darth Vader, 1/4 scale (#3200, 1992) 65.00
Yoda, 1/4 scale (Screamin #3300, 1992) 60.00
Han Solo, 1/4 scale (#3400, 1993). 65.00
C-3PO, 1/4 scale (#3500, 1993). 65.00
Stormtrooper, 1/4 scale (#3600, 1993) 65.00

Models

Luke Skywalker Vinyl Model Kit (Polydata 1995)

Chewbacca, 1/4 scale (#3700, 1994) 68.00
Boba Fett, 1/4 scale (#3800, 1994) 70.00
Tusken Raider, 1/4 scale (#3900, 1995) 68.00

Episode 1 Snap Fast (Ertl)
Naboo Fighter 1:48 (#30117). 10.00
Trade Federation Droid Fighter 1:48 (#30118) 10.00
Anakin's Podracer 1:32 (#30122) 20.00

Episode 1 Die-Cast Model Kit
Naboo Starfighter 1:48 (#30130) 18.00

STEEL MODELS

Star Wars Steel Tec Model Kits (Remco)
Millennium Falcon (#7140, 1995) $25.00
X-Wing Fighter (#7141, 1995) 25.00

FLYING MODELS

Original Star Wars Flying Rocket Model Kits (Estes)
R2-D2 (#1298, 1979) $25.00
T.I.E. Fighter (#1299, 1979) 30.00
X-Wing Fighter, Outfit Kit (#1302, 1979) 30.00
Proton Torpedo, Outfit with Launching Kit, Darth
     Vader picture box (#1420, 1979). 50.00
X-Wing Fighter, with Launching Kit (#1422, 1979) 50.00

New Flying Model Rocket Starter Sets (Estes)
X-wing (#1490, 1996) battery operated. 35.00
A-wing (#1491, 1996) battery operated. 35.00
Y-wing (#1492, 1996) battery operated. 35.00
Death Star (#1493, 1996) battery operated. 35.00
Luke Skywalker X-wing Fighter and Darth Vader TIE
     Fighter Starter Set (Estes #1801, 1998) 50.00

New Flying Model Rockets (Estes)
R2-D2 (#2142, 1997) 15.00
Death Star (#2143, 1997). 15.00
Darth Vader's TIE Fighter, 16½" (#2144, 1997). 15.00

Chewbacca and C-3PO Vinyl Model Kits (Screamin' 1996)

Models

Millennium Falcon (#2146, 1997) 15.00
Star Destroyer (#2147, 1997) 15.00
Shuttle *Tyderium* (#2148, 1997) 15.00

Flying Model Rockets with Recovery Parachute (Estes)
TIE Fighter, 9" (#2102, 1997) 24.00
X-wing, 10¾" (#2103, 1997) 18.00
R2-D2, 9" (#2104, 1997) 29.00

Ready-Built Flying Model Rocket (Estes) carded
Red Squadron X-wing Starfighter (#01810, 1998) 6.00

Star Wars Flying Model Rocket Launchers (Estes)
Darth Vader TIE Fighter (#01820, 1997) 30.00
Y-wing Starfighter (#01821, 1997) 30.00
Red Squadron X-wing Fighters, two (#01822, 1997) . . . 30.00
R2-D2 (#01823, 1997) 30.00

Episode 1 Flying Models (Estes 1999)
Naboo Fighter (#01832) 10.00
Trade Federation Droid Fighter (#01833) 10.00
Naboo Royal Spaceship (#01834) 10.00

Episode I Flying Model Rocket Starter Sets (Estes 1999)
Naboo Fighter (#01842) 20.00
R2-D2 (#01844) 20.00

Episode I Action Model Rockets (Estes 1999)
Trade Federation Droid Fighter (#01837) 30.00
Trade Federation Battleship (#01828) 20.00
Sith Infiltrator (#01829) 20.00

Balsa Model Glider Kits (Estes 1995–97)
Star Destroyer Flying model kit (#05020) 8.00
A-wing Fighter Catapult Flying model kit (#05021) 8.00
X-wing Fighter Flying model kit (#05022) 6.00
Y-wing Fighter Flying model kit (#05023) 6.00

Control Line Aircraft (Estes Cox)
X-wing Fighter kit, with Cox engine (#9310) 60.00
Darth Vader's TIE Fighter kit, with Cox engine (#9330) . 60.00

Models

Naboo Royal Starship Flying Action Model Rocket (Estes 1999)

Snowspeeder kit, with Cox engine (#9320). 60.00
Death Star Battle Station with X-wing Fighter kit, with
    Cox engine, Radio Controlled (#9420) 150.00
Landspeeder Radio Control Vehicle kit, with Cox
    engine (#9430). 100.00
Star Wars Combat Set, flying 13.6" wingspan
    X-wing Fighter and 9.5" wingspan TIE fighter
    with motor and control lines (Estes #9410, 1997) 100.00
X-wing Sterling Model Kit Fighter, 13" wingspan
    (Estes #6760, 1997) requires Cox engine 25.00
Y-wing Sterling Model Kit, 10¾" wingspan (Estes
    #6761, 1997) requires Cox engine 25.00

Deluxe Rocket Kits (Estes)
X-wing Fighter North Coast Rocketry high powered
    model rocket, 20" long, 18" wingspan, with
    recovery parachute (Estes #3540, 1997) 100.00

LEGO SYSTEM

Episode 1 Legos (1999)
Lightsaber Duel, 50 pieces (#07101) $6.00
Droid Fighter, 62 pieces (#07111). 6.00
Desert Skiff, 53 pieces (#07104) 6.00
Speeder Bikes, 90 pieces (#07128) 10.00
Gungan Patrol, 77 pieces (#07115) 10.00
Flash Speeder, 105 pieces (#07124) 10.00
A-wing Fighter, 123 pieces (#07134) 15.00
Anakin's Podracer, 134 pieces (#07131). 15.00
Snowspeeder, 212 pieces (#07130) 20.00
Slave 1, 165 pieces (#07144) 20.00
Naboo Fighter, 174 pieces (#07141). 20.00
X-wing Fighter, 263 pieces (#07140) 30.00
Sith Infiltrator, 243 pieces (#07151) 30.00
Gungan Sub, 375 pieces (#07161). 50.00
Mos Espa Pod Race, 894 pieces (#07171). 90.00

Episode 1 Lego Technic
Pit Droid, 217 pieces (#08000) 20.00
Battle Droid, 328 pieces (#08001) 30.00

Episode 1 Lego MindStorms
Droid Developer Kit, 657 pieces (#9748) 100.00

Anakin's Podracer (Lego 1999)

PAPER

This section includes all kinds of miscellaneous paper collectibles which don't fit in other sections; Books, Comics, Trading Cards, and Wall Art (posters, lithos, etc.) are all covered in their own sections; and Customizable Card Games can be found at the end of the GAMES section.

BOOKMARKS AND BOOKPLATES

Many bookmarks and bookplates contain attractive art work; but as collectibles, they are associated with books, and book collecting is *not* the driving force behind *Star Wars* collecting. This has kept the price of these items at, or near, original retail price.

Bookmarks

Return of the Jedi bookmarks (Random House 1983) each. $4.00
Star Wars Trilogy bookmarks (1997) each . . . . 2 to 3.00
Episode I bookmarks (1999) each . . . . 2 to 3.00

Bookplates

Return of the Jedi bookplates (Random House 1983) each. 5.00
Star Wars Trilogy bookplates (1997) each 3.00
Episode I bookplates (1999) each 3.00

CALENDARS

Calendars were only made for a few years when the movies first appeared. Since 1995, calendars have been sold

Star Wars 1991 Calendar (Cedco 1990)

every year and you can bet this will continue. Calendars appear in about July of the year before the year printed on the calendar, and by December they are available at discount and by January they are discounted heavily. If you intend to collect them, wait to get them at half price and don't unseal them. Opened calendars are worth about one-half of sealed.

Calendars (Ballantine Books 1977–84) sealed
The 1978 *Star Wars* Calendar (#27377) orig. $4.95 . . $30.00
1979 *Star Wars* 20.00
1980 *Star Wars* 20.00
1981 *The Empire Strikes Back* 25.00
1984 *Return of the Jedi* 15.00
Return of the Jedi, 1984 Ewok Calendar, with stickers . 15.00

Calendars (1990s)
Star Wars calendars, 1990–2000, sealed . . . . cover price
     Open . . . . half cover price

CATALOGS

Kenner issued two kinds of catalogs which covered *Star Wars* toys. The best known are the small pocket or consumer catalogs included in most of the vehicle packages. They were issued for all three movies and contain interesting pictures and early information which is not always accurate to what was actually produced. The larger retailer catalogs were given to the stores to get them to order *Star Wars* toys. Catalogs such as this are issued every year, or more frequently, by just about every toy company, and are often available at Toy Fair, at least to the press and retailers. As you might expect, the earlier catalogs sell for more than the later ones.

Every toy company with a *Star Wars* license has a catalog, but most of the collector interest focuses on Kenner. The Kenner Fall 1977 *Star Wars* catalog features the Early Bird

The Empire Strikes Back consumer mini-catalog (Kenner 1980)

Certificate Package and naturally pre-dates it. This makes it the very first Kenner collectible, but hardly the first *Star Wars* collectible. After all, the paperback book and the first Marvel comics appeared *before* the movie premiere. Sears Wish Books (Christmas Catalogs) are also interesting because they feature the Sears exclusives, which are some of the most valuable collectibles.

One of Kenner's more interesting *Star Wars* catalogs is from the 1986 Toy Fair. This is the last one to contain *Star Wars* merchandise until the mid 1990s revival of the line. The 1986 catalog covers the Droids and Ewoks lines and includes pictures of a number of figures which were never actually released.

Consumer Mini Catalogs (Kenner)
Star Wars 1977, logo cover, list 12 figures $20.00
Star Wars, X-Wing cover, lists eight new figures
(1978–79) 15.00
Other Mini-Catalogs (1980–84) each 10.00

Retailer Catalogs (Kenner)
"*Star Wars* Toys and Games Available Fall 1977"
featuring the Early Bird Certificate Package 75.00
Star Wars 1978 Catalog, features the first nine figures . 50.00
Star Wars 1979 Catalog, features the Boba Fett
rocket firing backpack. 35.00
Star Wars Collector Series 1984 Catalog 30.00
Kenner 1986 Toy Fair Catalog 25.00

GREETING CARDS

Star Wars Birthday Cards, etc (1994–99) each $2.00

LOBBY CARDS

Lobby cards are large prints containing scenes from a movie, or pictures of the stars which, as the name implies,

Kenner 1986 Toy Fair Catalog and Don Post Masks 1997 Catalog

Lobby Card from The Empire Strikes Back *(LucasArts 1980)*

were designed for display in the lobby of a movie theater. They are 11" x 14" in size and come in sets of eight different cards. *Star Wars* lobby cards, photo cards, and similar items can generally be acquired from dealers who specialize in lobby cards and posters from movies. Popular movies like *Star Wars* play for a long time, in a lot of theaters and are re-released too, meaning that more lobby cards, photo cards, and similar items are produced, and that more are saved by collectors.

Star Wars
Set of eight lobby cards, 11" x 14" (1977) $125.00
Set of eight photo cards, 8" x 10" (1977) 100.00

The Empire Strikes Back
Set of eight lobby cards, 11" x 14" (1980) 90.00
Set of eight photo cards, 8" x 10" (1980) 75.00
Return of the Jedi
Set of eight lobby cards, 11" x 14" (1983) 75.00
Set of eight photo cards, 8" x 10" (1983) 60.00

MAGAZINES

There have been several magazines devoted exclusively, or almost exclusively, to *Star Wars*—almost as many as Leonardo DiCaprio has today. The only surprising part is that some of these magazines were started more than a decade after the last movie had come and gone. Magazines covering collectibles, general interest, and humor are covered immediately following those which exclusively featured *Star Wars*.

BANTHA TRACKS
Lucasfilm

#1 to #4, each $15.00
Combined reissue #1–#4 . . . . 10.00

#5 to #9.	6.00
#10 to #19.	5.00
#20 to #33.	4.00
#34	7.50
#35 10th Anniversary, last issue.	6.00

LUCASFILM FAN CLUB MAGAZINE
The Fan Club (1987–94)

# 1 Anthony Daniels interview, 14 pages (1987)	$10.00
# 2 thru 6, 14pgs (1988–89), each	4.00
# 7 Harrison Ford interview	6.00
# 8 Steven Spielberg interview,	4.00
# 9 Sean Connery interview	9.00
#10 (1990)	3.00
#11 *The Empire Strikes Back* 10th Anniv.	8.00
#12 & 13 (1990).	3.00
#14 Billy Dee Williams interview (1991)	6.00
#15 (1992).	5.00
#16 *Star Wars* comics (1992).	6.00
#17 George Lucas Interview (1992)	7.50
#18 Art of Drew Struzan (1993)	7.50
#19 *Return of the Jedi* 10th Anniv., 30 pages.(1993)	10.00
#20 34 pages.(1993)	10.00
#21 36 pages (1994)	10.00
#22 TIE Fighter video game (1994)	5.00

Becomes:

STAR WARS INSIDER
The *Star Wars* Fan Club (1994–99)

#23 56 pages, Obi-Wan photo cover (1994)	$9.00
#24 Ralph McQuarrie cover, 60 pages (1995)	10.00
#25 James Earl Jones interview, 72 pages (1995)	5.00
#26 George Lucas interview, 80 pages (1995)	6.00
#27 Luke and Landspeeder cover, 80 pages (1996)	8.00
#28 to present (1996–99) each	5.00

Paper

Lucas Film Fan Club #13 (1990) and Star Wars Insider #33 (1997)

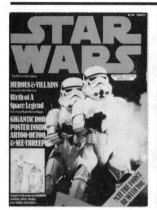 

Star Wars Official Poster Monthly #1 (Paradise Press 1978) and
Star Wars Technical Journal #2 (Starlog 1994)

OFFICIAL POSTER MONTHLY

Star Wars
#1 Stormtrooper cover $10.00
#2 thru #10, each. 5.00
#11 through #18, each 10.00
The Empire Strikes Back
#1 through #5, each. 5.00
Return of the Jedi
#1 through #4, each. 5.00

STAR WARS GALAXY MAGAZINE
Topps (1994–97)

#1 Fall 1994, *Star Wars* Widevision SWP3 card $7.50
#2 thru #13 (1995–98) bagged with cards, each. 5.00
Becomes:
STAR WARS GALAXY COLLECTOR
Topps (1998)

#1 Feb. 1998 Drew Struzan poster, SW2 prequel card . . 6.00
#2 thru present, each 5.00
Boba Fett one-shot special (April 1998) 5.00

STAR WARS: TECHNICAL JOURNAL
Starlog (1993–94)

#1 *Star Wars*: Technical Journal of the Planet
    Tatooine (1993) $9.95
#2 *Star Wars*: Technical Journal of the Imperial
    Forces (1994) 6.95
#3 *Star Wars*: Technical Journal of the Rebel Forces . . . 6.95

MAGAZINES: COLLECTIBLES

    Many collector magazines have run *Star Wars* covers.
They frequently come in two different versions, a hobby shop
or comic store version with *Star Wars* promos polybagged

Paper

with the magazine, and a newsstand version without promos. Magazines with their original promos can be worth a lot more money, depending on the collectibility of the item, but they can often be found, bagged and complete, at reduced prices in comics shops or at shows.

The following is a sampling of collector and distributor magazines with *Star Wars* covers. There are many others. Since they are primarily sold to collectors, the covers are usually pictures of *Star Wars* toys or trading cards, or art supplied by the manufacturers.

Advance Comics (Capitol City Distribution)
Issue #82 Empire's End cover $10.00

Cards Illustrated (Warrior Publications)
Issue #20 Star Destroyer and *Millennium Falcon* cover . 3.00
Issue #25 C-3PO and R2-D2 cover 3.00

Collect! (Tuff Stuff Publications)
Jan. 1995 Issue Darth Vader (McQuarrie art) cover 7.50
Oct. 1996 Issue Shadows of the Empire, Darth
    Vader cover (Hildebrandt art) 7.50
March 1997, May 1998 and others, each 5.00

Collectible Toys and Values (Attic Books)
Issue #15 Kenner figures cover 7.50
Issue #35 Yoda cover 5.00

Combo (Century Publishing Company)
Issue #27, Han and Jabba cover 3.00

Hero Illustrated (Warrior Publications)
Issue #26 Dave Dorman art cover 4.00
1994 Science Fiction Annual C-3PO with gun cover 4.00

Lee's Action Figure News & Toy Review (Lee Publications)
Issue #6 Micro Collection cover 7.00
Issue #15 . . . . 10.00
Issue #23 R2-D2 cover 7.00

*Lees Action Figure News & Toy Review #75 (Lees 1998)
and Triton #3 (Attic Books 1995)*

Paper

Issue #31 *Millennium Falcon* cover 7.00
Issue #32 TIE Fighter cover. 7.00
Issue #43 Galoob AT-ST cover 10.00
Issue #45 Boba Fett cover. 9.00
Issue #49 Luke Stormtrooper cover 9.00
Issue #50 Galoob TIE Fighter Pilot playset cover 7.00
Issue #56 Kenner Cinema Scenes Han, Luke and
 Chewbacca cover. 8.00
Later issues, each 6.00

Non-Sport Update (Roxanne Toser Non-Sport Enterprises)
Volume 4, No. 2 Ken Steacy art cover 5.00

Tomart's Action Figure Digest (Tomart Publications)
Issues #27, #32, #39, #40, #45 and others, each 6.00

ToyFare (Wizard Press)
Issue #1 AT-AT Cover 3.00

Triton (Attic Books)
Issue #3 *Star Wars* Galaxy card art cover 5.00

White's Guide to Collecting Figures (Collecting Concepts)
 "Comic Cover Version"
Issue #1. . . . . 7.50
Issues #8, #13, #26, #30, #34 and otheres, each 6.00

Wizard (Wizard Press)
Sci-Fi Invasion 1997 Boba Fett cover. 3.00

MAGAZINES: GENERAL

Mass market Collectible #3 is the issue of *Time* magazine (May 30, 1977) which appeared a few days before the
movie opened and featured a two-page spread praising the
movie as the best picture of the year. The value of old magazines generally depends on the cover photo or painting. The
Star Wars movies have generated hundreds, perhaps thousands, of magazine covers. When something is popular,

People Magazine, August 14, 1978 and Starlog #118 (1987)

everybody wants it on their cover. Many recent magazines are available from the publisher through back-issue ads, often at or near cover price.

Cinefantastique
Vol. 6 No. 4 The Making of *Star Wars* $20.00
Vol. 7 No. 1 The Making of *Star Wars* 20.00
Feb. 1997 *Star Wars* 20th Anniversary. 5.00
Cinescape (MVP Entertainment)
March/April 1997 X-wing cover. 5.00
Star Wars Special, March 1997 . . . . 5.00
Famous Monsters (Warren)
Issue #148 Darth Vader cover 5.00
People Magazine
July 18, 1977 C-3PO cover 10.00
Aug. 14, 1978 Carrie Fisher cover 10.00
Starlog (Starlog Group)
Issue #7, X-Wing and TIE Fighter 35.00
Issue #13 David Prowse 10.00
Issue #14 SF Matte painting cover 10.00
Issue #21 Mark Hammil 10.00
Issue #31 Empire Strikes Back. 10.00
Issue #35 Billy Dee Williams 10.00
Issue #99 C-3PO and R2-D2 . . . . 8.00
Time Magazine (Time Warner)
May 30, 1977. . . . . 20.00
May 19, 1980 Darth Vader cover 10.00
Recent Magazines (1997–99) each . . . . cover price

MAGAZINES: HUMOR

Personally, I enjoy humorous take-offs of the movies and TV shows that I like. The quintessential humor magazine (of course I mean *Mad Magazine*) has done quite a few *Star Wars* issues. As with any magazine, it is the appearance of *Star Wars* on the cover that makes it a *Star Wars* collectible.

Mad Magazine
Issue #196, Jan. 1978, Newman as Darth Vader $10.00

*Boss Nass cover, TV Guide, June 12 1999
and Mad Magazine #220 (1981)*

Paper

Issue #203, Dec. 1978, *Star Wars* musical cover 9.00
Issue #220, Jan. 1981, Newman as Yoda cover 7.00
Issue #242, Oct. 1983, *Return of the Jedi* cover 7.00
Cracked
Issue #146, Star Warz spoof cover 5.00
Crazy
Issue #37, Darth Vader cover 5.00

STAMPS

***Star Wars* Postage Stamps**, issued by St. Vincent
    and the Grenadines
    Metallic Stamp gift pack, folder containing nine-
        stamp sheet, plus a souvenir sheet with
        three triangular stamps printed on metallic foil $25.00
    First Day Covers stamp set, three covers, box-
        ed, with certificate of authenticity 15.00

POINT OF PURCHASE DISPLAYS

Before a *Star Wars* product gets to the consumer, it has
to be designed, manufactured, packaged, shipped, and dis-
played for purchase in your local store. Just about every part
of this process produces something that could be, and frequently is, collected.

Point of Purchase displays and store signs are much
more interesting. They are designed to attract your attention,
so they are colorful. They display the product just as nicely in
your room as they did in the store. And, best of all, they are
items that were never intended to be sold to the general public in the first place, so not everybody has one.

Empire Strikes Back 32-figure store display(Kenner 1981)

Paper

Generally, point of purchase items are not collected so as to acquire an entire set. Rather, a few are acquired to form a backdrop or focal point for the display of one's collection.

STORE DISPLAYS

Kenner, and every other large manufacturer, makes displays to promote their products at the point of purchase. If they have a contest or giveaway promotion, they will want to let you know about it. These come in all sizes and shapes, and are frequently made of cardboard. They are hanging or standing or sitting on or over the rack where the toy or other items are selected, or in the store's window. Over the years a lot of them have been produced, and many more are to come. Size and art work are important components of their collectible value, along with the importance of the product they promote. Displays for Kenner's action figures rank at the top.

Since the displays go to stores, it helps to work there if you want to collect them. Undoubtedly many displays are damaged in use, or simply thrown away at the end of the promotion; however, there are thousands of stores that sell action figures, and each store gets a reasonable supply, so initial print runs have to be 25,000 to 50,000 minimum for ordinary items. This tends to keep the price within reason. Signs and displays that are flat look very nice when framed, and make a handsome addition to your collection.

Star Wars Action Figure sign (1978–1980) depending on size. $100–250
The Empire Strikes Back Action Figure sign (1980–1982) depending on size 75–125
Return of the Jedi Action Figure sign (1983–1984) depending on size 40–90

The most valuable store display is quite recent. In the fall of 1997, many Toys "R" Us stores got a four-foot hanging *Millennium Falcon*, made in plastic and looking just like a scaled up version of the toy. Only 500 were supposed to be

Empire Strikes Back Store Display (Kenner 1980)

made, and they were given away in a drawing by Rosie O'Donnell. The contest entry forms estimated the value of the item at $500.00, but I would think $2,000.00 would be closer. When you entered, did you think where you would store the item if you won? Of course not, because you just wanted to win one. The store display for the contest is a nice consolation collectible. It shows the *Falcon* in a reversed picture.

PORTFOLIOS AND BLUEPRINTS

The Empire Strikes Back promo art portfolio. $40.00
Star Wars Intergalactic Passport & Stickers
    (Ballantine 1983) 10.00
Star Wars Blueprints, includes 15 prints, 13" x 19" in
    vinyl pouch (Ballantine 1977) 15.00
    Reprint: $6.95 (Ballantine 1992) 7.00
Star Wars Portfolio by Ralph McQuarrie, 11" x 14"
    (Ballantine Books #27382, 1977) 20.00
The Empire Strikes Back Portfolio by Ralph
    McQuarrie, Ballantine Books (1980) 15.00
Return of the Jedi Portfolio by Ralph McQuarrie,
    Ballantine Books (1983) 15.00
Star Wars Power of the Force Planetary Map, set,
    issued as a mail-in. 20.00
Star Wars/*The Empire Strikes Back* Portfolio, six
    11" x 14" plates (#875-007, 1994). 12.00
Star Wars Trilogy Print Portfolio set, eight 11" x 14"
    moviecards (Zanart #SW-1 1996). 12.00
Star Wars Post-Art portfolio, 11" x 14" (Classico
    #02762, 1995) 15.00
Star Wars Trilogy Moviecard Portfolio, eight 11" x 14"
    movie cards plus 8" x 10" ChromArt card of the
    Millennium Falcon (Zanart 1994) 14.00

PRESS KITS

Original *Star Wars* kit (1977). $150.00

Return of the Jedi Portfolio by Ralph McQuarrie (Ballantine 1983)

Star Wars Theater Program (1977)

Star Wars kit (1978)	100.00
Holiday special kit (1978)	175.00
NPR Presents kit (1979).	35.00
The Empire Strikes Back kit (1980).	60.00
Introducing Yoda kit (1980).	35.00
NPR Playhouse kit (1981)	30.00
Return of the Jedi kit (1983)	30.00

PROGRAMS

Star Wars Movie Program (1977) limited quantity offered in 1994	$75.00
The Empire Strikes Back Official Collector's Edition (Paradise Press)	15.00
The Return of the Jedi Official Collector's Edition (Paradise Press)	10.00

PROOFS

A few header card proofs are made for every action figure, so that design personnel, company executives, and others can check the graphics, weigh the sales appeal of the package, and generally bless the product. Everybody wants to get into the act and justify their job, so changes are frequent and often the proof is not quite like the final package. This makes them quite interesting collectibles. The most valuable proofs are those for products that were never made, or where the design was changed in some significant way. After that, the value of proofs varies with the value of the final figure.

ACTION FIGURE CARD PROOFS

The most famous of these changes in the *Star Wars* world was the retitling of the third movie from *Revenge of the Jedi* to *Return of the Jedi*. No product was actually released

Paper

Yoda, Revenge of the Jedi action figure card proof (Kenner 1982)

with a *Revenge of the Jedi* package, but the original name is mentioned on a number of packages, and in magazines, and action figure card proofs exist which have the *Revenge of the Jedi* logo. These are the most highly sought of the card proofs.

OTHER PROOFS

Just about every *Star Wars* product ever made has generated some kind of printing proof, sample, prototype or similar item. Maybe they even want to throw them away or give them away. Ask around in your area. Don't forget to check the local stores for signs. The right trash can make a very nice collectible.

STAND-UPS
Advance Graphics (1993–98)

Standees are near lifesize cardboard figures, designed as store displays and sold by Advanced Graphics. Comic shops and other stores buy them and some dealers get them to highlight their table at shows. Nobody seems to collect them, but if you want one, they are available for their retail price of about $25.00 (maybe a little less for smaller figures, like R2-D2 and Yoda.)

RECORDINGS

AUDIO—MUSIC—VIDEO

All of the movies have been adapted as radio plays, and many of the new novels and even a few of the comic books have become books on tape. There is collector interest in the former, particularly in the National Public Radio dramatizations. It is not yet clear whether books on tape are collected, in the sense that older tapes will go up in value, or whether *Star Wars* fans buy tapes to play, in which case newer formats with the next generation of sound quality enhancements will always be more desirable than older tapes.

AUDIO

Movie Adaptations for National Public Radio (Highbridge)
Star Wars: The Original Radio Drama (1993) 7 CDs. . $65.00
    Same, 6 cassettes 35.00
The Empire Strikes Back: The Original Radio
    Drama, National Public Radio (1993) 5 CDs 55.00
    Same, 5 cassettes 30.00
Star Wars/The Empire Strikes Back Limited Edition
    CD set (1993) 12 CDs 125.00
Complete *Star Wars*/Empire CD set (Lucasfilm
    #114-1, April 1995) 12 CDs 100.00
Return of the Jedi: The Original Radio Drama,
    (1996) 3 CDs 35.00
    Same, 3 cassettes 25.00
Star Wars Complete Trilogy (1996) 15 CDs 125.00
    Limited Edition Collector's Trilogy (1996) 175.00
Star Wars Trilogy CD Set, 9 CDs 75.00

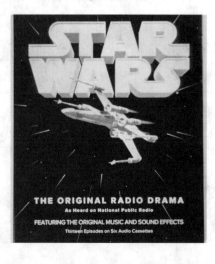

Star Wars, *The Original Radio Drama (Highbridge 1993)*

New Story Adaptations
  Various stories (1994–2000) each 15.00

Juvenile Adaptations, Read Along Books and Records
Star Wars (Buena Vista Records). 15.00
The Empire Strikes Back (Buena Vista Records #451) . 15.00
Return of the Jedi (Buena Vista Records #455, 1983) . 15.00
Ewoks Join the Fight (Buena Vista Records 1983) 25.00
Droid World (Buena Vista Records 1983) 30.00
Planet of the Hoojibs (Buena Vista Records 1983) 30.00

Other Juvenile Adaptations (1990s)
  Various book & recording combos, each . . . . cover price

MUSIC SOUNDTRACKS

    If you can't hum the *Star Wars* theme by John Williams
you probably bought this book by mistake. While you can get
the various movie soundtracks on eight-track tape, on cas-
settes, and in other formats, the collectible items are the original soundtrack LP albums. Obviously you would like to get
ones that were never played and are still in their original
shrink wrap. Just about every other format and every other
record, whether performed by the Boston Pops, the Utah
Symphony Orchestra, the Biola University Symphony Band,
or the Electric Moog Orchestra can be had for under $20.00.
Of course, if it has a colorful insert, its worth a little more.

Albums and CDs
Star Wars LP Soundtrack album, Music by
  John Williams, Performed by the London
  Symphony Orchestra, two records, insert and
  poster (20th Century Records 1977). $30.00
The Empire Strikes Back LP Soundtrack album,
  Music by John Williams, Performed by the

The Empire Strikes Back Soundtrack Record Insert (1980)

Recording

London Symphony Orchestra, two records
(RSO Records 1980) romantic art. 40.00
Return of the Jedi LP Soundtrack album, London
Symphony Orchestra, one record, with four
page color insert (RSO Records, 1983) 25.00
Star Wars Trilogy Special Edition soundtrack CD
with Bonus Darth Vader shaped single, CDs
set laser engraved with picture, plus 20
pages of liner notes (1997) 110.00

VIDEO TAPES

The three *Star Wars* movies are available in original
and special editions, and in letterbox and pan-and-scan for-
matted for your television set, which, as you should know, has
a much different aspect ratio than a widescreen movie. Like
all special effects movies, *Star Wars* is much better seen in a
movie theater than on TV. Video tapes were released over the
years with different box art and they can be collected for the
art, but few people do so. Collectors who have videotapes of
the movie got them to watch, not collect. Collectors who have
Droids and Ewoks video tapes got them for their kids to
watch, not themselves. My grandson likes the Ewok tape I
found for a buck. He's four years old. Hey! Start 'em young.

Boxed Videotapes
Star Wars (CBS/Fox Home Video 1991). $20.00
The Empire Strikes Back (CBS/Fox Home Video 1991)   20.00
Return of the Jedi (CBS/Fox Home Video 1991). 20.00
Star Wars Trilogy (CBS/Fox Home Video 1991)
boxed set. 60.00

From *Star Wars* to Jedi: The Making of a Saga
(CBS/Fox Home Video #1479, 1992) 10.00
Star Wars Video Trilogy Letterbox Collectors
Edition, with documentary tape and book (Fox
Video 1993) in holographic gift box. 100.00
Star Wars: A New Hope Special Edition (1997) 20.00
The Empire Strikes Back Special Edition (1997). 20.00
Return of the Jedi Special Edition Video (1997) 20.00

Recording

Star Wars, Return of the Jedi and The Empire Strikes Back
(Fox Video 1993)

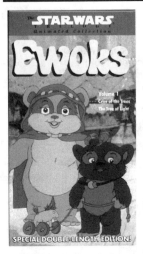

Ewoks Cartoon Video Tape (J2 Communications 1990)
and Episode I THX video tape (1999)

Star Wars Trilogy Special Edition Boxed Set (1997)
    Pan & Scan format (#2930) 50.00
    Widescreen (letterbox) format (#2934) 60.00
Droids: The Pirates and the Prince, (CBS/Fox Home
    Video #8467, 1996) 10.00
Ewoks: The Haunted Village (CBS/Fox Home Video
    #8466, 1996) 10.00
Droids or Ewoks cartoon tapes, each 5.00
Episode I, The Phantom Menace video tape (2000) . . . 15.00

STILLS

FILM FRAMES
Willitts Designs (1995–97)

    Film Frames are a full screen, letterbox movie image,
with a one-of-a-kind 70mm film frame, in a 7½" x 2¾"
acrylic holder. They are sold by Willitts Designs, who also
produced the limited edition lithographs by Ralph McQuarrie
(listed under WALL ART). The retail price of these strips is
$24.95, but we have seen dealers offering them for as little as
$15.00. They are the only way that a collector can own an
actual piece of the film. Each "edition" is numbered and limited to 9,500 sets, but each frame is unique since only a single 70mm print of the film was cut up.

Star Wars: A New Hope (1995)
12 different, each $25.00

The Empire Strikes Back (1996–97)
11 different, each 25.00

Return of the Jedi
13 different, each 25.00

Recording

Star Wars Film Frame, Ben Kenobi Edition (Willitts Designs 1995)

PHOTOS

Photos of your favorite star from *Star Wars* are also available from a variety of sources. Their value depends on their movie star status as of today, not on their role in the movie; i.e. Harrison Ford's autographed photo is expensive, but not the others. The price list below is designed to give you a baseline for evaluating any photo that you wish to purchase, or sell. They are for standard 8" x 10" photos, double-matted and ready for framing, with a certificate of authenticity. If the item you are considering buying at a dealer's table, or from and advertisement or cable TV show, is reasonably priced, go ahead and buy it—but don't expect to sell it later at a huge profit.

Signed Photos

Harrison Ford.	$150.00
Mark Hamill	50.00
Carrie Fisher	40.00
Sir Alec Guiness	50.00
David Prowse	45.00
Peter Cushing	50.00
George Lucas	95.00
Just about anyone else	under 50.00
Return of the Jedi Mark Hamill autographed photo plaque (1993)	100.00
The Empire Strikes Back Anthony Daniels autographed photo plaque (1993)	80.00
Darth Vader David Prowse autographed photo plaque, limited to 2,500 pieces (1997)	70.00
Darth Vader/David Prowse signed photo collage, matted (Timeless 1993)	30.00
Star Wars Movie Photos	5.00
The Empire Strikes Back Movie Photos	4.00
Return of the Jedi Movie Photos	3.00

Recording

ROLE PLAY TOYS

Role play toys include weapons, communicators, armor, utility belts, and similar items which are full size, or sized for a kid to play with. With all the different weapons used in the trilogy, it's a miracle there aren't a lot more *Star Wars* role play weapons. There are lightsabers, pistols, and laser rifles. The first Chewbacca Bowcaster arrived in mid 1997, and there are no weapons yet for any of the bounty hunters or Mos Eisley Cantina aliens, although Boba Fett's armor is already a collector's item. Maybe it's just as well. I suppose we'd lose too many little sisters if Kenner made a life-size Carbon-Freezing Chamber. On the other hand, Kenner could do well in the adult market with Princess Leia bondage gear.

With so little product, collector interest in the few classic items is quite high. As yet, there has been little collector interest in the 1990s items, and they can all be acquired for around their original retail prices.

Classic Weapons battery powered (Kenner 1978–84)
Star Wars Light Saber, inflatable, 35" long, light-up
    (#38040, 1997) boxed $90.00
    Loose 40.00
Droids Lightsaber (Green) (1984) 100.00
    Loose. 50.00
Droids Lightsaber (Red) (1984) 200.00
    Loose. 75.00
3-Position Laser Rifle, (#69310, 1978)
    Original *Star Wars* package. 250.00
    Loose, with *Star Wars* logo. 75.00
    Reissue as Electronic Laser Rifle (1980) in
        The Empire Strikes Back package 250.00
    Loose, with *The Empire Strikes Back* logo 75.00
Laser Pistol (#38110, 1978)
    Original *Star Wars* package 125.00
    Loose, with *Star Wars* logo. 25.00
    Reissue *The Empire Strikes Back* package. 100.00

3-Position Laser Rifle (Kenner 1978)

Loose, with *The Empire Strikes Back* logo 20.00
Reissue *Return of the Jedi* package 75.00
Loose, with *Return of the Jedi* logo. 15.00
Biker Scout Laser Pistol, (#71520, 1983)
Original *Return of the Jedi* package 75.00
Loose. 25.00

New Weapons (Kenner, 1995–98)
Electronic Luke Skywalker Lightsaber (#69795, 1996) . 20.00
Electronic Darth Vader Lightsaber (#69796, 1996)
Original orange box 25.00
Reissue, green box 20.00
Chewbacca's Bowcaster (#27734, 1997) 8.00
Electronic Heavy Blaster BlasTech DL-44 (#27737,
1996) 15.00
Electronic Blaster Rifle BlasTech E-11 (#27738, 1996) . 20.00
Star Wars Electronic Blaster Lazer Rifle. 17.00
Star Wars Endor Blaster Pistol (#27737, 1998) 14.50
Star Wars Commando Blaster Laser Rifle (#27738,
1998) 20.00

Episode I Weapons (Hasbro 1999)
Electronic Tatooine Blaster Pistol (#57133) 15.00
Electronic Darth Maul Double Bladed Lightsaber
(#84103) 30.00
Electronic Qui-Gon-Jinn Lightsaber (#84102) 25.00
Electronic Battle Droid Blaster Rifle (#26237) 20.00
Qui-Gon Jinn's Lightsaber (Hasbro #26264). 8.00
Naboo Foam Firing Blaster (Hasbro #57127) 10.00

Other Lightsabers, battery powered (Rubies 1995)
Star Wars Lightsaber, (#1588) white, blue or red, each. . 7.50

Episode I Lightsabers, battery powered (Rubies 1999)
Darth Maul Lightsaber (#1613) 10.00
Obi-Wan Kenobi Lightsaber (#1643) 10.00
Qui-Gon Jinn (#1638) 10.00

Electronic Tatooine Blaster Pistol (Hasbro 1999)

Role Play

Battery Operated Water Blaster (Kenner 1996)

New Accessories

Luke Skywalker Utility Belt (Kenner #27735, 1997). . . . 15.00
Star Wars Imperial Walkie-Talkie (Tiger Electronics
    #88-061, 1997) reception up to 100 feet 13.00
Darth Vader Voice Changer Walkie Talkies (Tiger
    Electronics #88-062, 1997) reception to 200 feet . 20.00
Star Wars Rebel Alliance Long Range Walkie
    Talkies (Tiger Electronics #88-063, 1997)t 35.00
Electronic Com-Link Communicators (Kenner #27791) . . 15.00
Darth Vader and Chewbacca Walkie Talkie Masks
    (Micro Games of America #SW-3980, 1995). 50.00
Darth Vader and Stormtrooper Walkie Talkies (Micro
    Games of America #SW-WT920M, 1995) 23.00
Boba Fett Armor Set, with chest shield, blaster, arm
    gauntlets & face shield (Kenner #27796, 1998). . . 40.00

Episode 1 Accessories (Hasbro 1999)
Jedi Gear (#57128) 18.00

Water Pistol (battery powered)
Water Blaster BlasTech DL-44 (Kenner #8402-0)
       Silver color (March 1997) 15.00
       Black color (Fall 1997) 12.00

Episode I Blaster Water Pistols (Larami 1999)
Battle Droid Rifle Power Soaker (#84030) 4.00
Naboo Pistol Power Soaker (#84030). 4.00
Battle Mauser Power Soaker (#84030). 4.00
Queen Amidala Super Soaker Pistol (#84060). 10.00

***Star Wars* Space Shooters** (Milton Bradley 1997)
    Millennium Falcon Blaster 20.00
    Darth Vader TIE Fighter Blaster 20.00
Space Shooter Battle Belt, with 32 Foam Disks 10.00

Role Play

SCHOOL & OFFICE SUPPLY

You awaken from a sound sleep on your *Star Wars* sheets, and outfit yourself from head to toe with *Star Wars* clothing. Are you ready to go forth to do battle with the face-less minions of an evil empire? Are you? Okay, well in that case you will just have to go to school, or to work, and pre-tend that your teacher is Emperor Palpatine or your boss is Darth Vader. Actually, this may not be much of a stretch, in which case you will need to outfit yourself with an array of school and office supplies bearing *Star Wars* pictures and logos.

SCHOOL SUPPLIES

PENS, PENCILS, MARKERS, SHARPENERS
New & Episode I Pens & Pencils
Pens, pencils, markers & sharpeners, each . . . . . . orig. retail

ERASERS
Return of the Jedi Erasers (Butterfly Originals/
    Spindex 1983) nine different, each $5.00
Return of the Jedi Glow In The Dark Erasers,
    Millennium Falcon, Darth Vader and C-3PO on
    5" x 7" header card (reoffered 1996) 4.00
Episode I, Figurine Erasers (Impact 1999)
3-Pack with Anakin Skywalker, R2-D2 and Jar Jar
    Binks (#70043). 5.00
3-Pack with Watto, Darth Maul and Sebula (#70043) . . . 5.00
Single Figurine Erasers, six different, each 3.00
Starfighter Eraser (#70075). 3.00

Bib Fortuna Eraser (Butterfly 1983) and Anakin Fat Book (1999)

Lightsaber Eraser (#70608) 5.00
Episode I, Study Kit (Impact 1999)
Watto, Sebula, Anakin Skywalker and Jar Jar Binks
  Pencil Pouch, Sharpener, Eraser & Ruler (#70058) . 7.00
Darth Maul, Darth Sidious, Qui-Gon Jinn and Obi
  Wan Kenobi Pencil Pouch, Sharpener, Eraser
  & Ruler (#70058) 7.00

NOTEBOOKS, MEMO PADS & STUDY KITS, etc.
Notebooks, memo pads, study kits, each . . . . orig. retail

BACKPACKS & BELT BAGS
Classic Backpacks
Darth Vader & Imperial Guards (Adam Joseph 1983) . . 30.00
R2-D2 & C-3PO (Adam Joseph 1983) 30.00
Yoda Backpack, red (Adam Joseph 1983) 30.00
Return of the Jedi, blue canvas 30.00
New Backpacks & Beltbags
New Backpacks & Beltbags, each . . . . orig. retail

LUNCH BOXES
  Lunch boxes have their own groups of collectors, making these more valuable than other school related items.

Star Wars, space battle on front & Tatooine scene
  on reverse, *Droids* thermos (King Seeley-
  Thermos 1977) metal box 55.00
  thermos 20.00
Star Wars, red with Darth and Droids pictured on
  front, Droids thermos (King Seeley-Thermos 1978)
  plastic box 35.00
  thermos 15.00
The Empire Strikes Back, Millennium Falcon on
  front & Luke, Yoda and R2-D2 on back, Yoda
  thermos (King Seeley-Thermos 1980) metal box . 45.00
  thermos 15.00

The Empire Strikes Back Lunch Box (King-Seeley 1980)

School

*Jar Jar Binks, R2-D2, Anakin Skywalker & Sebula
Figurine Erasers (Impact 1999)*

The Empire Strikes Back, Dagobah scene on lid,
Hoth battle on back, Yoda thermos (King
Seeley-Thermos 1980) metal box 45.00
   thermos 15.00
The Empire Strikes Back, red, Chewbacca, Han,
Leia, and Luke on lid, Yoda thermos (King
Seeley-Thermos 1980) plastic box 30.00
   thermos 15.00
The Empire Strikes Back, photo cover with logo
and inset pictures, Droids and logo on thermos
(King Seeley-Thermos 1980) plastic box. 30.00
   thermos 15.00
Return of the Jedi, Luke in Jabba's Palace on lid
and space scene on back, Ewok thermos (King
Seeley-Thermos 1983) metal box. 40.00
   thermos 15.00
Return of the Jedi, red with Wicket and R2-D2 on
front, Ewok thermos (King Seeley-Thermos
1983) plastic box 25.00
   thermos 10.00

OFFICE SUPPLIES

The only problem with *Star Wars* office supplies is that
they favor the rebel alliance, while most offices resemble the
galactic empire. To be true to life, they should have faceless
Stormtrooper images. Why sell pens one at a time to individual rebels. I bet a carton of Gamorrean Guard pens, with a
bonus Jabba the Hutt pen for the boss, would sell better—at
least if the boss were doing the buying!

Pens
Star Wars Rebel Fighter Space Pen (Fisher 1995) . . . $15.00
Star Wars The Force Titanium Plated Space Pen
   (Fisher #86734, 1996) in plastic box 75.00
Star Wars Rebel Pen, Fisher Space Pen (1997). 20.00
Star Wars Stationery Set, three designs packaged
   as a paper/envelope set (#91022, 1997). 5.00

School

STATUES & REPLICAS

STATUES—MAQUETTES—
BUSTS—FINE REPLICAS

It would take an impressive bankroll to collect all of the items in this section, and I doubt that very many people do so. However, most collectors could afford to buy, save up for, or convince a relative to buy one (or a few) items, which then forms the centerpiece of their collection.

Don't buy these collectibles to make money. Buy them because you want one to look at and enjoy. There is not much extra demand for the first one produced, or any particularly scarce one. A collector with a spare $500 or $1,000 to spend will usually be just as happy to buy the next one produced, and as long as there are collectors willing to buy, the companies will produce new items. This may limit your price speculation, but not your enjoyment.

Maquettes

Yoda Maquette, 26" mounted on black wood base with1" x 4" brass plate, with certificate of authenticity, limited to 9,500 (Illusive Originals #672000, 1995) $750.00

Boba Fett Maquette, sculpted by Mario Chiodo, 15" tall, mounted on black wood base with 1" x 4" brass plate, with certificate of authenticity, limited to 10,000 (Illusive Originals #672001) . . . 250.00

Admiral Ackbar Maquette, sculpted by Mario Chiodo,11" tall, mounted on black wood base with 1" x 4"brass plate, with certificate of authenticity, limited to 10,000 (Illusive Originals #672003) listed as "retired" by the manufacturer. . 125.00

Jabba the Hutt Maquette, sculpted by Mario Chiodo, 27" long, mounted on black wood base with 1" x 4" brass plate, with certificate of authenticity limited to 5,000 (Illusive Originals #672004) . . 250.00

Chewbacca Maquette, sculpted by Mario Chiodo, 17" tall bust, mounted on black wood base with 1" x 4" brass plate, with certificate of authenticity, limited to 7,500 (Illusive Originals #672006) . 250.00

Han Solo in Carbonite Prop Replica, 7' tall, cast in fiberglass from the original mold, sculpted by Mario Chiodo, with 2½" x 8" brass plaque, with collector's brochure, limited to 2,500 (Illusive Originals #672008) 1,200.00

Darth Vader Reveals Anakin Skywalker Bust, 26" tall, 40" wide, 17½" deep, 3-piece mask/helmet opens to reveal life-size Anakin Skywalker sculpted head by Mario Chiodo, plus stand, limited to 9,500, with full color collector's

brochure and certificate of authenticity (Illusive
Originals #672009, 1998) 1,100.00
Rancor Creature Maquette, 21" x 7" x 24", mounted
on base, with 2" x 4" silver-plated brass plaque,
limited to 9,500 (Illusive Originals #672011) 600.00
Han Solo Special Edition Statue, Release from
Carbonite, cold-cast resin with built-in light
source, 2,500 pieces (Jan. 1998) 110.00

STATUES

Boba Fett Bronze Statue, sculpted by Randy
Bowen, 12½" tall, weighs 18 lbs, mounted
on black Spanish marble, with certificate of
authenticity (Dark Horse Comics, 1997) $3,000.00
Rancor Bronze Statue, sculpted by Randy Bowen,
15" tall, weighs 25 lbs, mounted on black
Spanish marble, limited edition of 50 numbered
copies, with certificate of authenticity (1998) . . 3,000.00
Darth Vader Bronze Statue, sculpeted by Randy
Bown, 14" tall, 1/6 scale, limited edition with
certificate of authenticity (1999) 3,000.00
Darth Vader Nutcracker, 18" tall, FAO Schwarz
exclusive limited to 5,000 pieces (Steinbach) . . . 225.00

Yoda Maquette (Illusive Originals 1995)

Statues

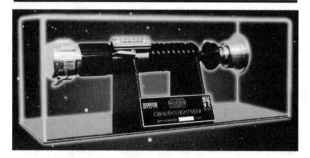

Obi-Wan Kenobi Lightsaber Replica (Icons 1997)

Luke & Leia pewter statue, FAO Schwarz exclusive
    limited to 1,000 pieces 450.00

REPLICAS

Icons Authentic Replicas

Authentic Darth Vader Lightsaber, die-cast metal
    and plastic prop replica, with numbered plaque,
    certificate of authenticity and plexi-glass
    display case, limited to 10,000 (Icons 1996) . . . $900.00
Authentic Obi Wan Kenobi Lightsaber, die-cast
    metal and plastic prop replica, with numbered
    plaque,certificate of authenticity and plexi-glass
    display case, limited to 10,000 (Icons) 1,000.00
Authentic Luke Skywalker Lightsaber, die-cast
    metal and plastic prop replica, with numbered
    plaque, certificate of authenticity and plexi-
    glass display case, limited to 10,000 (Icons) 900.00
TIE Fighter replica miniature, injected polyeure-
    thane with weathered appearances, with
    numbered plaque, certificate of authenticity
    plexi-glass and display case, limited to 1,977
    (Icons). 1,500.00
X-wing Fighter replica miniature, injected poly-
    eurethane with weathered appearances, with
    numbered plaque, certificate of authenticity and
    plexi-glass display case, limited to 1,977 (Icons
    1996) 1,500.00

DELUXE REPLICA HELMETS

Don Post Studios, cast from original movie prop
Deluxe Stormtrooper Helmet, 13" fiberglass helmet
    with lining (#82102) numbered edition of 1,000 . $950.00
Deluxe Scout Trooper Helmet, 13" fiberglass
    (#82114) numbered edition of 500 . . . . 950.00
Deluxe X-wing Fighter Helmet, 13" fiberglass helmet
    with lining (#82116) limited edition of 750 . . . . . . 950.00
Deluxe TIE-Fighter Helmet, 15" fiberglass helmet
    with lining (#82115) limited edition of 500. . . . . 1,200.00
Deluxe Darth Vader Helmet, 15" black fiberglass
    (#82100) 1,200.00
Deluxe Boba Fett Helmet, 15" fiberglass (#82101) . . . 950.00

Star Wars Chess Set (Danbury Mint 1995)

LIFE SIZE REPLICA STATUES

Don Post Studios Statues
Boba Fett Life Size Replica Statue, 6'½" fiberglass,
    cast from original props (#82023). $5,500.00
Stormtrooper Replica Statue, 6' fiberglass, cast
    from original props (#82022) limited to 500
    pieces. 5,000.00
Deluxe C-3PO Replica (#82031). 20,000.00
Deluxe R2-D2 Replica (#82030) 10,000.00

Rubies Figure
Darth Vader full 7' size Display Figure (Rubies 1997) 5,000.00

PORCELAIN BUSTS

Cold Cast Porcelain Busts
Emperor Palpatine bust sculpture, sculpted by Greg
    Aronowitz, box art by Drew Struzan, limited to
    3,000 (Legends in Three Dimensions, 1997). . . $125.00
Greedo bust sculpture, sculpted by Greg Aronowitz,
    9½" in box with art by Drew Struzan, limited to
    3,000 (Legends in Three Dimensions, 1998). . . . 140.00
Boba Fett bust sculpture, sculpted by Greg Arono-
    witz, box art by Drew Struzan, limited to 3,000
    (Legends in Three Dimensions, 1998) 160.00
Cantina Band Member 160.00
Tusken Raider. 150.00

OTHER FINE COLLECTIBLES

Star Wars Official Pewter Chess Set, 15" x 15" x 3"
    board plus 32 pewter figures on bases, sold
    at $19.95 per figure (Danbury Mint 1995) $650.00
Cinemacast Darth Vader statue, 15½" cold-cast
    porcelain (Kenner/Cinemacast 1995) 250.00
Life-Size Ewok Plush figure, 30" tall in sitting
    position, 12 lbs, 3,200 made, PepsiCo promo
    (Douglas Toys 1997) 500.00

Statues

TRADING CARDS

STAR WARS
Topps (1977)

Topps was the major producer of movie tie-in cards in the 1960s, 1970s, and 1980s. The standard that they created and followed with just about every movie set was 66 (or 88) cards, plus 11 (or 22) stickers. If the cards were successful, a second series of "all new" cards was produced. The cards and stickers came in colorful wax wrappers, and all three came in boxes of 36 packs. In those days there were no holograms, foils, autographed cards, 3-D redemption cards, and not even any promo cards, so collectors had nothing to collect except the cards, stickers, wrappers, and boxes.

Star Wars was very successful, so a total of five series of cards and stickers was produced. They are numbered consecutively, so as to form one large set of 330 cards and 55 stickers. Stickers came one to a pack, making a sticker set harder to assemble than a card set. Some stickers were even rumored to have been, (gasp!), peeled off and stuck to something, further reducing the number in circulation. Consequently, stickers are worth about $2.00 each, while the cards go for less.

The "best cards" from all three classic series have now been reissued in chromium as *Star Wars Chromium Archives*. Card series are listed in chronological order, so these cards are listed near the end of this section. Checklists of all the series through early 1998 are included in my previous book, *The Galaxy's Greatest Star Wars Collectibles Price Guide, 1999 Edition*.

Series 1, blue border with stars
Set: 66 cards/11 stickers $100.00
Pack: 7 cards + 1 sticker 7.50

Trade Card

Star Wars, *Series 1 card and sticker (Topps 1977)*

Star Wars, *Series 3 card and sticker (Topps 1978)*

Box: 36 packs	250.00
Box: Empty	15.00
Wrapper: C-3PO, black background	5.00

Series 2, red border

Set: 66 cards/11 stickers	75.00
Pack:	6.00
Box: 36 packs	150.00
Box: Empty	12.00
Wrapper: Darth Vader, yellow background	5.00

Series 3, yellow border

Set: 66 cards/11 stickers	75.00
Pack:	5.50
Box: 36 packs	130.00
Box: Empty	10.00
Wrapper: R2-D2, purple background	4.00

Card #207 (in Series 4) was originally printed (intentionally or unintentionally, depending on which story you believe) with C-3PO appearing to have a large but very un-droid-like male appendage. This would have been appropriate in the movie *Flesh Gordon*, but not in *Star Wars*. The card was reprinted, with the offending item removed. Collectors with warped minds have placed a high value on the card—I'm still looking for it at a better price. Maybe it will be included in some future series of *Star Wars Chromium Archives*, but somehow I doubt it.

Series 4, green border

Set: 66 cards/11 stickers	$65.00
Pack:	4.00
Box: 36 packs	110.00
Box: Empty	10.00
Wrapper: Obi-Wan and Luke, green background	3.00

Series 5, brown/orange

Set: 66 cards/11 stickers	60.00
Pack:	4.00

Trade Card

Star Wars, *Chewbacca and Jawa cards (Wonder Bread 1977)*

Box: 36 packs 110.00
Box: Empty 10.00
Wrapper: X-wing Fighter, purple background 3.00

OTHER EARLY STAR WARS CARDS

There were several other types of *Star Wars* cards,
stickers, and wrappers which appeared in the late 1970s and
early 1980s. The Wonder Bread series of 16 cards came one
per loaf of bread. General Mills cereals had two series of
stickers and Kellogg's had peel-away sticker cards in its cereal. Meanwhile, Topps produced sugar-free bubble gum with
distinctive wrappers and inside photos. Burger King gave out
three-card strips, while Hershey's candy bars could be pur-
chased in six-packs with a tray card.

STAR WARS
Wonder Bread (1977)

Set: 16 cards $25.00

STAR WARS
SUGAR FREE GUM WRAPPERS
Topps (1978)

Set: 56 wrappers $75.00
Wrapper: each 1.25
Box: empty 10.00

STAR WARS
General Mills Cereals (1978–79)

Set: 18 different large cards $50.00
Card: each 3.00

Trade Card

STAR WARS
ALBUM STICKERS
Panini (1977)

Set: 256 stickers with album.................. $35.00
Single sticker .... .25

STAR WARS AND
THE EMPIRE STRIKES BACK
"Everybody Wins Trading Cards"
Burger King (1980)

Set: 12 different strips $30.00
Set: 36 cards, cut.......................... 25.00
Card: cut .... .75
(Cards are unnumbered)

THE EMPIRE STRIKES BACK
Topps (1980)

While there were only three series of *The Empire Strikes Back* cards from Topps, there were more actual cards and stickers offered than for the previous movie. As before, stickers are more valuable than cards because there was only one sticker per pack. The packs also contained a stick of bubble gum, which is not a collectible and no longer edible. If you open a pack, save the wrapper and throw the gum away.

Series 1, grey and red border
Set: 132 cards/33 stickers $80.00
Pack: 12 cards.............................. 8.00
Box: 36 packs 90.00
Box: Empty 10.00
Wrapper: 2.50

The Empire Strikes Back *wrapper (Topps 1980)*

Trade Card

The Empire Strikes Back, Series 3 & Series 1 stickers and Series 2 rack pack (Topps 1980–81)

Series 2, grey and blue border
Set: 132 cards/33 stickers 65.00
Pack: 7.00
Box: 36 packs 70.00
Box: Empty 7.50
Wrapper: 2.50

Series 3, green and yellow border
Set: 88 cards/22 stickers 60.00
Pack 6.00
Box: 36 packs 65.00
Box: Empty 7.50
Wrapper: 2.00

THE EMPIRE STRIKES BACK
GIANT PHOTO CARDS
Topps (1980)

Test Issue Set: 60 Giant cards $85.00
Test Issue, single card 2.00
Regular Set: 30 cards 35.00
Regular Set Box. 50.00
Box: empty 5.00

THE EMPIRE STRIKES BACK
Hershey's (1980)

Cards appeared on six-pack candy bar trays
Set: 5 trays (with uncut cards) $8.00
Set: 5 cards cut from trays 5.00

Return of the Jedi, *Series 1, pack and card (Topps 1983)*

RETURN OF THE JEDI
Topps (1983)

There were only two series of *Return of the Jedi* cards and only about half as many total cards as in the previous two series. Stickers are again more valuable and each comes with two different backgrounds. While modern cards are of much higher quality than these and the previous Topps *Star Wars* cards, hardly anyone collects them! All the collecting action is in the promo cards and chase cards. At least these sets are collected.

Series 1, red border
Set: 132 cards/33 stickers $35.00
Pack: 10 cards, 1 sticker 2.50
Box: 36 packs 55.00
Box: Empty 5.00
Wrapper: 1.00
(Four different wrappers: Luke; Jabba; Ewok; Darth Vader)

Series Two, blue border
Set: 88 cards/22 stickers 25.00
Pack: 10 cards, 1 sticker, ... 2.50
Box: 36 packs 40.00
Box: Empty 5.00
Wrapper: 1.00
(Four different wrappers, Leia; Lando; C-3PO; Young Ewok; all say "New Series")

RETURN OF THE JEDI
ALBUM STICKERS
Topps (1983)

Set: 180 stickers with album. $20.00
Single sticker 25
Wax Box 40.00

Trade Card

STAR WARS GALAXY
Topps (1993, Art)

Star Wars Galaxy cards were the first new set of *Star Wars* cards in 10 years and the first to use art rather than pictures from the movies. The first section provides an all new look at the main characters, with art by Joe Smith. Variant cards with these images were used with the Just Toys Bend-Ems figures as well. A number of them also made their way onto T-shirts. The New Visions 60-card subset features full color illustrations from top comic book artists, including Gil Kane, Sam Keith, Dale Keown, Ken Steacy, Dave Stevens and Al Williamson. In addition, there are subsets covering the design of *Star Wars* and the art of *Star Wars*.

This first *Star Wars Galaxy* set is also an important element in the *Star Wars* marketing revival. New novels and comics had started in 1991, but very few other collectibles were being produced. This card series was heavily marketed and gave a good boost to the *Star Wars* revival.

Set: 140 cards $25.00
Pack: 8 cards. 2.00
Box: 36 packs 50.00
Millennium Falcon factory foil stamped set, plus
    holo-foil cards, plus Darth Vader 3-D holo-
    gram & #0 card & preview, in plastic ship model . 100.00
Millennium Falcon factory set, publishers proof,
    "limited to 500 sets" on sticker 125.00
Binder, with card SWB1 . . . . 18.00
Etched-Foil cards six different, #1 to #6, each 10.00
Autographed Cards 35.00
Six-card uncut-sheet (1:case). 50.00
Promo Cards
Boba Fett and Dengar (*Classic Star Wars* #8) 15.00
Jabba the Hutt, Oola and Salacious Crumb (*Star-
    log* #181 and *Wizard* #20) 10.00
Princess Leia (*Non-Sports Update* Vol. 4 #2) 10.00

Trade Card

Star Wars *Galaxy One, Boba Fett card and Princess Leia promo (Topps 1993)*

Dewback/Stormtrooper (*Non-Sports Update* Vol. 4 #2) . 10.00
Princess Leia & Dewback sheet (*Advance Comics* #52) . 6.00
Jabba the Hutt/Oola/Salacious Crumb sheet, from
   (*Previews*, & Comics Scorecard, Feb. 1993) 15.00
SWB1 binder card from *Star Wars Galaxy* Binder 10.00

STAR WARS GALAXY TWO
Topps (1994)

Set: 135 cards (#141-#275) $20.00
Pack: 8 cards 1.75
Box: 36 packs 40.00
Factory tin Set 100.00
Etched-Foil cards, (1:18) six different, #7 to #12, each . 9.00
Uncut Etched-Foil sheet 100.00
Autographed card (2000) 50.00
Six-card uncut sheet (1:case) 50.00
Album 16.00
Promo cards
P1 Rancor (*Cards Illustrated* #2) 15.00
P2 Lightsaber (*Non-Sports Update*, Vol. 5 #2) 15.00
P3 Yoda at Shrine, not released but samples exist . . unknown
P4 Jawas & C-3PO (Millennium Falcon *Factory* set) . . . 15.00
P5 Chewbacca & droid (Cards Illustrated #5) 15.00
P6 Boba Fett (Hero #12) 15.00
SWG1 promo 10.00
Tusken Raiders (*Classic Star Wars* #20) 10.00
Biker Scout/Ewok (*Triton* #3 variant card #266) 20.00
Promo sheet with P1 card (*Previews* Feb. 1994) 2.00

STAR WARS GALAXY THREE
Topps (1995)

Set: 90 cards: #276–#365 + #L1–#L12 . . . . $20.00
Pack: 5 cards + one 1st day issue and one insert 2.00
Box: 36 packs 40.00
First day set: 90 cards 75.00
First day card, each 1.00
Etched Foil Cards (1:12) six different, #13 to #18, each 9.00

Star Wars *Galaxy Two, Biker Scout/Ewok promo card
and regular series card (Topps 1994)*

Uncut Etched Foil panorama sheet. 100.00
Agents of the Empire Clearzone (1:18)
    Six different, E1 to E6, each. 10.00
Promo Cards
P1 promo, does not seem to exist
P2 Snowtroopers, convention give away 18.00
P3 Darth Vader (*Non-Sports Update*, Vol. 6 #4) 5.00
P4 Luke Skywalker (*Combo #7*). 5.00
P5 Snowspeeder and AT-AT (*Advance Comics* #83) . . . 5.00
P5 error promo 35.00
P6 cover of *Star Wars Galaxy Magazine* #5 (*Star
    Wars Galaxy Magazine* #5) 5.00
P7 Leia and twins (*Wizard* #52) 5.00
P8 Darth Vader and Boba Fett (*Cards Illustrated* #25) . . 5.00
No # Boba Fett (*Star Wars Galaxy II* factory set) 15.00
#000 Princess Leia promo (*Star Wars Galaxy Mag.* #4) . 5.00
One-Card sheet, card #000 (*Previews* Sept. 1995). 5.00

STAR WARS GALAXY—BEND-EMS
Topps (1993–95, Art)

Most of JustToys' Bend-Em figures came with trading cards from 1993 to 1995. The cards are variant *Star Wars Galaxy* cards, which are lettered on the back instead of numbered. Their earliest cards and figures matched, but the later ones were random, making it that much harder to complete a set of cards. Consequently, later cards are worth more than earlier cards. There are 28 cards in the set, plus three mail-in cards. The cards may very well be more collectible (and more valuable) than the figures.

Just Toys Bend-Ems variants (Joe Smith art)
0 Darth Vader mail-in card (Ken Steacy art) $15.00
00 Darth Vader mail-in card (Ralph McQuarrie art). . . . 15.00
Checklist card, variation of checklist card from
    series, mentions Series Two. 15.00
Cards A thru M, each 3.00
Cards M thru X, each 5.00
Star Wars Galaxy Series 2 cards
Cards Y thru BB, each 5.00

STAR WARS
Merlin (1997)

Set: 125 cards $30.00
Pack:. 1.50
Box:. 45.00
Chase Cards, oversize, three different, each 20.00

ACTION MASTERS
Kenner (1994)

Action Master die-cast figures came with trading cards that were unique to the figures, not promo cards for some card series. Because of this, they are generally overlooked by trading card magazines.

17 different cards from die-cast figures, each $3.00

Trade Card

Star Wars *Action Masters, Han Solo and Luke Skywalker cards*
(Topps 1994)

STAR WARS MASTERVISION
Topps (1995)

Topps Mastervision cards are large enough to be called wall art, and come on premium 24-point stock, UV-coated and foil-stamped.

Boxed Set: 36 cards 6¾" x 10¾"	$40.00
Card:	1.25
Promos	
No #	2.50
P2 promo (*Star Wars Galaxy* Mag. #5)	2.50

STAR WARS FINEST
Topps (1996)

This is an all-chromium set, subtitled "The character guide to the *Star Wars* universe." The cards feature text written by Andy Mangels and consist of 10 nine-card subsets by different artists.

Set: 90 Chromium cards	$60.00
Pack: 5 cards	3.50
Box: 36 packs	75.00
Topps Matrix Chase Cards (1:12) four different, each)	10.00
Embossed Chase Cards (1:9) six different, each	10.00
Topps Finest Refractor (1:12) 90 different, each	15.00
Refractor Set: 90 cards	1,100.00
Mastervisions Matrix redemption (1:360)	75.00
Mastervision Matrix mail-in	75.00
Album, with card	20.00
Album card	8.00
Promos	
SWF1 promo (*Star Wars Galaxy* Magazine #6)	4.00
SWF2 promo (*Star Wars Galaxy* Magazine #7)	4.00
SWF3 Luke on TaunTaun (*Non-Sports Update* Vol. 7 #3)	4.00
Refractor promo	40.00
Oversize Chromium Promo	15.00

Trade Card

Star Wars *Shadows of the Empire cards #32 & #52 (Topps 1996)*

STAR WARS:
SHADOWS OF THE EMPIRE
Topps (1996)

Shadows of the Empire cards are based on the novel, comic book, and video game "multimedia extravaganza" of the same name.

Set: 90 cards (#1 through #72 and #82 through #100) $15.00
Pack: 9 cards. 1.50
Box: 36 packs 50.00
Etched foil, gold gilt (1:9) six different, each 7.00
Foil Embossed (1:18) four different, each 10.00
Redemption card (1:200) 60.00
Autographed Mastervision mail-in redemption. 50.00
Promos
One card promo sheet, SOTE#3, 5¼" x 7". 5.00
SOTE1 Prince Xizor (*Star Wars Galaxy Magazine* #7) . . 3.00
SOTE2 Darth Vader (*Non-Sports Update* Vol. 7 #4) 3.00
SOTE3 Luke and Lightsaber (from *Star Wars* Topps
      Finest Series One box). 3.00
SOTE4 Dash Rendar (*Star Wars Galaxy* Magazine #8) . 3.00
SOTE5 Boba Fett (QVC and convention giveaway) 3.00
SOTE6 Guri (*Fan* #19). 3.00
SOTE7 R2-D2 and C-3PO (San Diego Con give-
      away, *Collect* Vol. 4, #9, *Combo* #24) 3.00

STAR WARS WIDEVISION
Topps (1995)

With Widevision cards, Topps went back to images from the movies. This time they had high quality and the same aspect ratio as the films (like the letterbox videotape version). The images were transferred directly from the original film master, not a second-generation version.

Set: 120 cards, 4½" $50.00
Pack: 10 cards. 5.00

Trade Card

Box: packs. 100.00
Topps Finest (1:11) 10 different, C1 to C10, each 20.00
Album, with #00 card 16.00
Promo Cards
SWP0 Han, Luke and Chewie (*Star Wars Galaxy* II
   factory set) 15.00
SWP1 Stormtroopers, Luke and Ben (*Non-Sport
   Update* Vol. 5 #6 and show give-away) 5.00
SWP2 *Millennium Falcon* cockpit (*Advance Comics* #72) 10.00
SWP3 TIE Fighters (*Star Wars Galaxy* Magazine #1) . . 10.00
SWP4 Exterior of Star Destroyer (*Wizard* #42) 5.00
SWP5 Darth Vader throttling Rebel (*Collect* Jan. 1995) 10.00
SWP6 Leia & C-3PO in Yavin IV (*Cards Illustrated* #14) 10.00
0 Luke and X-wing (*Star Wars* Widevision album) 8.00
No# sheet Han in gunport (*Previews* Oct. 1994) 10.00
Promos from Classic Edition 4-Pack action figures
K01 Int. Rebel Blockade Runner—Corridor 8.00
K02 Int. Millennium Falcon—Gunport 8.00
K03 Int. Millennium Falcon—Cockpit 8.00
K04 Int. Tatooine—Mos Eisley—Cantina 8.00

Star Wars, The Empire Strikes Back *Chromium cards*
C4 (Topps 1995)

(STAR WARS WIDEVISION)
THE EMPIRE STRIKES BACK
Topps (1995)

Set: 144 cards $45.00
Pack: 9 cards. 2.75
Two different packs
Box: 24 packs 80.00
Chromium cards (1:12) 10 different, C1 to C10, each . 13.00
Movie Poster Set (1:24) six different, each 8.00
Promos
#0 Darth Vader (*Star Wars Galaxy* Magazine #3) 3.00
P1 Han Solo (*Advance* #79) 10.00
P2 AT-AT (*Non-Sports Update* Vol. 6 #4) 10.00
P3 Luke, R2-D2 and Yoda (*Cards Illustrated* #20) 10.00
P4 Luke hanging by hands (*Combo* #7 & *Combo* #12) . 12.00
P5 Stormtroopers and Han Solo in Carbonite,
  (convention giveaway) 30.00
P6 Luke, Leia, C-3PO and R2-D2 (*Wizard* #48) 10.00
Three-card (P1, P2, P3) sheet (*Previews*, May 1995) . . . 4.00

Trade Card

(STAR WARS WIDEVISION)
RETURN OF THE JEDI
Topps (1996)

Set: 144 cards	$45.00
Pack: 9 cards	2.50
Box: 24 packs	60.00
Topps Finest Chromium (1:12) 10 different, each	11.00
Mini-Posters (1:box) six different, each	10.00
3-Di (1:case) Admiral Ackbar	50.00
Redemption card	30.00

Promo Cards

#0 Three dead Jedi Warriors at Ewok celebration, from *Star Wars Galaxy Magazine* #6	4.00
P1 Han, Luke and Lando (*Star Wars Galaxy Mag.* #5)	4.00
P2 Biker Scout and Luke (*Advance Comics* #83	4.00
P3 Stormtroopers, Han and Leia (*Non-Sports Update*, Vol. 7 #1)	4.00
P4 Emperor Palpatine (*Cards Illustrated.* #27)	4.00
P5 Jabba the Hutt and Bib Fortuna (*Wizard* #54)	4.00
P6 Han Solo, Luke and Chewbacca (giveaway)	50.00
One-card sheet (Card #0) (*Previews*, Nov. 95)	5.00

STAR WARS TRILOGY
WIDEVISION (RETAIL)
Topps (1997)

Set: 72 cards	$20.00
Pack:	2.00
Box:	50.00
Lasercut Set (1:9) six different, each	9.00

Promos

P0 Lasercut	10.00
P1 Stormtroopers (San Diego Comic Con giveaway)	5.00
P2 Jabba the Hutt (*Star Wars Galaxy Magazine* #10)	5.00
P3 X-wing Fighter Squadron (magazines)	5.00
P4 Sandcrawler (*Star Wars* 3-D I packs)	10.00
P5 Luke in Landspeeder (*Star Wars* 3-D I packs)	10.00
P6 *Millennium Falcon* & Stormtroopers (*Star Wars* 3-D I packs)	10.00
P7 Landspeeder in Mos Eisley (*Wizard Sci-Fi Special '97 Star Wars* Trilogy Special Edition promo)	5.00
P8 Jabba's Dancing Girls (*Combo*)	5.00

Star Wars *Trilogy Widevision (Retail) Lasercut #2 (Topps 1997)*

Trade Card

Star Wars *Trilogy Special Edition Widevision #69 (Topps 1997)*

STAR WARS TRILOGY
SPECIAL EDITION WIDEVISION
Topps (1997)

```
Set: 72 cards . . . . . . . . . . . . . . . . . . . . . . . . . . . . . . $25.00
Pack: 9 cards. . . . . . . . . . . . . . . . . . . . . . . . . . . . . . .   3.00
Box: . . . . . . . . . . . . . . . . . . . . . . . . . . . . . . . . . . . .  75.00
```
Lasercut Set (1:9) six different, each. 9.00
Holograms (1:18) two different, each. 20.00
Spec. Ed. 3D card (1:Box) X-wings Departing 15.00
Galoob MicroMachine Promos
    Five different, G1 to G5, each 3.00
Hasbro Vehicles Promos
    Four different, H1 to H4, each 5.00

STAR WARS WIDEVISION 3-D
Topps (1997)

This card set contains all new images from the first movie, and utilizes an exclusive, multi-level 3-D digital imagery technology. The technology is quite impressive, but also expensive.

```
Set: 63 cards . . . . . . . . . . . . . . . . . . . . . . . . . . . . . . $90.00
Pack: 3 cards. . . . . . . . . . . . . . . . . . . . . . . . . . . . . . .   4.00
Box: 36 packs . . . . . . . . . . . . . . . . . . . . . . . . . . . . . . 120.00
```
Chase Card (1:36)
1m Death Star 3-D Motion card 30.00
Promos
2m Swoops and Rontos (*Trilogy Special Edition* promo . 10.00
3Di 1 Darth Vader, Stormtroopers and Captain Piett . . . 10.00
3Di 2 Darth and Luke 25.00
P1 Darth Vader (*Star Wars Galaxy* #9) 10.00
P2 Luke and Darth Vader (2,500 made) 50.00
P1 AT-ATs, *The Empire Strikes Back*! promo. 20.00
Dm/o Admiral Ackbar *Return of the Jedi* promo 20.00

STAR WARS VEHICLES
Topps (July 1997)

The *Star Wars* Vehicle cards feature 50 comic art cards by Top Cow Studios, plus 22 cards with movie photos featuring ships. All of the cards come with back blueprints and specs by Bill Smith, author of *The Essential Guide to Star Wars Vehicles and Vessels*. All of the cards are on 20 point Mirror-bond card stock.

Set: 72 cards	$25.00
Pack: 5 cards.	2.00
Box: 36 packs	50.00
Cutaway cards, (1:18) four different, C1 to C4, each. .	15.00
3-D cards (1:36) Chris Moeller art, two different	25.00
Redemption card (1:360) for uncut pair of 3-D cards . .	60.00
Mail-in card	50.00
Promos	
P1 Speeder Bikes, refractor.	50.00
P2 *Shuttle Tyderium*, refractor	85.00

Star Wars *Chrome Archives card (Topps 1999)*

STAR WARS CHROME ARCHIVES
Topps (1999)

Set: 90 chromium cards	$90.00
Pack: 5 cards	5.00
Box: 36 packs.	150.00
Double Sided Chrome Insert (1:12) nine diff., each. . .	15.00
Clear Chrome (1:18) four different, each	20.00
Nine-card uncut sheet.	75.00
Promos	
P1 Darth Vader: "Hate Me Luke! Destroy Me!".	5.00
P2 Yoda: "Welcome, Young Luke!"	5.00

OTHER CARDS AND STICKERS

Trix *Star Wars* stickers, set: 4 stickers	$5.00
Lucky Charms *Star Wars* stickers, set: 4 stickers	5.00
Monster Cereals *Star Wars* stickers, set: 4 stickers	5.00
Cocoa Puffs *Star Wars* stickers, set: 4 stickers.	5.00
Big G trading cards, with *Star Wars* logo	
(General Mills 1978) set: 18 photos and wallet . . .	30.00
The Empire Strikes Back Sticker set and Album	
(Burger King)	10.00
3-D Ewok Perk-up sticker sets, each	5.00

Trade Card

Star Wars: A New Hope *Metal Cards and Star Wars Dark Empire*
(Metallic Images 1994 & 1995)

METAL CARDS
Metallic Images (1994–99)

Star Wars: A New Hope (1994)
Set: 20 tin cards in tin box with certificate. $40.00
Promo P1 . . . . 4.00
Star Wars: The Empire Strikes Back (1995)
Set: 20 tin cards in tin litho box with certificate 50.00
Promo P2 . . . . 4.00
Series 2
Set: 20 tin cards in tin litho box with certificate 50.00
Star Wars: Return of the Jedi (1995)
Set: 20 tin cards in tin litho box with certificate 50.00
Promo P3 . . . . 6.00
Star Wars: The Art of Ralph McQuarrie (1996)
Set: 20 tin cards in tin litho box with certificate 60.00
Star Wars: Dark Empire (1995)
Set: 6 metal cards in tin litho box 15.00
Series II (1996)
Set: 6 metal cards in tin litho box (36,000 made) 15.00
Star Wars: Shadows of the Empire (1997)
Set: 6 metal cards in tin litho box 20.00
Star Wars: Jedi Knight (1997)
Set: 6 metal cards in tin litho box 14.00

24K GOLD CARDS
Authentic Images (1997)

Gold Star Wars cards, limited to 1,000 units, in acrylic
holder, with black vacuum-formed jewel case:
Series One: *A New Hope*
Special Edition Ingot $75.00
Darth Vader. 100.00
Other cards, four different, each. 75.00
Series Two: *The Empire Strikes Back*
Boba Fett. 100.00
Other cards, four different, each. 75.00
Series Three: *Return of the Jedi*, five different, each . 75.00

Trade Card

Gold Gallery Series cards, limited to 500 units, in acrylic holder, with black vacuum-formed jewel case:

Gallery Series 1: *A New Hope*

Jabba the Hutt & Han Solo	350.00
Darth Vader & Ben Kenobi	550.00

Gallery Series 2: *The Empire Strikes Back*

Luke and Yoda	325.00
Luke and Darth Vader	400.00

24-karat gold card set, reproduction of three posters, 1,997 sets world-wide, JC Penney exclusive | 225.00

STAR WARS EPISODE I WIDEVISION
Topps (1999)

Series One (Hobby Edition)

Set: 80 cards	$30.00
Pack: 8 cards	3.00
Box	75.00
Expansion Cards (1:2)	
Expansion Set: 40 cards	40.00
Expansion Card	2.00
Chromium Inserts (1:12) eight different, each	20.00
Promos, three different, each	2.00

Series One (Retail Edition)

Set: 80 cards & 16 stickers	25.00
Pack: 8 cards	2.00
Box:	60.00
Stickers (1:2) 16 different, each	0.20
Foil Inserts (1:8) 10 different, each	8.00
Mega Chromes five different, each	15.00
Collectors Tin set: 8 cards	20.00
Hallmark Promos, H1–H3, each	3.00

Series Two (Hobby Edition)

Set: 80 cards	30.00
Pack: 8 cards	2.75
Box:	75.00
Embossed Foil Inserts (1:12) six different, each	10.00
Chrome Inserts (1:18) four different, each	15.00
Oversize Promos, 4" x 7½"	
OS-1 Dueling with Darth Maul	2.00
OS-2 A Time to Rejoice	2.00

Star Wars Episode I *card #56 (Topps 1999)*

Trade Card

VEHICLES

VEHICLES, CREATURES, PLAY-SETS AND ACCESSORIES

Vehicles are much more important in *Star Wars* than in most other action figure lines. The 3¾" size of the figures allowed the production of vehicles which were large enough to accommodate several figures, and so the larger vehicles became virtual playsets for the figures.

Today, many collectors have a large supply of loose figures, which they display with the appropriate loose vehicles, creatures, playsets, and accessories. This has helped to keep collector prices for these items at a high level. Vehicles, creatures, and accessories from the classic movies are listed first, followed by those from the new Power of the Force and Episode I, The Phantom Menace series.

VEHICLES
Kenner (1978–86)

Vehicles were released over the period of all three movies and many which originally came out in "*Star Wars*" boxes can be found in boxes from one or both of the later movies.

Star Wars Vehicles (1978–79)
Landspeeder, holds two figures (#38020, 1978)
    Original *Star Wars* box $75.00
    Reissue in Collector Series box (1983) 35.00
    Loose 25.00

Millennium Falcon *Spaceship (Kenner 1979)*

Imperial TIE Fighter (Kenner 1978)

X-Wing Fighter, 14" long, electronic (#38030, 1978)
 Original *Star Wars* box 125.00
 Reissue in *The Empire Strikes Back* box 200.00
 Loose. 45.00
Imperial TIE Fighter, 12" wide, electronic (#38040, 1978)
 Original *Star Wars* box 135.00
 Reissue in *The Empire Strikes Back* box 200.00
 Loose. 45.00
Darth Vader TIE Fighter, grey, 11" across, pop-off
 solar panels, electronic (#39100, 1979)
 Original *Star Wars* box 125.00
 Loose. 60.00
 Original *Star Wars* box with Battle Scene Setting 500.00
 Loose, with Battle Scene 150.00
 Reissue in Collector Series box (1983). 60.00
 Loose. 40.00
Millennium Falcon Spaceship, 21" long, 18" wide,
 with "Battle Alert Sound" (#39110, 1979)
 Original *Star Wars* box 325.00
 Reissue in *The Empire Strikes Back* box 225.00
 Reissue in *Return of the Jedi* box 175.00
 Reissue in Collector Series box (1983). 125.00
 Loose. 90.00
Radio-Controlled Jawa Sandcrawler, 17" long (#39270, 1979)
 Original *Star Wars* box 600.00
 Reissue in *The Empire Strikes Back* box 700.00
 Loose. 250.00
Imperial Troop Transporter, electronic (#39290, 1979)
 Original *Star Wars* box 100.00
 Reissue in *The Empire Strikes Back* box 100.00
 Loose. 45.00

Exclusive Vehicles (1979–80)
Sonic-Controlled Land Speeder, battery operated,
 JC Penney exclusive (#38540, 1979)
 Original *Star Wars* box 600.00
 Loose. 225.00

Vehicles

Imperial Cruiser, Sears exclusive (#93351, 1980)
    Original *The Empire Strikes Back* box. 100.00
    Loose. 40.00

The Empire Strikes Back Vehicles (1980–82)
Darth Vader's Star Destroyer, 20" long (#39850, 1980)
    Original *The Empire Strikes Back* box. 135.00
    Loose. 40.00
Twin-Pod Cloud Car, 10" wide, (#39860, 1980)
    Original *The Empire Strikes Back* box. 90.00
    Reissue in *The Empire Strikes Back* box with
        Bespin Security Guard (white) figure 125.00
    Loose, no figure. 40.00
AT-AT All-Terrain Armored Transport (#38810, 1981)
    Original *The Empire Strikes Back* box. 250.00
    Reissue in *Return of the Jedi* box. 200.00
    Loose. 100.00
Rebel Armored Snowspeeder, electronic (#39610, 1982)
    Original *The Empire Strikes Back* box. 90.00
    Reissue in *The Empire Strikes Back* box with
        Rebel Soldier (Hoth Battle Gear) figure 175.00
    Loose. 40.00
Slave I, Boba Fett's Spaceship, 12" long, including
    Simulated Frozen **Han Solo** (#39690, 1982)
    Original *The Empire Strikes Back* box. 90.00
    Reissue in *The Empire Strikes Back* box with
        Battle Scene Setting 275.00
    Loose. 40.00
Rebel Transport, 20" long, including 5 Hoth Back-
    packs and 4 Asteroid gas masks (#69740, 1982)
    Original *The Empire Strikes Back* box. 100.00
    Loose. 35.00
"Battle Damaged" X-Wing Fighter, electronic (#69780, 1981)
    Original *The Empire Strikes Back* box. 150.00
    Reissue in *Return of the Jedi* box. 100.00
    Loose. 35.00
Scout Walker (#69800, 1982)
    Original *The Empire Strikes Back* box. 80.00
    Reissue in *Return of the Jedi* box. 60.00
    Loose. 25.00

AT-AT All-Terrain Armored Transport (Kenner 1981)

Vehicles

Imperial TIE Fighter (Battle Damaged) blue (#71490, 1983)
    Original *The Empire Strikes Back* box 150.00
    Reissue in *Return of the Jedi* box 125.00
    Loose 40.00

Return of the Jedi Vehicles (1983–84)
Speeder Bike 8" long (#70500, 1983)
    Original *Return of the Jedi* box 30.00
    Reissue in *Power of the Force* box 20.00
    Loose 15.00
Y-Wing Fighter with Laser Cannon Sound (#70510, 1983)
    Original *Return of the Jedi* box 100.00
    Loose 50.00
B-Wing Fighter, 22" long, electronic (#71370, 1984)
    Original *Return of the Jedi* box 85.00
    Loose 40.00
TIE Interceptor, with Battle Sound and Flashing
    Laser Light (#71390, 1984)
    Original *Return of the Jedi* box 90.00
    Loose 50.00
Imperial Shuttle, 18" tall, electronic (#93650)
    Original *Return of the Jedi* box 350.00
    Loose 175.00

Power of the Force Vehicles (1984–85)
Tatooine Skiff, 12" long (#71540, 1985)
    Original *Power of the Force* box 625.00
    Loose 300.00

Droids Vehicles (1985)
A-Wing Fighter, electronic, with planetary map (#93700)
    Original *Droids* box 625.00
    Loose 300.00
ATL Interceptor Vehicle (#93900)
    Original *Droids* box 35.00
    Loose 15.00
Side Gunner with *Star Wars* Planetary Map (#94010)
    Original *Droids* box 50.00
    Loose 10.00

TIE Interceptor (Kenner 1984)

Vehicles

Electronic X-wing Fighter (Kenner 1995)

NEW VEHICLES
Kenner (1995–99)

Kenner (now Hasbro) has produced new vehicles right along with all the new action figures, and their boxes have followed the same color sequence—first red, then green, with a few purple boxes for *Shadows of the Empire* vehicles. There have been box variations as well, and many can be identified by the packaging variation number found near the bar code on most boxes.

In February 2000, Toys "R" Us sold Hasbro's excess stock of vehicles for $9.95 each. Many valuable vehicles were included, including AT-ATs and F/X Red-5 X-wing Fighters. They also sold deluxe creatures such as Rancors and Banthas for the same price. I hope you got the ones you needed, but if you didn't, your friendly neighborhood or internet dealer may have a few left—but not for $9.95! However, his price on some expensive vehicles may be a little softer than before.

Power of the Force Vehicles, red boxes (1995–96)
Landspeeder (#69770, 1995) $10.00
TIE Fighter (#69775, 1995) 20.00
Imperial AT-ST (Scout Walker) (#69776, 1995) 25.00
Electronic X-wing Fighter (#69780, 1995). 30.00
Electronic *Millennium Falcon* (#69785, 1995) 50.00

Power of the Force Vehicles, green boxes (1996–98)
Luke's T-16 Skyhopper (#69663, 1996) 20.00
Cruise Missile Trooper with Twin Proton Torpedo
    Launchers (#69653, 1997). 13.00
Darth Vader's TIE Fighter with Launcher Laser
    Cannons (#69662, 1997) 20.00
Electronic Rebel Snowspeeder with Topps wide-
    vision trading card (#69585, 1996) 25.00

Vehicles

A-Wing Fighter (Kenner 1997)

Power of the Force Vehicles with figures (1997–98)
A-Wing Fighter with **A-Wing Pilot** (#69737, 1997) 25.00
Electronic Imperial AT-AT Walker with **AT-AT Com-
mander** and **AT-AT Driver** (#69733, 1997)
     [.00] sticker over bottom of figures' photo 90.00
     Variation [.01] no sticker, full photo shown 75.00

Shadows of the Empire Vehicles (1996)
Boba Fett's *Slave I* (#69565, July 1996) purple box ... 30.00
Boba Fett's *Slave I*, including **Han Solo in Carbon-
ite** (#69565) reissue in green box............. 20.00
Dash Rendar's Outrider, with Topps widevision
     trading card (#69593, 1996) purple box 35.00
     Reissue in (#69814) green box............... 20.00

Speeder Bike Vehicles with figures (Asst. 69760)
Imperial Speeder Bike with **Biker Scout Storm-
trooper** (#69765, 1996) red box [none] 20.00
Swoop vehicle with **Swoop Trooper** (#69591,
     1996) purple box [none].................... 12.00
Speeder Bike with **Luke Skywalker** in Endor Gear,
     (#69651, 1997) [.00] two white gloves in photo... 20.00
     Variation [.01] wearing one black glove......... 12.00
Speeder Bike with **Princess Leia Organa** in Endor
     Gear (#69727, 1997) [.00] rocks in side photos... 20.00
     Variation [.01] moss airbrushed over rocks 15.00
Power Racing Speeder Bike with **Scout Trooper**
     (#60588, 1998) 12.50
Drawing Board Speeder Bike with **Biker Pilot** (#69760) 11.00

Expanded Universe Vehicles (Asst. #69620, 1998)
Cloud Car with **Cloud Car Pilot** (#69786, 1998)...... 15.00
Airspeeder with **Airspeeder Pilot** (#69774, 1998) 15.00
Speeder Bike with **Rebel Speeder Bike Pilot**
     (#69772, 1998)........................... 12.50

Vehicles

Electronic Power F/X Vehicle
Electronic Power F/X Luke Skywalker Red Five
    X-wing Fighter, electronic, plus non-removable
    Luke Skywalker and R2-D2 (#69784, 1998) 60.00

EPISODE I VEHICLES

Large Vehicles
Electronic Naboo Fighter (#84099, 1999)
    [.02] "with Lights and Sounds" 30.00
    [.03] "with Real Movie Lights and Sounds" 20.00
Femba with Shield Generator and **Gungan Warrior**
    (#84369) [.00] FAO Schwarz exclusive 75.00

Mid Size Vehicles (Asst. #84025)
Trade Federation Droid Fighters, including three
    Droid fighters (#84171, 1999) [.0100] 23.00

STAP and Battle Droid (Hasbro 1999)

Vehicles with figure (Asst. #84020)
Anakin Skywalker's Pod Racer with "Blast-Open
    Directional Vanes" and **Anakin Skywalker**
    (#84097, 1999) [.0200] 25.00
Sebula's Pod Racer with Spring-Out Spinning Blade
    and **Sebula** (#840 , 1999) 25.00

Vehicle
Flash Speeder with Launching Laser Cannon (#84191). 10.00

Vehicle and figure (Asst. #84135)
Stap and Battle Droid (#84139) [.00] 12.00
Sith Speeder and Darth Maul (#84141) [.0100] 12.00
Armored Scout Tank with Battle Droid (#84367) 10.00
Gungan Assaault Cannon with Jar Jar Binks (#84368) . 10.00

SHIPS
Kenner (1997–98)

    Ships differ from "vehicles" because ships are not
scaled to fit action figures, but vehicles are. Obviously

Vehicles

Kenner can't make a Star Destroyer that is the same scale as its other vehicles—it would be over 100 feet long!

Collector Fleet in try-me box (1997–98)
Electronic Blockade Runner (Kenner #27844, 1997). . $15.00
Electronic Star Destroyer (Kenner #27835, 1997). 15.00
Electronic Super Star Destroyer *Executor* (Kenner
    #27914, 1998) 33.00

Tauntaun (Open Belly Rescue) (Kenner 1982)

CREATURES
Kenner (1979–84)

Classic Creatures
Patrol Dewback, 10¼" long (#39240, 1979)
    Original *Star Wars* box $75.00
    Reissue in *The Empire Strikes Back* box 250.00
    Reissue in Collector Series box (1983) 50.00
    Loose. 25.00
Tauntaun, 8" tall (#39820, 1980)
    Original *The Empire Strikes Back* box 75.00
    Loose. 25.00
Tauntaun, with Open Belly Rescue Feature (#93340, 1982)
    Original *The Empire Strikes Back* box 75.00
    Loose. 25.00
Wampa, Snow Creature from Hoth, 6¼" tall (#69560, 1982)
    Original *The Empire Strikes Back* box pictur-
        ing Rebel Commander 60.00
    Reissue as **Hoth Wampa** in *The Empire
        Strikes Back* box picturing Luke Skywalker. . . . 35.00
    Reissue in *Return of the Jedi* box. 40.00
    Loose. 20.00
Jabba the Hutt Action Playset, including Jabba and
    Salacious Crumb molded figure (#70490, 1983)
    Original *Return of the Jedi* box 60.00
    Reissue in *Return of the Jedi* box (Sears). 40.00
    Loose. 30.00

Vehicles

Rancor Monster, 10" high (1984)
      Original *Return of the Jedi* box 75.00
      Reissue in *Power of the Force* box 60.00
      Loose 35.00

NEW CREATURES
Kenner (1997–99)

The first three creature and figure combination boxes arrived in August 1997. The figures are all based on the new footage from the first movie. A lot of them were produced, and Hasbro's overstock was available in early 2000 at Toys "R" Us at $4.95 each. Distribution of the 1998 figures was poor, and local stores rarely had them available, but a few showed up in 2000 with the original three.

Creature and Figure Combos (Asst. #69645, 1997)
Ronto and Jawa (#69728) [.00] $15.00
Dewback and **Sandtrooper** (#69743) [.00] Galactic
      Empire and Unaffiliated logos on front 17.00
      Variation, [.01] Galactic Empire logo only 15.00
Jabba the Hutt and **Han Solo** (#69742) [.00] Galactic
      Empire and Rebel Alliance logos, Han pictured
      to Jabba's right 25.00
      Variation [.01] Han pictured to Jabba's left 15.00
      Variation [.02] Unaffiliated & Rebel Alliance logos . 15.00

Second Batch (May 1998)
Tauntaun with Han Solo in Hoth Gear (#84107) [.00] . . . 15.00
Luke Skywalker and TaunTaun (#69729) [.00] 15.00
Wampa and Luke Skywalker (in Hoth Gear)
      (#69768) [.00] 15.00

Deluxe Creatures and Figure (Asst. #69655, May 1998)
Rancor and Luke Skywalker, with "Exclusive Battle-
      worn **Jedi Luke**" (#69771) [.00] 30.00
Bantha and Tusken Raider, "includes exclusive
      Tusken Raider with Gaderffii Stick" (#69769)
      [.00] 30.00

Rancor and Luke Skywalker (Kenner 1998)

Episode I Creature and Figure (1999)
Kaadu and Jar Jar Binks with "Energy Ball Atlatl"
    (#84094) 15.00
Opee and Qui-Gon Jinn, with "Snapping Jaws"
    (Opee) and "Articulated Ankles for Swimming"
    (Qui-Gon Jinn) (#84096) [.0000] warning on sticker 15.00
Femba with Shield Generator and Gungan Warrior
    (#84369) [.00] FAO Schwarz exclusive 75.00

PLAYSETS
Kenner (1979–85)

Star Wars Playsets (1979)
Death Star Space Station, 23" high (#38050, 1979)
    Original *Star Wars* box $225.00
    Loose. 60.00
Creature Cantina Action Playset (#39120, 1979)
    Original *Star Wars* box 125.00
    Loose. 40.00
Land of the Jawas Action Playset (#39130, 1979)
    Original *Star Wars* box 160.00
    Reissue in *The Empire Strikes Back* box 225.00
    Loose. 50.00
Droid Factory with 31 plastic robot parts (#39150, 1979)
    Original *Star Wars* box 125.00
    Reissue in *The Empire Strikes Back* box 175.00
    Loose. 50.00

The Empire Strikes Back Playsets (1980–82)
Imperial Attack Base, Hoth scene (#39830, 1980)
    Original *The Empire Strikes Back* box. 125.00
    Loose. 30.00
Hoth Ice Planet Adventure Set (1980, 1980)
    Original *The Empire Strikes Back* box. 150.00
    Reissue in *The Empire Strikes Back* box, with
       Imperial Stormtrooper (Hoth Battle Gear). . 200.00
    Loose, no figure. 50.00

Ewok Village Playset (Kenner 1983)

Vehicles

Dagobah Action Playset (#38820, 1981)
>   Original *The Empire Strikes Back* box. 55.00
>   Loose. 25.00

Turret & Probot Playset, with **Probot** (#38330, 1981)
>   Original *The Empire Strikes Back* box. 150.00
>   Loose. 60.00

Rebel Command Center Adventure Set, with **R2-D2**, **Luke Skywalker** and **AT-AT Commander** (#69481, 1981)
>   Original *The Empire Strikes Back* box. 225.00
>   Loose. 100.00

Return of the Jedi Playset (1983)
Ewok Village Action Playset, 2-story playset (#70520, 1983)
>   Original *Return of the Jedi* box. 75.00
>   Loose. 25.00

Ewok Playset (1984)
Ewok Family Hut, 12" high, with 15 accessories and four non-poseable figures (Kenner Pre-school, 1984)
>   Original *Ewoks* box 50.00
>   Loose. 15.00

Cloud City Playset, Sears Exclusive (Kenner 1981)

Exclusive Playsets
Cantina Adventure Set (Sears' promotional set) with Greedo, Hammerhead, blue Snaggletooth, and Walrus Man (#38861, 1979)
>   Original *Star Wars* box 700.00
>   Loose. 300.00

Cloud City Playset (Sears' exclusive) with Han Solo in Bespin outfit, Ugnaught, Lobot, Dengar, and Boba Fett (#38781, 1981)
>   Original *The Empire Strikes Back* box. 375.00
>   Loose. 150.00

The Jabba the Hutt Dungeon Action Playset (Sears exclusive) Variation #1, including Klaatu, Nikto, and 8D8, red box (#71381, 1983)
>   Original *Return of the Jedi* box 130.00
>   Loose. 60.00

Vehicles

Variation #2, including EV-9D9, Amanaman,
    and Barada, green box (#59262, 1984)
Original *Return of the Jedi* box 325.00
Loose. 200.00

Episode I Playsets
Theed Generator Complex with Battle Droid (#26222) . . 20.00
Theed Hangar Playset, Motorized (#84173). 30.00
Electronic Naboo Royal Starship Blockade Cruiser/
    Playset (#84146) with red R2 unit 100.00

ACCESSORIES AND MINI-RIGS
Kenner (1981–84)

Some of the accessories listed in this section were
called "playsets" or "one-figure vehicles" on their boxes.
What places them in this category is their small size.

Accessories
Vehicle Maintenance Energizer (#93430, 1983)
    Original *The Empire Strikes Back* box. $20.00
    Reissue in *Return of the Jedi* box. 15.00
    Loose. 9.00
Radar Laser Cannon (#93440, 1983)
    Original *The Empire Strikes Back* box. 20.00
    Reissue in *Return of the Jedi* box. 15.00
    Loose. 7.50
Tri-Pod Laser Cannon (#93450, 1983)
    Original *The Empire Strikes Back* box. 20.00
    Reissue in *Return of the Jedi* box. 15.00
    Loose. 9.00
Ewok Assault Catapult (#71070, 1984)
    Original *Return of the Jedi* box 18.00
    Loose. 8.00
Ewok Combat Glider (#93510, 1984)
    Original *Return of the Jedi* box 18.00
    Loose. 8.00
Ewok Battle Wagon, 12" long with *Star Wars* Planet-
    ary Map (#93690, 1984)

Vehicle Maintenance Energizer and Radar Laser Cannon
(Kenner 1982–83)

Vehicles

Original *Power of the Force* box	225.00
Loose.	75.00

Imperial Sniper Vehicle, one-figure vehicle (1984)
Original *Power of the Force* box	75.00
Loose.	35.00

Security Scout, one-figure vehicle (1984)
Original *Power of the Force* box	250.00
Loose.	60.00

One-Man Sand Skimmer, one-figure vehicle (1984)
Original *Power of the Force* box	75.00
Loose.	30.00

Ewok Fire Cart, accessories plus two non-poseable figures (Kenner Preschool, 1984)
Original *Ewoks* box	40.00
Loose.	15.00

Ewok Woodland Wagon (Kenner Preschool, 1985)
Original *Ewoks* box	75.00
Loose.	20.00

MINI-RIGS

Mini-Rigs were one-man "crawling, climbing, flying" accessories for the action figures, that were too small to be part of the regular vehicle line-up. They came in a box with a hanging flap, and the best graphics are on the back of the package.

None of these mini-rigs never appeared in the three movies, but a few showed up in the animated Droids series. These days Kenner packages such items with a figure and sells them as a "Deluxe" figure.

Mini Rig 1-Figure Vehicles, 6" x 4½" boxes (1981-83)
MTV-7 Multi-Terrain Vehicle (#40010, 1981)
Original *The Empire Strikes Back* box.	$35.00
Reissue with **AT-AT Driver** figure.	60.00
Reissue in *Return of the Jedi* box.	25.00

INT-4 Mini-Rig (Kenner 1982)

Desert Sail Skiff (Kenner 1984)

Loose, without figure	9.00
MLC-3 Mobile Laser Cannon (#40020, 1981)	
Original *The Empire Strikes Back* box	25.00
Reissue with **Rebel Commander** figure	60.00
Reissue in *Return of the Jedi* box	25.00
Loose, without figure	9.00
PDT-8 Personnel Deployment Transport (#40070, 1981)	
Original *The Empire Strikes Back* box	30.00
Reissue with **2-1B** figure	60.00
Reissue in *Return of the Jedi* box	15.00
Loose, without figure	9.00
INT-4 Interceptor (#69750, 1982)	
Original *The Empire Strikes Back* box	30.00
Reissue with **AT-AT Commander** figure	60.00
Reissue in *Return of the Jedi* box	15.00
Loose, without figure	9.00
CAP-2 Captivator (#69760, 1982)	
Original *The Empire Strikes Back* box	30.00
Reissue with **Bossk** figure	60.00
Reissue in *Return of the Jedi* box	20.00
Loose	9.00
AST-5 Armored Sentinel Transport (#70880, 1983)	
Original *Return of the Jedi* box	15.00
Loose	7.00
ISP-6 (Imperial Shuttle Pod) (#70890, 1983)	
Original *Return of the Jedi* box	20.00
Loose	9.00
Desert Sail Skiff (#93520, 1984) mini rig	
Original *Return of the Jedi* box	15.00
Loose	10.00
Endor Forest Ranger (#93610, 1984) mini rig	
Original *Return of the Jedi* box	15.00
Loose	10.00

Vehicles

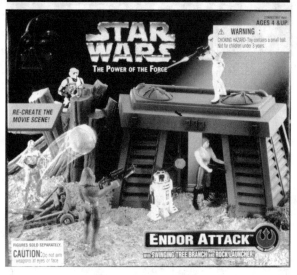

Endor Attack (Kenner 1997)

NEW ACCESSORIES
Kenner (1996–99)

First Batch (Asst. #27597, Oct. 1996)
Detention Block Rescue (#27598) $15.00
Death Star Escape with "Firing Cannon and Remov-
    able Bridge" (#27599). 15.00

Second Batch (Asst. #27857, Aug. 1997)
Hoth Battle with "Rotating Gun Turret and Shooting
    Laser" (#27858) 18.00
Endor Attack with "Swinging Tree Branch and Rock
    Launcher" (#27859) 18.00

VANS AND RACERS
    A less authentic toy than a *Star Wars* van would be hard
to design. Not only are there no cars or vans in the movies,
there aren't even any roads.

Star Wars Van Set, two toy vans, 7" in length, black
    van with Darth Vader picture; white van with
    good guys, plus 12 barrels, four pylons and
    two T-Sticks (Kenner #90170, 1978) $150.00
Darth Vader SSP (Super Sonic Power) Van, black,
    with Blazin' Action, gyro powered (Kenner
    #90160, 1978) 50.00
Star Wars Heroes SSP (Super Sonic Power) Van,
    white, with Blazin' Action, gyro powered
    (Kenner #90160, 1978) 50.00
Star Wars Duel at Death Star Racing Set, 19" x 20"
    box (Fundimensions 1978) 200.00

Vehicles

WALL ART

Wall art includes just about every kind of picture, poster or other item that is designed to be framed and/or hung on a wall. Calendars are covered under PAPER.

ANIMATION CELS
Royal Animation (1995–97)

Royal Animation makes sericels from the "Droids and Ewoks" animated TV series. Sericels are silk-screened from the original cel, with an added lithograph background. Each comes with a certificate of authenticity and a Lucas Films seal. The sericels are double-matted and 14" x 18" in size.

Droids Sericels
R2-D2 & C-3PO, Best Friends (DR-1) $90.00
Battle Cruiser (DR-2) 90.00
R2-D2 & C-3PO Stranded (DR-3). 90.00
Bounty Hunter, Boba Fett and Stormtroopers (DR-4) . . 90.00

Ewoks Sericels
The Big Hug (EW-1). 90.00
Celebration (EW-2) 90.00

CHROMART

ChromArt prints are 8" x 10" in an 11" x 14" matte. They are made with acrylic, foil, and etching to give an illusion of depth. The enhancements make them quite striking.

ChromArt Prints (Zanart Entertainment)
20 different prints from Posters, Video Game covers
     and other sources, each. $12.00
Second Series
     Nine different ChromArt Prints, each 13.00
Star Wars Trilogy Movie Cards. 14.00

*Star Wars One-Sheet Poster & Dark Forces Chromart Prints
(Zanart 1995)*

Third Series
    Eight different Blueprint AchromArt prints, each . . . 12.00

Fourth Series (1997)
    Six diff. framed 11" x 14" Chromart prints, each . . 20.00

Other Prints
Star Wars Trilogy International Release ChromArt
    print, John Alvin art, three prints, matted in
    wood frame (SWI-3W, 1996) limited to 2,500
    copies 250.00

LITHOGRAPHS

Many *Star Wars* limited edition lithographs were created by well-known science fiction and *Star Wars* artist Ralph McQuarrie. They are 18" x 12" in size, framed and matted, and each comes with an Illuminated 70mm Film Frame.

Many other prominent *Star Wars* artists have also produced lithographs, including Boris Valejo, Drew Struzan, the Bros. Hildebrandt, and Dave Dorman. Lithographs fall in the realm of fine art, and the high prices that they command are based on this, rather than being driven up by collector demand. They make excellent gifts.

Star Wars, A New Hope (Ralph McQuarrie art, limited edition)
The Cantina on Mos Eisley (Willitts Designs) $150.00
Millennium Falcon (Willitts Designs) 180.00
Rebel Attack on the Death Star (Willitts Designs) 200.00
Rebel Ceremony (Willitts Designs) 150.00

Empire Strikes Back (Ralph McQuarrie art, limited edition)
Rebel Patrol of Echo Base (Willitts Designs) 150.00
Luke Skywalker & Darth Vader Duel (Willitts Designs) 150.00
Battle of Hoth (Willitts Designs) 150.00
Cloud City of Bespin (Willitts Designs) 150.00

Star Wars Teaser Poster (1976) and
Empire Strikes Back Advance One-Sheet Poster (1980)

Wall Art

Return of the Jedi (Ralph McQuarrie art, limited edition)
Jabba the Hutt (Willitts Designs). 175.00
The Rancor Pit (Willitts Designs) 175.00
Speeder Bike (Willitts Designs) 175.00
Death Star Generator (Willitts Designs) 175.00

Other Lithographs (Various artists, limited editions)
Star Wars 15th Anniversary Serigraph, by Melanie
    Taylor Kent, 20¼" x 30½" (1992) 1,750.00
Star Wars Lithograph by Ken Steacy, 17" x 24"
    signed and numbered (Gifted Images 1994) 600.00
In a Galaxy Far, Far Away, limited, signed lithograph
    by Michael David Ward, 20" x 30", signed by
    Anthony Daniels and Kenny Baker 175.00
Luke Skywalker Limited Edition Lithograph by Al
    Williamson, 22½" x 23" in 29" x 29" frame (1996) 300.00
Darth Vader Limited Edition Lithograph by Al
    Williamson, 24" x 24" in 30" x 30" frame (1996) . 300.00
Star Wars R2-D2 Remarked Lithograph by the
    Bros. Hildebrandt, signed, 24" x 18" 175.00
Star Wars Luke and Yoda Lithograph by Boris
    Vallejo, signed and numbered, 30" x 36" 600.00

Star Wars, Limited Edition Lithographs by Dave Dorman
Star Wars Dewback Patrol, 34" x 16" (1997) 75.00
Star Wars Battle of Hoth, 34" x 16", (1997). 75.00
Star Wars Tales of the Jedi, Freedon Nadd Uprising
    18" x 22", (1997) 75.00
Star Wars Star's End, 18" x 22" (1997). 75.00
Star Wars Princess Leia (Boushh) 16" x 22" (1997) . . . 75.00
Star Wars Throne Room of Jabba, 32" x 14" (1997) . . . 75.00

POSTERS

There are many types of posters, from those sold in toy
stores to those that come in magazines and as fast food give-
aways, but the most valuable by far are the theatrical posters
that were issued to promote the movie. These had no initial

*The Empire Strikes Back Domestic One-Sheet Poster and
Style B Domestic One-Sheet Poster (1980)*

Wall Art

price—they were sent to movie theaters or given away at shows. Their value is entirely collector driven. There are a considerable number of general movie poster collectors who compete with *Star Wars* collectors for these posters, keeping the prices high. Posters are most valuable when they are rolled, not folded, and should never be put on your wall using thumb tacks. As a practical matter, this will make it hard to show it to your friends in order to impress them. If your poster is worth $150 or more, you should probably have it professionally framed, which will cost you close to $100, but at least you can then hang it on your wall and show it off.

POSTERS—THEATRICAL

Star Wars
Advance A One-sheet, "A long time ago in a galaxy
    far far away..." $250.00
Star Wars advance, 2nd version. 150.00
Style A One-sheet, Tommy Jung art 175.00
Star Wars, style A, with record promo 175.00
Star Wars advance, style B 150.00
Star Wars, style C 150.00
Style D One-sheet (Circus poster) 325.00
Anniversary One-sheet (1978) theater give-away 600.00
'79 Re-release One-sheet, "It's Back!" 100.00
'81 Re-release One-sheet 60.00
'82 Re-release One-Sheet 50.00

The Empire Strikes Back
Advance One-sheet 200.00
Style 'A' One-sheet (Love Story) Rodger Kastel art. . . 200.00
Style 'B' One-sheet Tommy Jung art. 75.00
'81 Re-release One-sheet, Tommy Jung art 50.00
'82 Re-release One-sheet, Tommy Jung art 40.00

Revenge of the Jedi
Advance Revenge of the Jedi One-sheet, 41" x 27"
    with release date 350.00

Revenge of the Jedi Advance One-Sheet Poster (1983) and
Star Wars Episode One The Phantom Menace Teaser Poster (1999)

Variation, no release date. 400.00

Return of the Jedi
Style 'A' One-sheet 35.00
Style 'B' One-sheet 40.00
Return of the Jedi, 1985 reissue 50.00

Special Edition One-sheets (1997)
Star Wars Trilogy Special Edition Advance One-sheet . 30.00
Version 'B' *Star Wars: A New Hope* Drew Struzan art. . 30.00
Version 'C' *The Empire Strikes Back* Drew Struzan art . 30.00
Version 'D' *Return of the Jedi* , Drew Struzan art 30.00

POSTERS–SPECIAL EVENTS

The Art of *Star Wars*, Center for the Arts $50.00
Caravan of Courage. 60.00
Immunization Poster 10.00
Star Tours Poster. 5.00
Public Radio Drama poster. 150.00
Vintage Action Figures Photo poster 15.00

POSTERS–COMMERCIAL

Star Wars 10th Anniversary Poster, 27" x 41" (1987)
    by Drew Struzan. $10.00
Star Wars 10th Anniversary Poster, signed , limited . . 100.00
Star Wars 15th Anniversary poster by Melanie Tay-
    lor Kent, 20" x 30" (1992) 25.00
Star Wars 15th Anniversary Movie Poster, by Greg &
    Tim Hildebrandt (Collector's Warehouse 1992) . . . 15.00
    Deluxe, signed edition of 1,000 . . . . 50.00
The Empire Strikes Back 10th Anniversary Poster,
    by Larry Noble, 27" x 41" (1990). 15.00
Return of the Jedi 10th Anniversary Advance
    Poster, 27" x 40" (1993) 15.00
    Deluxe version, gold foil border 50.00
Return of the Jedi 10th Anniversary Style A poster,
    27" x 40" by Kazo Sano (1994). 15.00
Star Wars Checklist Poster, 27" x 40" (Killian Enter-
    prises 1995) full color reproductions of all
    movie one-sheet posters and variants 15.00
Star Wars Radio Poster (1993) 15.00
Star Wars Cutaway Posters (1997) each 20.00
Star Wars Cutaway Posters, signed and numbered . . . 40.00
Almost all other commercial posters, each. 5.00
A few larger or fancier commercial posters, each. up to 15.00

Episode I Commercial Posters (At-A-Glance, 1999)
    Several different, each 5.00

Food Premium Posters
Burger Chef Premiums (1978) four different, each 10.00
General Mills Premiums (1978) four different, each . . . 10.00
Proctor and Gamble Premiums (1978) three diff., each. 10.00
Nestea Premiums (1980) two different, each 8.00
Burger King Premiums (1980) three different, each 5.00
The Empire Strikes Back montage by Boris Vallejo
    (Coca Cola 1980). 20.00

Wall Art

Proctor and Gamble Premiums (1980) four diff., each . . 5.00
Dixie Cups Story card poster (1981) 15.00
Hi-C *Return of the Jedi* poster (1983). 8.00
Oral-B *Return of the Jedi* poster (1983). 8.00
Star Wars Trilogy Special Edition Pepsi mail-in
    posters, 24" x 36", each 5.00

PRINTS

Dave Dorman prints (Rolling Thunder Graphics 1995–96)
Shadows of the Empire signed print, 24" x 36" $40.00
Boba Fett: Bounty Hunter Print, signed 65.00
Star Wars: Smuggler's Moon Print, signed 65.00
Star Wars: Dark Empire II Print, signed). 65.00
Obi-Wan Kenobi Art Print, signed. 65.00

TIN SIGNS
Tin Signs International

Embossed Movie Posters
Star Wars, tin litho, 15" x 24" $25.00
The Empire Strikes Back, tin litho, 15" x 24". 25.00
Return of the Jedi, tin litho, 15" x 24" 25.00

1997 Batch
Star Wars: A New Hope, tin litho, 12" x 17" 13.00
Star Wars: A New Hope, tin litho, horizontal 17" x 12" . 13.00
The Empire Strikes Back, tin litho, 12" x 17". 13.00
Return of the Jedi, tin litho, 12" x 17" 13.00

HOLOGRAMS

Darth Vader Hologram Picture, 5" x 3" in 8" x 10"
    matte (A.H. Prismatic #1021/99, 1994) $30.00
Millennium Falcon Hologram Picture, 3" x 2" in 5" x 7"
    matt (A.H. Prismatic #1020/33, 1994) 15.00
Star Wars Deluxe Fight Scene Limited Edition 3-D
    Hologram (Fantasma 90MT-MLF, 1993) in
    deluxe 8" x 10" Black Matte 30.00
Millennium Falcon Deluxe Hologram Picture
    3½" x 5" in a 8" x 10" matte (90MT-MLF, 1994) . . 25.00

***Star Wars* Holograms** (A.H. Prismatic, 1997)
    Darth Vader matted (#1021-99PM, 1997) 30.00
    Millennium Falcon on Acrylic Stand
        (#1020-33AS, 1997) 17.00
    Millennium Falcon matted (#1020-33PM, 1997) . . 17.00

LIGHTED POSTERS

Star Wars Neon Movie Poster (Neonetics 1993)
    framed $200.00
Darth Vader Neon Framed Picture (Neonetics 1995) . 225.00
Star Wars Millennium Falcon Neon Framed Picture
    (Neonetics 1994) 225.00
Star Wars Millennium Falcon LED Framed Picture
    (Neonetics 1994) 140.00

Wall Art

INDEX